Applied Functional Programming in Scala

*Architecting composable systems with Scala
higher-order functions, algebraic data types,
and advanced functional patterns*

Virendra Kumar Mishra

bpb

www.bpbonline.com

First Edition 2025

Copyright © BPB Publications, India

ISBN: 978-93-65891-294

To View Complete
BPB Publications Catalogue
Scan the QR Code:

www.bpbonline.com

Dedicated to

My father, mom, brother, sister
my sister-in-law and my cute niece Choobie
my all mentors and my all friends

About the Author

Virendra Kumar Mishra is a senior architect at *SAP*, with over 18 years of industry experience designing and delivering complex, scalable systems. He holds B.Tech in computer science, graduated in 2008, and has since built a career rooted in engineering principles, practical design, and continuous learning. He has worked with leading global IT organizations, including *CenturyLink*, *Sapient*, and now *SAP*, where he has led end-to-end implementations across domains. His core expertise lies in Java/Spring, Node.js, Scala, and other languages (Go, Haskell, etc) with reactive programming, and modern functional programming practices. His interest in category theory grew out of a desire to understand the deep abstractions behind code and how they can simplify real-world complexity when applied correctly.

Known among peers for his clear thinking and hands-on approach, Virendra also enjoys mentoring developers and engaging in architectural discussions that blend theory with practical trade-offs. He believes software development is not just about solving problems but about solving them elegantly.

Outside of work, he enjoys spending time with his family, reading about mathematics and philosophy, and taking long, reflective walks. This book is a culmination of years of experience, curiosity, and a passion for bridging the gap between abstract theory and pragmatic code.

About the Reviewers

❖ **Nishant Joshi** is an individual contributor and founding engineer of *Hyperswitch* specializing in type-safe payment infrastructure. He exhibits expertise in Rust programming while maintaining proficiency across full-stack technologies and multiple languages. His professional portfolio encompasses contributions to over 100 public repositories, demonstrating commitment to open-source development.

❖ **Viktar Tsikhmanovich** is an experienced engineering manager and development team lead with a strong background in JavaScript and UX/UI. He has extensive hands-on experience with frontend frameworks like AngularJS, Angular platform, and ReactJS (Next.js), complemented by backend expertise in Python and cloud platforms such as AWS and Azure. Viktar is well-versed in object-oriented and functional programming, with a solid understanding of GOF and GRASP principles. In his current role as tech lead and solution architect for a medical project, Viktar leads cross-functional teams to deliver scalable and impactful solutions.

Acknowledgement

I would like to express our sincere gratitude to all those who contributed to the completion of this book.

First and foremost, we extend our heartfelt appreciation to our family and friends for their unwavering support and encouragement throughout this journey. Their love and encouragement have been a constant source of motivation.

I would like to extend our special thanks to the following individuals for their valuable input and contributions to this project: Mudasir Rasool Najar, Heena Mushtaq, and Mudasir Ahmad Wani. Your insights and feedback have been instrumental in shaping the content and improving the quality of this book. Thank you for your invaluable support.

I am immensely grateful to BPB Publications for their guidance and expertise in bringing this book to fruition. Their support and assistance were invaluable in navigating the complexities of the publishing process.

I would also like to acknowledge the reviewers, technical experts, and editors who provided valuable feedback and contributed to the refinement of this manuscript. Their insights and suggestions have significantly enhanced the quality of the book.

Last but not least, we want to express our gratitude to the readers who have shown interest in our book. Your support and encouragement have been deeply appreciated.

Thank you to everyone who has played a part in making this book a reality.

Preface

Functional programming has steadily evolved from a theoretical curiosity into a practical and powerful paradigm for building modern software systems. With the growing complexity of applications and the increasing need for reliability, concurrency, and maintainability, the core tenets of functional programming, immutability, pure functions, composability, and type-safety have become more relevant than ever. This book is a comprehensive journey through the principles, patterns, and tools that empower developers to build robust and scalable applications using functional programming in Scala.

The book begins by laying the theoretical foundations of functional programming, introducing concepts like pure functions, higher order functions, and immutability. It builds on these ideas with an exploration of category theory, showcasing its importance as a mathematical backbone for functional abstractions such as monads, functors, and applicative functors. We then transition into hands-on Scala development, covering the language's features, Cats and ZIO libraries, and their use in managing side effects in a principled way.

The chapters lead readers through advanced functional patterns, the use of optics, and the implementation of real-world systems using web frameworks such as http4s, Tapir, and ZIO HTTP. Each chapter builds on the previous one, ultimately guiding the reader in developing functional web applications that are composable, testable, and scalable. This book is designed for developers who want to take their knowledge beyond theory and apply functional programming techniques to address real-world software challenges.

Ultimately, theory and practice converge in a comprehensive case study that integrates all previously learned tools and techniques. A functional toy e-commerce application is designed and implemented from scratch, covering everything from user registration and product catalog to order management, security, and analytics. Architectural diagrams, service design patterns, database schemas, and API endpoints offer a complete view of how functional programming principles are applied to a real-world system.

Chapter 1: Fundamentals of Functional Programming - This chapter introduces the fundamentals of functional programming, rooted in lambda calculus, and contrasts it with imperative and object-oriented paradigms. It covers core principles like pure functions, immutability, and lazy evaluation. Using Scala, it highlights function composition, modularity, and benefits like testability, concurrency, and code predictability in real-world applications.

Chapter 2: Implementation of Category Theory - This chapter presents category theory as the mathematical foundation for structuring functional programming concepts. It explains categories as collections of objects and morphisms with properties like identity and associativity. Core abstractions such as semigroups, monoids, functors, applicative functors, and monads are covered, along with practical types like reader, writer, and state. The chapter also introduces optics for precise data manipulation, linking theory to real-world functional programming in Scala.

Chapter 3: Introduction to Scala - This chapter introduces Scala, a statically-typed language on the Java Virtual Machine that blends object-oriented and functional programming. It covers Scala's functional features such as higher order functions, lambda expressions, closures, currying, and partial application. Readers learn about Scala installation, integrated development environment setup, version differences, and functional error handling with Option, Try, and Either. The chapter emphasizes treating functions as first-class citizens and Scala's alignment with functional programming principles.

Chapter 4: Understanding Cats - This chapter explores the Cats library, a powerful Scala toolkit grounded in category theory to support functional programming. It introduces core type classes like functor, monad, applicative, and traverse for modular, reusable code, along with advanced abstractions like contravariant and bifunctor. It covers semigroup, monoid, comonads, and useful data types like Validated and Writer, emphasizing Cats role in creating composable, type-safe, and effect-safe functional applications.

Chapter 5: Understanding ZIO - This chapter introduces ZIO library, a type-safe, purely functional framework for building concurrent, asynchronous, and testable Scala applications. It explains ZIO's core type, effect aliases, control flow, structured error and resource management, and concurrency with fibers and STM. Features like ZLayer for dependency injection and zio.test for effectful testing are highlighted, showcasing ZIO's power in creating scalable, modular, and maintainable applications.

Chapter 6: Effects Implementation in Pure Way - This chapter clarifies the difference between effects and side effects, highlighting the challenges side effects pose to functional purity. It explores strategies for managing them using pure functions, immutability, and abstractions like monads. Libraries like Cats Effect and ZIO offer tools for safe, type-safe I/O and exception handling. Practical examples demonstrate building scalable, maintainable applications by isolating side effects through functional design principles.

Chapter 7: Functional Pattern Implementation - This chapter covers functional design patterns for building composable, scalable, and effect-safe Scala applications. It introduces domain-specific languages using ADTs and improves them with tagless final encoding for better modularity. It explores free monads and functors to separate computation from execution, and explains ZIO layer for dependency injection, highlighting modularity, testability, and resource safety in functional architectures.

Chapter 8: Functional Tools - This chapter introduces essential Scala functional tools for building robust, type-safe, and composable applications. It covers Monocle for immutable data manipulation, Monix for reactive programming, Caliban for type-safe GraphQL, Circe for JSON handling, and ZIO scheduling for concurrency. Additionally, it presents PureConfig for configuration, FS2 for streaming, and Cats collections and retry for functional data structures and retry policies, enabling practical, real-world functional solutions.

Chapter 9: Web Implementation in Functional Way - This chapter covers building web applications with functional programming principles like immutability, pure functions, and composability. It highlights functional programming benefits in web development such as easier state management, concurrency, and testability. Key Scala libraries including http4s, Tapir, ZIO HTTP, and sttp are introduced. A to-do app example demonstrates functional HTTP routing and response handling, setting the stage for subsequent functional database integration.

Chapter 10: DB Implementation in Functional Way - This chapter covers functional database operations in Scala, emphasizing immutability, pure functions, and side-effect control using monads like IO. It compares four Scala libraries: Slick (type-safe, composable queries), Quill (compile-time query generation), doobie (pure functional raw SQL with Cats Effect), and Skunk (PostgreSQL-focused, highly type-safe). Practical examples include a to-do app with Skunk and guidance on choosing the right library for functional DB access.

Chapter 11: Functional Streams for Scala - This chapter explores functional streams in Scala, highlighting their lazy, composable, and resource-efficient handling of large or infinite data sequences. It covers transformations like map, filter, and reduce while maintaining immutability and side-effect isolation. The chapter introduces FS2 and ZIO streams libraries, comparing their features, concurrency support, and use cases such as real-time analytics and reactive applications, guiding developers to build scalable, efficient data pipelines.

Chapter 12: Case Study on Functional Toy E-commerce Site - This chapter presents a case study on building a toy e-commerce site using functional programming principles and tools. It covers user management, product catalog, cart, checkout, order processing, payments, inventory, reviews, analytics, customer support, and security within a layered architecture. Using Scala, Skunk, and React, the design emphasizes modular, composable services with type-safety, immutability, and effectful computations, illustrating the practical and scalable development of functional applications.

Code Bundle and Coloured Images

Please follow the link to download the
Code Bundle and the *Coloured Images* of the book:

https://rebrand.ly/zoiq3iu

The code bundle for the book is also hosted on GitHub at
https://github.com/bpbpublications/Applied-Functional-Programming-in-Scala.
In case there's an update to the code, it will be updated on the existing GitHub repository.

We have code bundles from our rich catalogue of books and videos available at
https://github.com/bpbpublications. Check them out!

Errata

We take immense pride in our work at BPB Publications and follow best practices to ensure the accuracy of our content to provide with an indulging reading experience to our subscribers. Our readers are our mirrors, and we use their inputs to reflect and improve upon human errors, if any, that may have occurred during the publishing processes involved. To let us maintain the quality and help us reach out to any readers who might be having difficulties due to any unforeseen errors, please write to us at :

errata@bpbonline.com

Your support, suggestions and feedbacks are highly appreciated by the BPB Publications' Family.

Piracy

If you come across any illegal copies of our works in any form on the internet, we would be grateful if you would provide us with the location address or website name. Please contact us at business@bpbonline.com with a link to the material.

If you are interested in becoming an author

If there is a topic that you have expertise in, and you are interested in either writing or contributing to a book, please visit www.bpbonline.com. We have worked with thousands of developers and tech professionals, just like you, to help them share their insights with the global tech community. You can make a general application, apply for a specific hot topic that we are recruiting an author for, or submit your own idea.

Reviews

Please leave a review. Once you have read and used this book, why not leave a review on the site that you purchased it from? Potential readers can then see and use your unbiased opinion to make purchase decisions. We at BPB can understand what you think about our products, and our authors can see your feedback on their book. Thank you!

For more information about BPB, please visit www.bpbonline.com.

Join our Discord space

Join our Discord workspace for latest updates, offers, tech happenings around the world, new releases, and sessions with the authors:

https://discord.bpbonline.com

Table of Contents

CHAPTER 1
Fundamentals of Functional Programming

Introduction

This chapter explains the meaning of functional programming. It extends upon the paradigm shift from an object-oriented approach to a functional approach to solving problems, talking about the different characteristics of functional programming and the benefits it offers.

It gives us a bird's eye view of how you think of solutions in a functional way and their implementation. Towards the end, we will provide the difference between object-oriented and functional approach, for implementing the same problem.

Structure

In this chapter, we will cover the following topics:

- Functional programming
- Function as first-class citizen
- Pure function
- Referential transparency
- Immutability
- Lazy evaluation

- Function composition
- Higher order function
- Statements versus expressions
- Advantages and usage of functional programming
- Difference between functional and object-oriented approach

Objectives

By the end of this chapter, readers will become familiar with functional programming core features. This chapter explains what functional programming is and what its features or basic pillars are that make it so special. It also provides a programming implementation that is modular, easy to reason about, composable, and thread safe, which comes as a free fruit by following this functional paradigm.

Functional programming

In 1930, there was research on how we can define a formal system that could advocate computations. *Alonzo Church*, a B.S. degree holder from *Princeton University* devised a formal system for computations using the function application. This formal system was called **lambda calculus**.

It expresses the computations based on function abstraction and application. It consists of three types of expression:

- **Variables**: x, y, and z etc.
- **Abstractions(functions)**: $\lambda x.\ M$, where x is a variable and M is a lambda term.
- **Applications**: $(M\ N)$ where M and N are lambda terms.

Examples:

- **Identity function**: $\lambda x.\ x$
- **Constant function**: $\lambda x.\ \lambda y.\ x$ (always return the first argument)

Church numerals:

As lambda calculus expresses computations using functions. In the same way, Church numerals represent natural numbers as functions in lambda calculus. The number n is represented as a function that applies another function n times.

- **Church numeral for 0**: $\lambda f.\ \lambda x.\ x$ (apply f 0 times to x)
- **Church numeral for 1**: $\lambda f.\ \lambda x.\ f x$ (apply f 1 time to x)
- **Church numeral for 2**: $\lambda f.\ \lambda x.\ f\,(f\,x)$ (apply f 2 times to x)
- **Church numeral for n**: $\lambda f.\ \lambda x.\ f\,(f \dots (f\,x)\dots)$ (apply f n times to x)

Arithmetic operations in lambda calculus:

- **Successor function (SUCC)**: The successor function takes a Church numeral n and returns $n + 1$:

$$SUCC = \lambda n.\ \lambda f.\ \lambda x.\ f\,(n\,f\,x)$$

  - n is a Church numeral
  - f is the function to apply
  - x is the initial value
  - $f\,(n\,f\,x)$ applies f one more time than n does

- **Addition function (ADD)**: Addition of two Church numerals m and n is defined as applying $SUCC$ m times to n.

$$ADD = \lambda m.\ \lambda n.\ \lambda f.\ \lambda x.\ m\,f\,(n\,f\,x)$$

  - $m\,f\,(n\,f\,x)$ applies f m times to the result of applying f n times to x

- **Multiplication function (MUL)**: Multiplication of two Church numerals m and n is defined as applying n m times.

$$MULT = \lambda m.\ \lambda n.\ \lambda f.\ m\,(n\,f)$$

  - $m\,(n\,f)$ applies $n\,f$ m times

Hence, lambda calculus influenced the core pillars of a functional programming, that is:

- Functions as first-class citizens
- Immutability
- High ordered function
- Recursions

This inspiration became the foundation of functional programming.

This was a little history of functional programming. Let us now understand closely what it is, for better clarity.

As per Scala website,

Functional programming is a programming paradigm where programs are constructed by applying and composing functions. It is a declarative programming paradigm in which function definitions are trees of expressions that each return a value, rather than a sequence of imperative statements which change the state of the program.

In functional programming, functions are treated as first-class citizens, meaning that they can be bound to names (including local identifiers), passed as arguments, and returned from other functions, just as any other data type can. This allows programs to be written in a declarative and composable style, where small functions are combined in a modular manner.

Firstly, dissect the preceding definition and try to understand it in an easier way. There are some important terms in the preceding definition, and we need to understand these terms better. Let us take it one by one and understand the functional scope in isolation. We will then combine all of it to get the final meaning.

There are lots of functional programming evaluated from lambda calculus, that is, List (1958), Haskell (1990), Scala (2004). In this book, we will be focusing on Scala language to understand functional programming keys ideas and its implementations using Scala.

The Scala expressions can be invoked on Scala **Read-Evaluate-Print-Loop** (**REPL**), as follows:

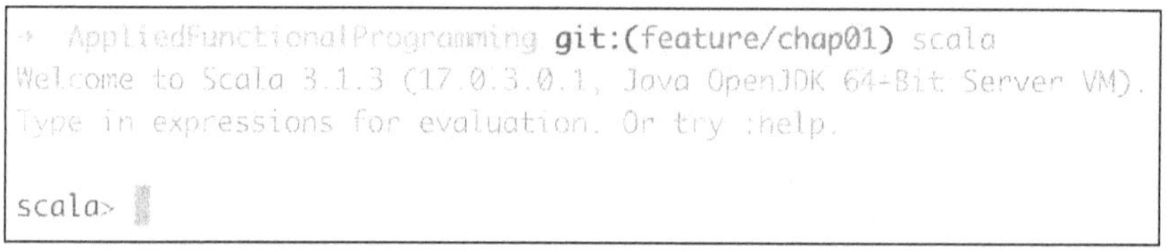

```
›  AppliedFunctionalProgramming git:(feature/chap01) scala
Welcome to Scala 3.1.3 (17.0.3.0.1, Java OpenJDK 64-Bit Server VM).
Type in expressions for evaluation. Or try :help.

scala> ▌
```

Figure 1.1: Scala REPL to try quick function evaluation

NOTE: Scala REPL is a console provide by Scala, by default, in order to run Scala expressions without creating any Scala main method program. It is basically used to try out small expressions easily. It can be started directly on Console as shown in Figure 1.4.

Let us understand it better using example.

Given a list of integers, we need to double them and fetch those which are less than 40.

input = {35, 1, 4, 25, 6, 30, 8, 15, 24}

Firstly, take an example of an imperative language such as Java. To achieve our goal, we have the following pseudo-code statement.

Get a list of integers as input, and follow the given steps:

1. Iterate through the list.
2. Multiply each element with 2.
3. Check if it is less than 40.
4. If yes, store in result list and leave in case it is greater than 40.

Refer to the following code:

```
1.    List<Integer> multiplyBy2FetchNumbersLessThan40 (List<Integer> input){
2.    Int number;
3.    List<Integer> result = new ArrayList<>();
4.    for(int i=0; i< input.length; i++) {
5.        number = input.get(i) * 2 ;
```

```
6.          if(number < 40 ){
7.            result.add(number);
8.          }
9.  }
10. return result;
11. }
```

As it can be seen in the preceding code, each step-by-step control sequence is detailed in order to get the result.

On the other hand, in declarative programming, only components are defined declaratively; not the control sequence.

Refer to the following code:

```
1. def multiplyBy2(number: Int): Int = number * 2

2. def lessThan40(number: Int): Boolean = number < 40

3. val input = List(35, 1, 4, 25, 6, 30, 8, 15, 24)

4. val result =input.map( multiplyBy2) .filter(lessThan40)
```

Figure 1.2 is a pictorial representation of functions used and how they are linked with each other to become a functional pipeline:

functional composition   functional composition

(map multiply By 2)   (filter less than 40)

Figure 1.2: *Functional pipeline linked together*

As described previously, there are two independent functions created, namely **mulitplyBy2** and **lessThan40**, which are independent components. They are then used in *line 4* to get the required result.

Table 1.1 tabulates the data for this example. It describes how input data gets changes changed step-by-step by a pipeline of function application and results in outcome:

input	mutiplyBy2	lessThan40	result
{35, 1, 4, 25, 6, 30, 8, 15, 24}	{70, 2, 8, 50, 12, 60, 16, 30, 48}	{70, 2, 8, 50, 12, 60, 16, 30, 48}	{2,8,12,16,20}

Table 1.1: *Step-by-step functional application*

Programming paradigm

Paradigm is a pattern of achieving solution. When we talk about programming paradigms, it speaks of how to structure different programming constructs for solving a problem.

For example, in object-oriented programming, we define sequence of control to solve a problem.

In above example of doubling and picking less than 40, step is defined as per sequence of control proceeds to get the desired result.

The steps defined are as follows:

1. Initialization of result array.
2. For loop to iterate over the input number list.
3. Inside for loop:
   a. Double the number
   b. Check if doubled number is less than 40
   c. If yes adding it in result list
4. After looping with complete list, we will have the result list with desired number.

As you can see in above steps, it is defined as **execution control** proceeds step over steps and calculates the desired numbers.

In the functional world, functions are defined to achieve a low-level task and we then combine those functions with each other to solve the desired problem. Hence, we do not describe the control sequence.

In same way, achieving the desired double number which is less than 40 task, functional approach defined small modular functions `multiplyBy2` and `lessThan40` which are not in sync with execution control. Instead, those functions are combined with `map` and `filter` function to achieve the desired outcome.

Applying and composing functions

Application of function means using a function by calling the function and providing the required parameter as well. The tough part however, is composing functions. We will learn this by taking an example from mathematics.

Let us assume we have two functions, as follows:

$$f(a) : A \rightarrow B$$

Here, function f takes a as input and produces b as output. Let us assume we have another function g, as follows:

$$g(b): B \rightarrow C$$

It takes b as input and produces c as output.

If we have the preceding two functions and our problem statement is to produce c when you have a as input using $f(a)$ and $g(b)$, then, the solution is function composition:

$$g \circ f(a) : A \rightarrow C \text{ [Composed function using f and g]}$$

This simply tells us to use function *f* first and provide the input. Then whatever be the output, provide it to *g* as input. So, *g ∘ f* is a composed function which takes *a* as input and produces *c* as output.

Declarative programming

Declarative programming describes code that tells us what to achieve instead of how to achieve it. It is used in imperative programming to direct the control sequence as a step-by-step expression to solve a given problem.

In declarative programming, code structure is provided but it does not dictate how and what should be the sequence of control to execute the statements.

As you can see, we have not directed the control. Independent components are defined and then they are associated in specific way to get the result.

Trees of expression

Trees of expression can be understood as group of expressions to achieve a single dedicated task which the function is designed for. For example, doubling and picking which is less than 40, we have **multiplyBy2** and **lessThan40** expressions are combined using **map** and **filter** to achieve the required result.

```
def multiplyBy2(number: Int): Int = number * 2

def lessThan40(number: Int): Boolean = number < 40

val input = List(35, 1, 4, 25, 6, 30, 8, 15, 24)

val result =input.map( multiplyBy2) .filter(lessThan40)
```

Map values

Mapping values means transforming it to another value, using some transformation function. For example, **multiplyBy2** function is a transformation function which is used with **List.map**, which is transforming each element of a list by using said transformation function, as follows:

List.map(multiplyBy2)

Table 1.2 tabulates the data for this example:

Before transformation	After transformation
{35, 1, 4, 25, 6, 30, 8, 15, 24}	{70, 2, 8, 50, 12, 60, 16, 30, 48}

Table 1.2: Input transformation by function application

Figure 1.3 features how a function transforms the domain to its codomain set:

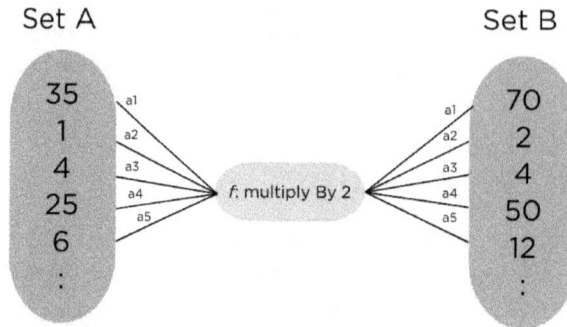

Figure 1.3: *Functional mapping between domain and its codomain*

Sequence of imperative statements

The sequence of imperative statements is a series of statements maintained in a particular order, to be executed to achieve the desired result. This statement association order shows the same control flow during execution of those statements.

Figure 1.4 features the sequence of statements executed for our problem:

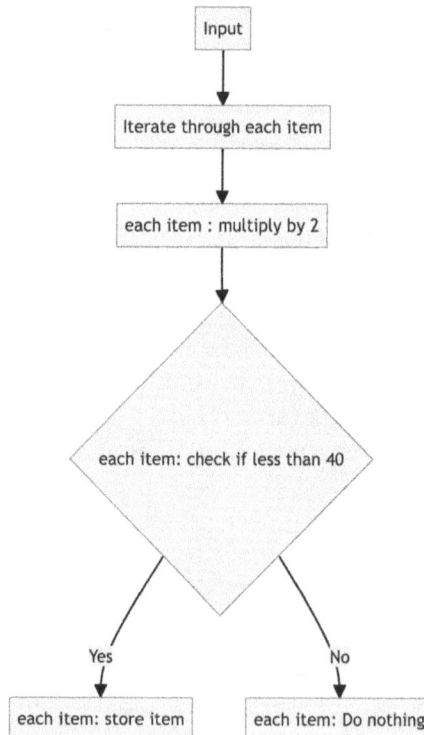

Figure 1.4: *Sequence of statements for our problem*

Update running state of program

During the application execution, the state of application is directly changing. This change in application state is the outcome of running sequence of statements as in impetrative programming, in contrast with functional programming where this state change is achieved by applying or composing the different independent functions created.

In the following example, state is the result of integers which are multiplied by 2 and then less than 40:

```
End State: {2, 8, 12, 16, 30}
```

Function as first-class citizen

Functional programming uses function as a core tool to achieve the required result. Generally, in other programming style, functions are declared to represent a specific logic and then they are called wherever that logic is required with parameters. It also returns a value if required. Refer to the following example:

Function declaration:

```
<return value> functionName (<parameters> … ){
// it contains the logic which takes parameters and return a value
}
```

Function call:

```
<variable> = functionName(<parameters>…)
```

To be a first-class citizen, it should comply with the behavior that other basic data types (integer, string, double and so on) reflect. These behaviors are as follows:

- It can be used as values.
- It can be defined and used in its literal form like other string, integer data type without being assigned to any variable.
- It can be passed in and return from any other function.
- It can be stored in data structure (list, map) like other values.
- It has type associated like any other values contains.

It should reflect all the characteristics which any normal values do. Now, let us understand how function in functional programming shows these characteristics with Scala language. Refer to the following code:

```
1. val multiplyBy2 = (number: Int) => number * 2
2. val multiplyBy2: Int => Int = Lambda$1328/0x0000000800549410@66863941
```

Line 1 represents a function, whereas *line 2* shows how this function is represented in language. You can see that it has type associated **Int => Int** and represented as value:

```
scala> multiplyBy2(10)
val res0: Int = 20
```

Function as literal

The following example shows how functions can be used:

```
1. input.map((number : Int) => number * 2 )
```

As you can see, the function literal **((number: Int) => number * 2** multiplies each element in the list, by **2**. It is directly added inside the map as a function literal.

Function as input parameters

Function can be used directly as an input parameter, as shown in the following example:

```
1. val multiplyBy2 = (number: Int) => number * 2
2. input.map(multiplyBy2)
```

Here, the **multiplyBy2** function is used as a parameter to **map** function for achieving the same logic as previously.

Function as return value

A Function can also be returned as an output, as shown in the following code:

```
1. scala> val multiplyBy2 = (number: Int) => number * 2
2. val multiplyBy2: Int => Int = Lambda$1324/0x0000000800584208@e6e5da4
3.
4. scala> val returnFunction = (number: Int) => multiplyBy2(number)
5. val returnFunction: Int => Int = Lambda$1471/0x00000008005d1208@7ec5
   aad
6.
7. scala> returnFunction(10)
8. val res0: Int = 20
```

Here in *line 4*, the **multiplyBy2** function is being returned, and when **returnFunction** is called with a parameter, the returned function **multiplyBy2** is called again. The provided parameter will be **10** and it will be multiplied by **2**. The result is **20**.

Functions stored in data structures

Function can also be stored in data structures as values. The following example describes how different functions are defined first, and then those functions are stored in a list named **functionList**:

```scala
1. scala> val multiplyBy2 = (number: Int) => number * 2
2.        | def multiplyBy3 = (number: Int) => number * 3
3.        | def multiplyBy6 = (number: Int) => number * 6
4.        | def multiplyBy10 = (number: Int) => number * 10
5.             | val functionList = List(multiplyBy2, multiplyBy3,
   multiplyBy6, multiplyBy10)
6.
7. val multiplyBy2: Int => Int = Lambda$1557/0x00000008005f8000@4ba1f425
8. def multiplyBy3: Int => Int
9. def multiplyBy6: Int => Int
10.def multiplyBy10: Int => Int
11.val          functionList:       List[Int        =>         Int]        =
   List(rs$line$4$$$Lambda$1557/0x00000008005f8000@4ba1f425,
   rs$line$4$$$Lambda$1560/0x00000008005f83f0@550574cb,
   rs$line$4$$$Lambda$1561/0x00000008005f87e0@1e7113f8,
   rs$line$4$$$Lambda$1562/0x00000008005f8bd0@3e149513)
```

Above code is executed in scala REPL (interactive interpreter) from *lines 1* to *5* where all functions defined in *lines 1, 2, 3* and *4*, are stored inside list as in *line 5*, with type **Int =>** **Int**. *Line 7* to *11* describe the output of *line 1* to *5*.

Pure function

Pure functions are same as mathematical functions, which always produce the same output for same provided inputs. For example, the sum function which takes two numbers as inputs, always produces the same output, that is, the sum of two inputs.

In the same way, the function which takes inputs and always produces the same output without creating any side-effects, are called **pure functions**. Here, side-effects are all those side (extra) actions which are not directly contributing to the evaluation of result or changing some state outside of its functional or local scope.

The following are treated as side-effects:

- Any interaction with console during function execution.
- Any interaction with input/output or socket.
- Changing global variables and so on.

In other words, pure function has the following properties:

- **Total**: Returns a value for every possible input.
- **Deterministic**: Returns the same value for the same input.
- **Inculpable**: No (direct) interaction with the world or program state.

Example of impure functions are as follows:

- `System.currentTimeMillis()`
- `Calendar.get(Calendar.DAY_OF_WEEK)`
- `Calendar.get(Calendar.HOUR_OF_DAY)`
- `Calendar.get(Calendar.MINUTE)`

The abovementioned functions are all impure functions because they are not deterministic, meaning, the same method call will give different outputs. These functions are dependent upon the time (outside of functional/local scope) when it is executed.

Examples of pure functions are as follows:

- `Math.max(int a, int b)`
- `Math.min(int a, int b)`
- `Math.abs(int a)`

The above-mentioned functions are all pure functions because all methods are total and deterministic. It will always produce the same result for same inputs.

Referential transparency

A function is said to be referentially transparent if we can replace it with its corresponding value, without changing the behavior of the program.

It can be done using pure functions as they neither depend upon the outside world state for its evaluation nor update the outside world during evaluation, they depend upon inputs provided and always produce the same output for the same inputs. Hence, they can be replaced by their output, and this will not change the program's behavior. Let us better understand it by an example.

```
1. def add(a: Int, b: Int): Int = a + b
2. val result = add(2, 3)  // result will always be 5
```

As in the above example, **add(2, 3)** can safely replace with 5 anywhere in your program. It has no side effects and always returns the same output for the same input — making it referentially transparent.

This property helps to reason about code with the same reasoning that occurs in mathematics to validate the overall function verification. Let us say that your code is made up of 4 functions $(f1, f2, f3, f4)$ which are all dependent upon each other using the following relation to produce output:

$$f1 \rightarrow f2 \rightarrow f3 \rightarrow f4$$

Here, → represents dependency relation.

A reasoning about the preceding implementation would be easy for given input. Refer to the following steps:

1. Select suspect function and replace it with its expected output.
2. Add output in the preceding relation and run it again.
3. Repeat *step 1* and *step 2* until we get the erroneous function.

Since, referential transparency provides the same capability of replacing the code with its expected output, it is very easy to reason about the code and locate the erroneous code easier.

Immutability

Immutability means that something that cannot be changed. In the programming world, it is said that immutable objects are the objects that cannot be changed after its properties get initialized after creation.

This is one of the core concepts behind functional programming. Immutability provides a strong foundation to functional programming and inherits it from the mathematical world. All mathematical expressions exhibit immutability. For example, if we multiply two numbers, the expression *5 * 8* is immutable and it cannot be updated.

Immutability provides great benefits in thread-safety and holds strong surety that it would not produce wrong result in concurrent processing. The reason behind the production of wrong result in a concurrent scenario, happens when more than one thread tries to update the same set of data. Let us try to understand the same by example.

There is one bunch of integers available in list and there are two threads T1, T2 which are using the same mutable list.

- **T1**: Responsible for doubling the values.
- **T2**: Responsible for deducting 4 from every value.

10	5	4	7	12	11	13	15	6	16

The right result from both threads, if they allow to work with list independently, are as follows:

T1:

20	10	8	14	24	22	26	30	12	32

T2:

6	1	0	3	8	7	9	11	2	12

Now, let us see what happens when we try to run both threads simultaneously, with the following ordering of T1 and T2.

As shown in *Figure 1.5*, T1 thread is represented by orange color and T2 thread is represented by red color. Time is represented by the *x* variable where:

$$x1 < x2 < x3 < x4 < x5 < x6 < x7$$

Figure 1.5 describes the importance of immutability which make very easy to work in multithreaded environment and requires least effort to make program functionally correct. This graph depicts two threads working on a single list and its context switch which makes sometimes wrong output with different threads context switches:

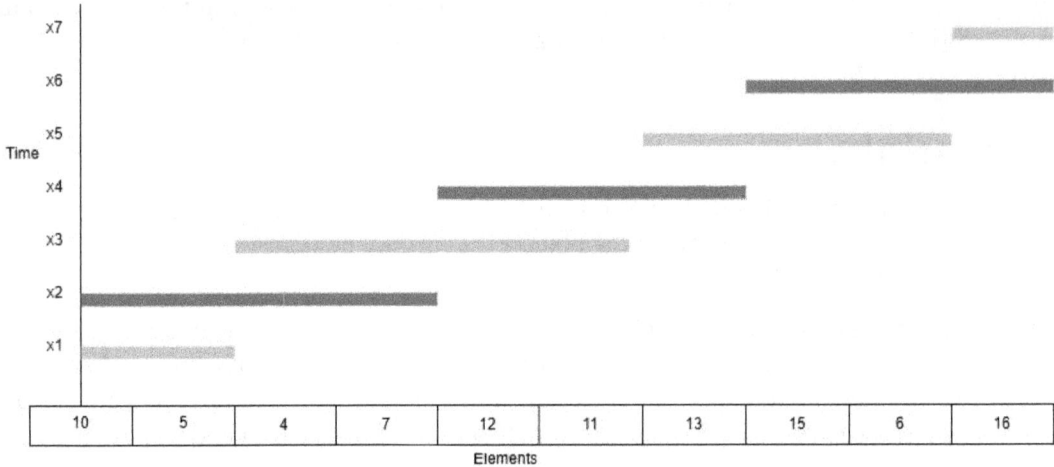

Figure 1.5: Context switch graph for two threads execution on mutable list

This means that both T1 and T2 threads get a chance to work on list indexes, as follows:

1. list[0] and list[1] on *x1* time by T1 thread.

   Input list:

10	5	4	7	12	11	13	15	6	16

   T1 list:

20	10								

2. list[0], list[1] , list[2] and list[3] on *x2* time by T2 thread.

   Input list:

20	10	4	7	12	11	13	15	6	16

   T2 list:

16	6	0	3						

3. list[2], list[3], list[4] and list[5] on *x3* time by T1 thread.

   Input list:

16	6	0	3	12	11	13	15	6	16

T1 list:

16	6	0	6	24					

4. list[4], list[5] and list[6] on $x4$ time by T2 thread.

Input list:

16	6	0	6	24	11	13	15	6	16

T2 list:

16	6	0	6	20	7	9	15	6	16

5. list[6], list[7] and list[8] on $x5$ time by T1 thread.

Input list:

16	6	0	6	20	7	9	15	6	16

T1 list:

16	6	0	6	20	7	18	30	12	

6. list[7], list[8] and list[9] on $x6$ time by T2 thread.

Input list:

16	6	0	6	20	7	18	30	12	16

T2 list:

16	6	0	6	20	7	18	26	8	12

7. list[9] on $x7$ time by T1 thread.

Input list:

16	6	0	6	20	7	18	26	8	12

T1 list:

16	6	0	6	20	7	18	26	8	24

Hence, the result produced by T1 and T2 thread, would be as follows:

16	6	0	6	20	7	18	26	8	24

This is not even close to what we needed to achieve with T1 and T2 threads.

Thus, you can see with the preceding example that the list was mutable, and each thread was able to change the value from the provided one and another thread picked new value as its input instead of the one provided in input list. If the list was immutable, then both threads had read the inputs and there was no chance to update the list because of its immutability. Thus, each thread would have always read the right input.

Immutability provides strong emphasis on the fact that data would never be changed. So, data would always be read and then a new set of value generated instead of updating the original one. Hence, it provides thread-safety and ensure the right results in case of concurrent scenarios without any extra effort.

Lazy evaluation

Lazy evaluation is an execution strategy that delays the execution of code until it is required. Generally, there are two types of execution strategies being used in programming languages:

- Eager evaluation
- Lazy evaluation

As obvious from the naming, strict evaluation does the execution as soon as it encounters the code. It is a very common execution strategy among many programming languages. Let us understand in depth, what it means by strict evaluation or execution of code as soon as it encounters.

Optimization

In lazy evaluation, there are major spaces for optimization to be done by the compiler. As functional programming uses referential transparency and lazy evaluation does not evaluate the code in-place, it could be able to investigate the patterns inside the usage. For example, if the same function was called many times with same input, then compiler would have the option to evaluate one method call and replace all other method calls with its output obtained from the first call.

It is possible because of referential transparency, the method call could be replaced with its output with impacting program output.

If there are 10 function calls and each function call take around 20 seconds, then strict evaluation would run all 10 methods call and would run in 10 * 20 = 200 seconds.

Whereas same lazy evaluation technique will allow the function to be called once and replace other function call with its output. Hence, it would take the following time:

$$1*20 = 20 \ seconds$$

Thus, it is a 10-fold performance improvement of lazy evaluation over strict evaluation in the preceding example.

Let us take a very basic example of Fibonacci sum defined as the following function:

1. fib(n) = fib(n-1) + fib(n-2)
2. fib(1) = 1
3. fib(0) = 0

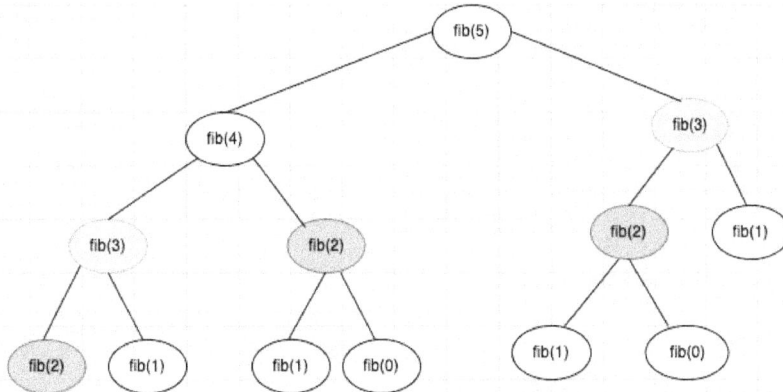

Figure 1.6: *Execution tree that shows how to execute fib(5)*

If we need to calculate **fib(5)**, then it will be:

fib(5) = fib(4) + fib(3)   ------------a

Further, we get two smaller problem **fib(4)** and **fib(3)**:

fib(4) = fib(3) + fib(2) ---------------b
fib(3) = fib(2) + fib(1) ---------------c

Further,

fib(2) = fib(1) + fib(0) ----------------d

As per above execution tree, you can see that **fib(5)** need **fib(4)** and **fib(3)** is to be evaluated, but **fib(4)** and **fib(3)** both need **fib(2)** further to calculate individual result. The same color box represents the same problem, which is iteration in different branches of the execution tree. **fib(4)** need **fib(3)** which is also required in right branch of **fib(5)**. Same as of **fib(2)**, which is used many places in above execution tree.

If it is strict evaluation, then **fib(3)** and **fib(2)** will be calculated as many times as it appears in execution tree because it executes problems as it gets statement or expressions and cannot check whether the same expression would be evaluated further.

Whereas, lazy evaluations work like exploring first the whole expression like generating execution tree first and hence get benefitted by optimizing and reusing the same problems. In the above example, during the exploration, it is quite evident that **fib(3)** and **fib(2)** are executing many times, so evaluating them once and storing their results will optimize the solution. This optimized saving would be large for bigger Fibonacci number for example, **fib(50)**.

User defined control structures

It is possible to implement new user-defined control structures using functional programming.

Let us take an example of a control structure which will allow to execute the code when conditional statement provided evaluates too false, that is, opposite of **if**.

Infinite data structures

Before looking into lazy evaluation benefits over implementing infinite data structures, let us first understand what infinite data structure means.

For example, if a program needs to be evaluated over all-natural numbers, then it is not possible in strict evaluation to create an infinite list of natural numbers and limitation is the main memory. Strict evaluation tries to hold all data in main memory before performing on that data so it becomes impossible for strict evaluation to work with infinite list.

On the other hand, lazy evaluation works on different techniques to represent infinite data structure. It does not create all-natural numbers at all to represent this infinite list. It only carries starting natural number and information that all exist. If all generated numbers got used, then, it creates the next set of numbers. Hence, it represents the infinite list but generates numbers on the fly when it will be used.

```
Natural_number_list = {0,1,2,3…}
```

 After usage of **1, 2, 3** it again becomes the following:

```
Natural_number_list = {4,5,6,7,…}
```

Function composition

Let us say we have the following two functions:

$$f(a) \rightarrow A \rightarrow B$$

Here, function f takes a as input and produces b as output. Let us say we have another function g, as follows:

$$g(b): B \rightarrow C$$

It takes b as input and produces c as output.

If we have the preceding two functions, and our problem statement is to produce c when you have a as input using $f(a)$ and $g(b)$, the solution is function composition.

$$g \circ f(a) : A \rightarrow C \; [\textit{Composed function using } f \textit{ and } g]$$

Let us now understand it more closely. Assuming, we have three functions for a bank account update:

```
1. deposit( moneyTobeAdded : Int ): Int
2. withdraw( moneyTobewithdraw : Int ): Int
3. //composed function of deposit and withdraw
4. val depositThenWithdraw: Int => Int = withdraw compose deposit
5. runInTransaction( fnList : List[Int => Int]) : void
```

If we want to deposit $100 to an account and then withdraw $50 in a transaction, then we need to be of type **Int => Boolean** which is required by the third function. We could combine the **deposit** and **withdraw** function together and then provide it to the third function as follows:

```
1. val depositThenWithdraw = withdraw compose deposit
2. runInTransaction( List(depositThenWithdraw ))
```

As **deposit** and **withdraw** got composed, new function **depositThenWithdraw** of type **Int => Int** is created and added in list to be run in transactions.

Higher order function

When a function takes another function as input to produce result or produce function as result, then it is called as **higher order function**. It would only be possible when the function is first-class citizen.

Higher order function introduces generic programming. When a function takes another function as input, it becomes more abstract and generic in the sense that the called **main** function could provide any definition to higher order function. It works in an abstract way and provides more concrete implementation when input parament is provided.

Let us understand it better, using the following example.

The following is a definition of **map** function of **List** (immutable) in Scala language:

```
1. final def map[B](f: (A) => B): List[B] // builds n new list by
    applying a function 'f' to all elements of the given list
```

It takes a function as a parameter. The **map** function is more generic in the sense that the **map** method maps each element of a list from type **A** to type **B**.

Achieving it depends on the caller intention about how to convert given type **A** to **B**. **map** function takes this definition as input and extends it to complete list transformation from type **A** to type **B**.

This is the power that comes from higher order function, which makes function be more abstract or generic, based on details provided by user, in a variety of scenarios.

Statements versus expressions

Statements are instructions to be executed to perform actions, as they execute in-place actions and does not return value. Hence, it causes side-effects. Many statements in Java programming language are made as statements. These are part of control statements. For example, **if** then **else**, **switch**, **for**, **while**, **do-while**, **continue**, **break**.

If these statements are executed, then they do not return any value. Instead, they provide instructions to do some specific and dedicated actions, as follows:

```
1. if(logic == true ) {
2.    result= "true logic"
3. }
4. else {
5. result= "false logic"
6. }
```

The preceding code updates the **result** variable in-place and there is no way **if** then **else** could return value, based on **logic** instead of updating in-place.

This is the source of side-effects as it is updating the variable inside function instead of returning the value and hence not favorable in functional programming.

Another important difference between statements and expressions is composition. As expression always return values, it can be composed with other expressions where first output becomes the input for another expression. This can go further with many expressions. On the other hand, the statement gets executed in-place and create side-effects, which is possible to combine with another statement without any other support. Effects can be used to capture statements or side-effect and put them inside the container to provide functional compositions over effect. We will learn this in later chapters.

Advantages and usage of functional programming

The preceding concepts provide many advantages to functional programming, which helps in easier, modular, concurrent, and testable software implementations. The benefits of functional programming could be divided majorly into the following points.

Unit testing

Functional programming advocates pure functions, where functions are only allowed to evaluate the inputs provided to them to generate output. There is no other relation with other states outside of function, and no other side effects are allowed. Hence, it becomes ideal for unit testing where inputs are provided without setting external state, and outputs are validated against generated output.

Concurrency

It comes by default with functional programming without making any extra effort because of its immutability. In other programming paradigms, it always gets tough to implement concurrency. When two or more threads try to update the same data, and other execution logic is dependent upon the same data, then it becomes a nightmare to align all thread access of the data in the required order. Sometimes, it creates scenarios which are difficult to reproduce and when it comes in production environment, very time-consuming.

The main reason for all complexity comes as your data is immutable. If it was immutable, so no thread would be able to update it accidently and all problems of having strict right order of threads would go away. This immutability solves all concurrency problems from its root. This is where functional programming shines where immutability is in its core pillar.

Debugging

When the function output is only dependent upon its input and logic of processing of inputs, and there is no dependency on global state of program, then it is always easy to locate the erroneous code inside the function. As functional programming emphasizes on immutability and no side-effects (no dependency on global state), it makes it easy for debugging inside functional programming. Furthermore, if a function is dependent upon more than one function, then some functions could be replaced with its required output using referential transparency to locate the erroneous code.

Easier to reason about

The same concepts work as mentioned previously, in the reasoning of code. This reasoning comes from a mathematical background, which is the basis of functional programming. For example, if $A = B$ and $B = C$ then $A = C$ using mathematical reasoning.

The same reasoning could be applied for functions in functional programming. If function $f1:A{\rightarrow}B$ and function $f2:A {\rightarrow}B$, then we could have a function easily, which would be a composition of both *fcomp*: $A{\rightarrow}C$ *(f1 compose f2)*.

All reasoning is available to validate the truthfulness of program by virtue of pure functions and immutability.

Some other benefits of functional programming are as follows:

- Pure functions are easier to reason about.
- Testing is easier, and pure functions lend themselves well to techniques such as property-based testing.
- Programs are more bulletproof.
- Programs are written at a higher (abstract) level and are therefore easier to comprehend.

- Function signatures are more meaningful.
- Parallel/concurrent programming is easier.
- Function signatures are more like documentation to the code.

Difference between functional and object-oriented approach

There are fundamental differences between functional programming and object-oriented approaches. Both paradigms differ in the manner in which they tackle a problem.

Functional programming focuses on pure functions with immutable data, which is used to achieve program output. It thinks in a totally different way when designing a solution. The program is divided into individual tasks. Pure functions are developed for each task, and then they are composed with each other to formulate the program's intention.

The key concepts used in functional programming are as follows:

- Function as first-class citizens
- Pure functions
- high order functions
- Recursions
- Immutability

On the other hand, the object-oriented approach focuses on data (classes and objects). Data contains required behavior in form methods. In this paradigm, the problem is divided into the entities being used and each entity and its behavior is developed as class. Then, each class interacts with each other to solve the program intention.

The key concepts used in object-oriented programming are as follows:

- Encapsulation
- Abstraction
- Inheritance
- Polymorphism

Conclusion

In this chapter, we discussed about the fundamentals of functional programming, traits of functional programming and how it differs from object-oriented approach.

In the next chapter, we will look at those traits in more detail, as well as the benefits that they provide, for better software implementation which would be more robust, high performant, concurrent, resource safe, testable and more resilient.

CHAPTER 2
Implementation of Category Theory

Introduction

This chapter discusses a mathematical branch, category theory. It digs deeper into category theory, what problem it focuses on solving, and how it is related to functional programming. We will further explore different abstracted mathematical structures that category theory provides and the relationship among them. This chapter also includes some terminology specific to category theory. You should come back to it after reading the next chapters, since it would relate more to the abstract category theory mechanism.

We will discuss each of the concepts in the upcoming chapters with finer details, and more practical examples to use the concepts defined here.

Structure

In this chapter, we will cover the following topics:

- Introduction to category theory
- Morphism
- Sets
- Semigroup
- Monoid
- Functors

- Applicative functor
- Foldable
- Traversable
- Monad
- Optics

Objectives

By the end of this chapter, readers will be familiar with category theory and its importance for a better understanding of functional programming. This chapter explains different abstracted mathematical structures and their properties. It also contains the laws that these structures follow. Further, we will also discuss how these structures are used for problem solving.

Introduction to category theory

Category theory provides a mathematical framework to study categories, which comprises any object and its morphism (relationship or transformer). These morphisms have one fundamental property; they transform an object into another object in the same category, but they always preserve its structural properties. There are many ways these objects could be transformed using the morphism defined, and hence, studying its relationships and properties. It focuses on how these morphisms could be composed any number of times to create new morphism, which again apply on the object and preserve its structural property.

Let us understand it more closely; the concept of category and what type of relationship exist among them. Categories represents common types, and its relationships called **morphisms**.

Category = Same structure objects + morphisms (relationship)

Let us take some examples to understand it better. A collection of all integer numbers (objects here are integers which share the commonality that all are whole numbers with their counterparts) and all the operations that could be applied on integer numbers and generate the integer number only become morphisms of this *Integer Category*(Z). (If morphism does not evaluate to non-integer number, then it points to another object which lies in another category). Morphisms are generally denoted with arrow, where the left hand of the arrow conveys input and the right-hand side indicates its result.

The following figure shows a pictorial form of a *Integer Category*(Z) and its *sum* (+) morphism:

Objects – natural numbers + negative counter parts

Morphism – sum (+)

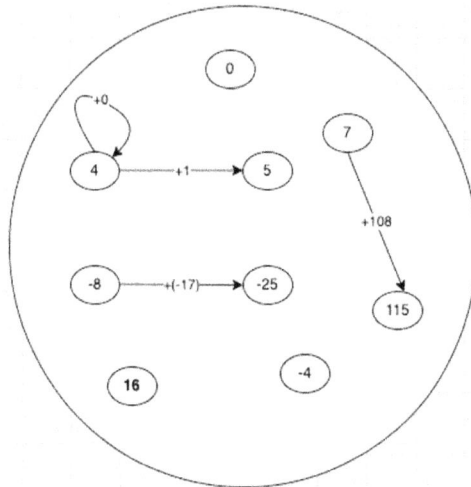

Integer Category

Figure 2.1: *Integer category with sum as morphism (+)*

Category

The concept of category, comprising object and structural-preserving morphisms can be applied to any domain (mathematics, computer programming etc.). By defining these categories in such a way, it abstracts out their inner (specific details) and hence, they can focus on common hidden patterns among different categories.

Formally, a category C can be defined, as follows:

- **Objects**: It is the main component of the category with defined category properties and characteristics. These objects could be dependent on the domain or field being studied. The following are examples of objects used for different areas of focus:

  o Sets

  o Mathematical structures

  o Types

  o Process or systems

  o Geometric spaces

  o Mathematical objects

- **Morphisms:** These are the relationships, connections, or transformations abstractions among the objects inside the category. These notions of morphisms define how one object of category can be transformed to another object.

Properties

The following are the properties of a category:

- **Associativity**: The composition of morphisms are associative. It means that for morphisms $f:A{\rightarrow}B$, $g:B{\rightarrow}C$ and $h:C{\rightarrow}D$, the following compositions hold true:

$$(h \circ g) \circ f = h \circ (f \circ g)$$

- **Identity**: Every object in the category must have identity morphisms which transforms it to self. For example, identity morphism for A is $id\_A: A \rightarrow A$, identity morphism of B is $id\_B: B \rightarrow B$, and if there is one morphism $f:A \rightarrow B$ then, the following compositions of identity morphism holds:

$$id\_A \circ f = f$$
$$f \circ id\_B = f$$

The following figure is a category showing object identity morphism id_A and id_B for object A and B respectively:

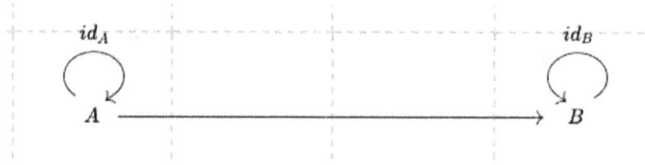

Figure 2.2: Identity morphism id_A and id_B for object A and B respectively

Laws

These laws ensure that category structure always preserves the fundamental properties of composition and identity. Categories are bounded to the following laws:

- **Associative law**: Associativity over composition must hold among the category morphisms. This means that the result must be independent of how morphisms are composed. Either way of composition should result in the same transformations.

  For $f:A{\rightarrow}B$, $g:B{\rightarrow}C$, and $h:C{\rightarrow}D$, the following compositions hold true:

$$(h \circ g) \circ f = h \circ (f \circ g)$$

- **Identity law**: There must always be an identity morphism in the category, which when applied to an object always maps to the same object. It is also composed to another morphism resulting to the same morphism, that is, If $id\_A:A{\rightarrow}A$ and $f:A{\rightarrow}B$ then, the following equations hold true for the identity morphism:

$$id\_A \circ f = f$$
$$f \circ id\_B = f$$

- **Unital law**: It combines associativity and identity laws. For any morphisms, $f:A \rightarrow B$, $g:B \rightarrow C$, and $h:C \rightarrow D$, the following equations always stand true:

$$f \circ id\_A = f \text{ (left Identity)}$$

$$id\_C \circ f = f \text{ (right identity)}$$

Category theory generalizes all the concepts in terms of above defined categories, irrespective of objects and morphisms (relationship among objects) among them.

Morphism

A morphism is a relationship between objects that describes the transformation that modifies one object into another object in the same category. Its fundamental property is that it preserves the structure from the input object to the output object. Its details are generally hidden, so that it could be studied in an abstract way and be able to get its hidden or higher-level patterns among the objects. It is defined as arrows ($\rightarrow$) between two category objects A and B with morphism f.

An example is as follows:

$$f:A \rightarrow B$$

The read as object A can be transformed to object B using morphism f. The same is described in *Figure 2.3*, where category A is transformed to category B using morphism f:

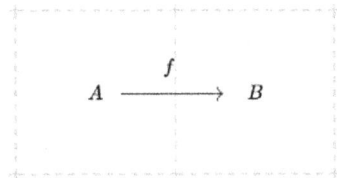

Figure 2.3: Depiction of morphism from category A to B

Since it is an abstract notion of relationship or transformation between objects, its exact properties and behavior will be known when it is applied on specific category.

Common types of morphisms

The following are some common types of morphisms:

- **Monomorphism**: It is also known as **injective morphism**. It preserves distinctness. A morphism $f: A \rightarrow B$ is known as monomorphism when $f(x) = f(y)$ is only true for $x=y$. These morphisms are often used to represent inclusion relationships between objects.

  As depicted in *Figure 2.4*, each object in category A is transformed to distinct object of category B. This is also called **one-to-one mapping**:

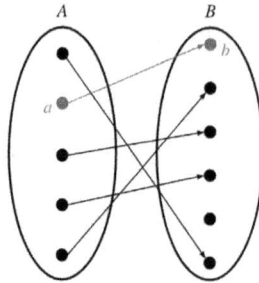

Figure 2.4: Injective function mapping for domain A and codomain B

- **Epimorphism**: It is also known as **surjective morphism**. It covers all the elements of its codomain. If $f: A \rightarrow B$; meaning that, if morphism $f:A \rightarrow B$ is epimorphism, then every element of codomain B is mapped to domain A.

  As depicted in *Figure 2.5*, all objects in category B are mapped to at least one object of category A. It means that one object of category B could be mapped to more than one object of category A.

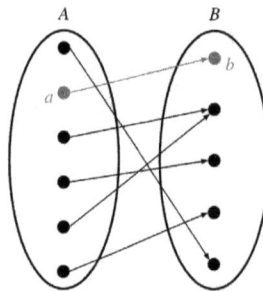

Figure 2.5: Surjective function mapping for domain A and codomain B

- **Isomorphism**: It represents a specific morphism which is invertible, meaning that it has both left and right inverse. If there exist a morphism $f:A \rightarrow B$, then there must be an inverse morphism (domain and codomain gets swapped) $g:B \rightarrow A$, such that, $f \circ g = id\_B$ and $g \circ f = id\_A$.

- **Endomorphism**: This is a morphism which connects to self. If there an object A in category C, then the morphism $f: A \rightarrow A$ is called **endomorphism**. It is generally used to depict the transformation that can be applied to same object.

  Figure 2.6 describes this relationship where each category is mapped to itself using id_A or id_B:

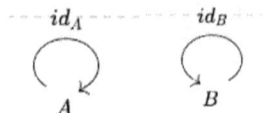

Figure 2.6: Endomorphism, connection to self id_A and id_B for A and B respectively

- **Automorphism**: It is an isomorphism from an object to itself. If there an object A in category C, then isomorphism of $f: A \rightarrow A$. It is generally used to depict symmetries that preserve the structure of an object.

- **Homomorphism**: It is a morphism that preserves the structures of an object. If a morphism $f: A \rightarrow B$ represent homomorphism between two objects A and B in same category, then it preserves the operations and relations between element of the objects.

Composition of morphisms

One of the key features of category theory is the composition of morphisms. Given two morphisms, $f: A{-}{>}B$ and $g: {-}{>}C$, their composition, denoted as $g \circ f$, represents the chaining of the mappings. It means that the output of the morphism f is used as the input for the morphism g. It helps to chain the morphisms to create the new morphism between the objects.

The composition of morphisms is associative, meaning that $(h \circ g) \circ f = h \circ (g \circ f)$.

Figure 2.7 describes this composition of morphisms. It shows that if we compose h and g morphisms and further compose the result to f which will establish a morphism from category A to category D. It is exactly the same if we first compose g and f morphisms and compose the result with morphism h.

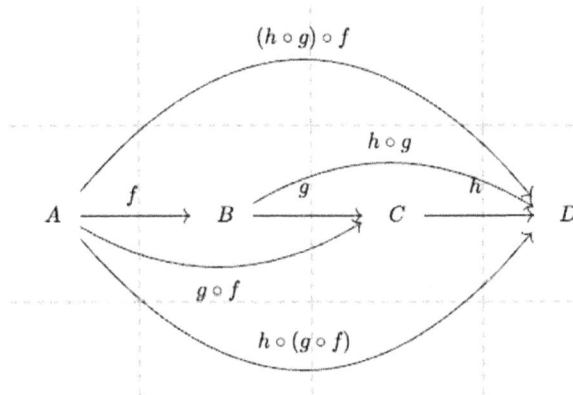

Figure 2.7: *Depiction of composition of morphisms*

Identity morphisms

Every object in a category has an identity morphism associated with it. The identity morphism, denoted as id_A, represents a do-nothing mapping from an object A to itself. It serves as the neutral element with respect to morphism composition. For any morphism $f: A{-}{>}B$, we have the identities $id\_A \circ f = f$ and $f \circ id\_B = f$. Refer to *Figure 2.2* for identity configuration.

Identity morphisms ensure that every object in a category can be connected to itself, and they play a crucial role in maintaining the structure and coherence of the category.

Sets

In category theory, it is the category whose objects are sets. The arrows or morphisms between sets A and B are the total functions from A to B, and the composition of morphisms is the composition of functions.

Usage

The following are the applications of the set category in different domains:

- **Mathematical reasoning**: It allows to study and analyze properties of sets and functions in a general and abstract manner.

- **Functional programming**: The concepts of functions, composition, and immutability in functional programming languages align with the morphisms and composition in the set category.

- **Database theory**: Sets can represent entities, and functions can represent relationships or transformations between these entities. The study of relational databases and query languages, such as SQL, is influenced by the concepts of sets and functions from the set category.

- **Type theory and programming language semantics**: The set category plays a role in type theory and the semantics of programming languages. It provides a foundation for understanding the relationship between types and functions, and it allows for the formalization of type systems and the reasoning about program behavior.

- **Topology and analysis**: The set category is closely related to topology and analysis. The concepts of continuous functions, open sets, and topological spaces can be described in terms of the set category.

- **Abstract algebra**: The set category serves as a starting point for studying abstract algebraic structures, such as groups, rings, and fields.

- **Programming language design**: The concepts and abstractions from the set category often inform the design and implementation of programming languages. Category theory provides a way to reason about the behavior and composition of programs, leading to the development of more expressive and powerful programming languages.

The abstract and general nature of category theory allows its concepts to be applied in various domains, providing a unifying framework for studying structures, relationships, and computations.

Semigroups

In mathematics, a semigroup is an algebraic structure consisting of a set together with an associative internal binary operation on it.

Figure 2.8 describes the relationships of algebraic structures:

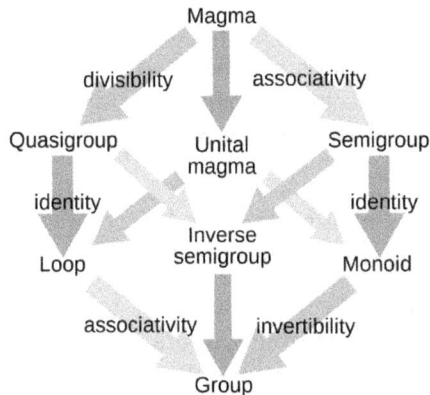

Figure 2.8[1]*: Algebraic structure*

Definition

A semigroup is defined, as follows:

- **Set**: A semigroup is defined over a set, which represents the objects or elements of the semigroup.

- **Binary operation**: A semigroup has an associative binary operation, denoted as <> (or sometimes denoted as ∘), which takes two elements of the set and produces a new element of the same set. For any three elements a, b, and c in the set, the operation satisfies the associativity property: $(a <> b) <> c = a <> (b <> c)$.

Usage

Semigroups are widely used in functional programming for various purposes, including data manipulation, validation, concurrency, and more. The following are some common use cases and benefits of using semigroups:

- **Data manipulation**: Semigroups are useful for combining and merging data structures. For example, if you have two lists, you can use a semigroup operation to concatenate them.

1. By Ethaniel, Own work, extended from File:Magma_to_group3.svg: complete the cube with Unital magma, CC0, https://commons.wikimedia.org/w/index.php?curid=95944694

- **Validation and error handling**: Semigroups are often used in validation to accumulate and combine validation results. Each validation step can produce a result or an error, and semigroup operations are used to combine these results or errors into a final result or error. This allows you to perform multiple validations and collect all the errors encountered during the process.

- **Concurrent and parallel programming**: Semigroups are useful for combining results in concurrent or parallel computations.

- **Log aggregation**: Semigroups can be used to combine logs using a semigroup operation to merge or concatenate them into a single log. This is particularly useful in distributed systems or scenarios where logs need to be aggregated for analysis or monitoring purposes.

- **Monoid construction**: Semigroups are a key component in constructing monoids, which are semigroups with an identity element.

Semigroups provide a flexible and composable way to combine values of the same type. They allow you to define custom combining operations for your data structures, enabling powerful transformations and computations. By leveraging semigroups, you can write code that is more expressive, reusable, and modular in functional programming.

Monoid

A monoid is a set equipped with an associative binary operation and an identity element. For example, the nonnegative integers with addition form a monoid, the identity element being 0.

In functional program, the set of strings built from a given set of characters is a free monoid.

Definition

A set S equipped with a binary operation $S \times S \rightarrow S$, which we will denote •, is a monoid if it satisfies the following two axioms:

- **Associativity**: For all a, b and c in S, the equation $(a \bullet b) \bullet c = a \bullet (b \bullet c)$ holds.

- **Identity element**: There exists an element e in S such that for every element a in S, the equalities $e \bullet a = a$ and $a \bullet e = a$ hold.

Usage

Monoids are widely used in functional programming for various purposes, offering benefits such as composability, abstraction, and code reuse. The following are some common use cases and benefits of using monoids:

- **Data aggregation**: Monoids are often used for aggregating data structures. For example, you can use a monoid to compute the sum or product of a list of numbers, concatenate strings, etc. The identity element acts as a starting point for the aggregation, and the binary operation combines the values iteratively.

- **Folding and reducing**: Monoids provide a convenient way to fold or reduce data structures into a single value. By using the monoid's binary operation, you can combine the elements of a collection into a single result. This is commonly used in functional programming to compute summaries or to process large datasets efficiently.

- **Validation and error handling**: Monoids are useful for validating and handling errors in functional programming. By combining monoidal values that represent validation results or errors, you can collect and accumulate the results or errors. This allows you to perform multiple validations and obtain a final result or error that summarizes the outcome.

- **Functional composition**: Monoids enable function composition. You can compose multiple functions into a single function. This composability allows you to build complex computations from smaller, reusable components.

- **Concurrency and parallelism**: It can be used to combine results in concurrent or parallel computations. If you have multiple computations running concurrently or in parallel, you can use a monoid operation to combine their results into a single result. This allows you to aggregate the outcomes efficiently and process them further.

- **Abstracting over computations**: It provides a level of abstraction that allows you to write generic code that works with various types. By relying on the monoid interface, you can create reusable functions and libraries that operate on monoidal values without being tied to specific data structures or implementations. This promotes code modularity and extensibility.

By leveraging monoids, you can write code that is more expressive, modular, and reusable in functional programming. They provide a powerful abstraction for combining values and computations, enabling concise and efficient solutions to a wide range of problems.

Functors

In category theory, a functor is a mapping between categories that preserves the structure and relationships of objects and morphisms. Functors provide a way to relate categories and establish connections between them.

Figure 2.9 describes the specificity of functors, applicative functors and monads. Applicative functors are specialized functors which provides ability to sequence different functorial computations. Further, monads are more specialized version of applicative functors which provides ability to functorial computation to be dependent upon the result of other functorial computations.

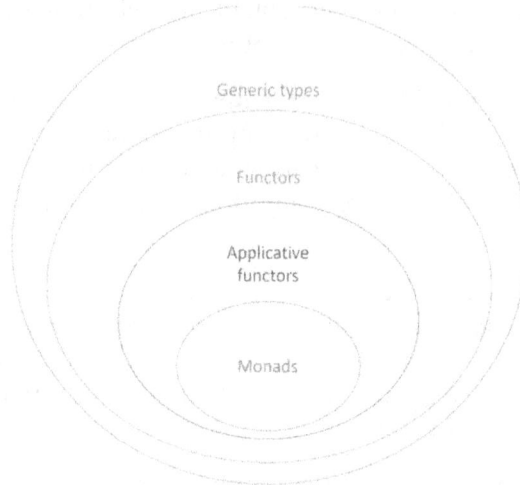

Figure 2.9: Relation between functors, applicative functors and monads

Definition

A functor *F: C -> D* is a mapping that associates each object in category *C* with an object in category *D* and each morphism in *C* with a morphism in *D*, while preserving the composition and identity properties.

Refer to the following figure:

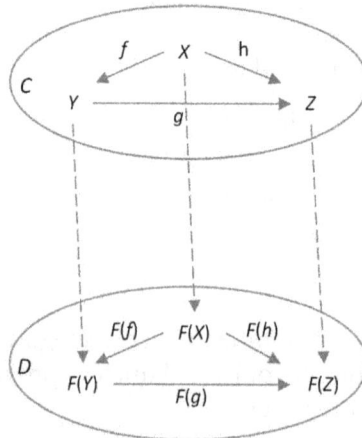

Figure 2.10: Dotted line represents functors F mapping object and morphism between category C and category D

For every object *A* in *C*, the functor assigns an object *F(A)* in *D*. Similarly, for every morphism *f: A -> B* in *C*, the functor assigns a morphism *F(f): F(A) -> F(B)* in *D*. The functor must satisfy the following conditions:

- **Preservation of identity**: For any object A in C, the functor must map the identity morphism $id\_A: A \rightarrow A$ to the identity morphism $id\_\{F(A)\}: F(A) \rightarrow F(A)$ in D. This ensures that the identity of objects is preserved.

- **Preservation of composition**: For any morphisms $f: A \rightarrow B$ and $g: B \rightarrow C$ in C, the functor must satisfy $F(g \circ f) = F(g) \circ F(f)$. In other words, the composition of morphisms in C is preserved under the functor.

Functors provide a way to translate concepts and structures from one category to another with structure-preserving mappings. They allow us to study and compare different categories by establishing relationships between their objects and morphisms.

Laws

There are two functors'[2] laws, as follows:

- Functor must preserve identity morphisms:

  ```
  fmap id = id
  ```

- Functor must preserve the composition of morphisms:

  ```
  fmap (g . h) = (fmap g) . (fmap h)
  ```

A binary tree may similarly be described as a functor:

```
1. data Tree a = Leaf | Node a (Tree a) (Tree a)
2. instance Functor Tree where
3.     fmap f Leaf         = Leaf
4.     fmap f (Node x l r) = Node (f x) (fmap f l) (fmap f r)
```

Usage

The following are some common use cases and benefits of using functors in functional programming:

- **Mapping over collections**: Functors allow us to apply a function to each element of a collection while preserving the structure of the collection. For example, we can map a function over a list, a Maybe value, or any other functor, modifying or extracting values in a consistent and uniform way.

- **Abstracting over effectful computations**: Functors provide a way to abstract over effectful computations, such as **input/output (I/O)** actions, Maybe computations, either computation, and more. By lifting a pure function into the context of a functor, we can apply it to values within that context. This abstraction allows us to write generic code that works with different types of effectful computations without being tightly coupled to a specific implementation.

---

2. https://hackage.haskell.org/package/base-4.21.0.0/docs/Data-Functor.html#t:Functor

- **Encapsulating side effects**: Functors allow to apply a function to the value it contains while preserving the structure of the functor. Hence it helps to run function which could create side effects inside the functional context which helps to encapsulate it inside functor context and still make it composable and predictable. For example, in the I/O monad in Haskell.

- **Building computational pipelines**: Functors, along with other abstractions like monads, allow us to build computational pipelines or chains of computations. By chaining multiple functor operations or combining functors with other monadic operations, we can create a sequence of computations that transform and process data step-by-step. This composability promotes code reuse, modularity, and clarity.

- **Enforcing laws and maintaining referential transparency**: Functors adhere to certain laws, such as the identity and composition laws, which ensure that the behavior of the functor operations is predictable and consistent. By following these laws, we can reason about our programs more effectively and maintain referential transparency, which is a key principle in functional programming.

- **Abstraction and generic programming**: Functors provide a level of abstraction that allows us to write generic code that works with various types. By relying on the functor interface, we can create reusable functions and libraries that operate on functors without being tied to specific data structures or implementations. This promotes code modularity and extensibility.

Overall, functors are a foundational concept in functional programming, providing a powerful mechanism for working with values within a context. They enable us to abstract over effectful computations, process collections of data, separate pure and impure code, and build composable and reusable code.

Applicative functor

An applicative functor is an intermediate structure between functors and monads. Applicative functors allow for functorial computations to be sequenced (unlike plain functors), but do not allow using results from prior computations in the definition of subsequent ones (unlike monads). Applicative functors are the programming equivalent of lax monoidal functors with tensorial strength in category theory.

Applicative functors[3] are also required to satisfy four equational laws, as follows:

- **Identity**: pure id <*> v = v
- **Composition**: pure (.) <*> u <*> v <*> w = u <*> (v <*> w)
- **Homomorphism**: pure f <*> pure x = pure (f x)
- **Interchange**: u <*> pure y = pure ($ y) <*> u

---

3. **https://hackage.haskell.org/package/base-4.21.0.0/docs/Control-Applicative.html**

Applicative functors can be used to combine values and functions within a functorial context. By leveraging the power of applicative functors, we can express complex computations that involve multiple values and effects in a concise and composable manner.

Applicative functors have a wide range of applications in functional programming, including parsing, concurrent programming, and dealing with effectful computations. They provide a convenient and compositional way to work with computations that involve multiple values and effects.

Usage

Applicative functors play a significant role in functional programming, providing a powerful tool for composing computations and working with effectful and container-like values. The following are some key aspects of applicative functors in functional programming:

- **Composing computations**: Applicative functors allow us to combine computations that involve multiple values or effects using composition to build complex computations from smaller, reusable components.

- **Working with effectful computations**: Applicative functors provide a way to lift functions that operate on plain values into the context of these effectful computations, enabling us to apply them to values inside the functors.

- **Validation and error handling**: By combining computations using the applicative operators, we can sequence multiple validations or computations and collect their results. If any validation fails or an error occurs, the overall result will reflect that.

- **Parsing and data manipulation**: Applicative functors are commonly used in parsing (for structured data like XML, JSON) and data manipulation tasks. Parser combinators often utilize applicative functors to combine smaller parsers into larger, more complex ones.

- **Concurrency and parallelism**: Applicative functors provide a way to express computations that can be executed concurrently or in parallel. By using the applicative operators, we can combine computations that are independent of each other, allowing them to be executed simultaneously.

- **Functor laws and compatibility**: Applicative functors adhere to a set of laws that govern their behavior, including identity, composition, and homomorphism laws. The adherence to these laws facilitates reasoning and ensures the correctness of programs.

Applicative functors provide a flexible and expressive way to work with computations involving effects, composition of functions, data manipulation, and more. They are a fundamental building block in functional programming and are widely used in various libraries and frameworks to facilitate the development of robust and composable code.

Foldable

In functional programming, the **Foldable** type class provides a way to abstractly fold or reduce a data structure into a single value by applying a combining function to the elements of the structure. The **Foldable** type class defines a set of common operations that can be performed on data structures, such as lists, trees, and other containers.

The **Foldable** type class is defined by the following methods:

- **foldr**: This method takes a combining function and a starting value, and it recursively combines the elements of the data structure from right to left.

- **foldl**: This method folds (operates) the elements from left to right.

- **foldMap**: This method applies a mapping function to each element of the data structure and combines the results using a monoidal operation.

Overall, **Foldable** provides a powerful abstraction for working with collections and performing generic folding operations, promoting code reuse and composability.

Usage

The following are some common use cases and examples of using **Foldable** in functional programming:

- **Folding a list**: The most common usage of **Foldable** is to fold or reduce a list into a single value.

- **Conversion to other data structures**: **Foldable** provides functions like **toList** and **toSet** that allow you to convert a data structure to a list or a set, respectively.

- **Concatenation and monoid operations**: **Foldable** provides functions like **concat** and **mconcat** that allow you to concatenate or combine the elements of a data structure. These operations are particularly useful when working with monoids, as **Foldable** leverages the **Monoid** type class to perform the combining operation.

- **Traversing and applying functions**: **Foldable** provides the **traverse_** and **sequenceA_** functions, which allow you to traverse a data structure and apply a function to each element. This is useful when you want to perform an action on each element of a structure, such as printing or logging.

- **Custom foldable instances**: You can define your own instances of the **Foldable** type class for custom data types. By implementing the **foldr**, **foldMap**, or **toList** functions for your data type, you can leverage the rich set of functions provided by **Foldable**.

Overall, **Foldable** provides a generic way to fold, traverse, and manipulate data structures in a functional and abstract manner. It allows you to write code that is more reusable and modular by relying on the common operations defined by **Foldable** rather than specific functions tailored to each data structure.

Traversal

In category theory, traversal refers to a concept that allows you to navigate and transform the components of a composite object within a category. Traversal is a generalization of the notion of traversing and modifying data structures in functional programming.

In category theory, a traversal is typically defined as a natural transformation between two endofunctors. It captures the ability to traverse and transform the components of a composite object in a structured and compositional manner. The traversal provides a way to navigate through the object and apply a transformation to each component while maintaining the overall structure.

A traversal consists of the following components:

- **Source endofunctor**: The source endofunctor represents the composite object or structure that you want to traverse. It maps objects within the category to themselves, while preserving the structure of the composite object.

- **Target endofunctor**: The target endofunctor represents the transformed composite object after applying the traversal. It also maps objects within the category to themselves, but with potential modifications to the individual components.

- **Natural transformation**: The traversal is realized as a natural transformation from the source endofunctor to the target endofunctor. This natural transformation captures the navigation and transformation of components within the composite object.

The key idea behind a traversal is to provide a way to modify the individual components of a composite object without changing the overall structure. It allows you to apply a given transformation or computation uniformly to each component while maintaining the relationships and connections between them.

Traversals have wide applications in various areas, including functional programming, data manipulation, and data analysis. They provide a way to traverse, modify, and transform complex data structures while preserving the structure and relationships within them.

Traversable type class in functional programming is associated with several properties and laws that ensure its consistent behavior and maintain the desired semantics.

Properties

The following are the key properties of **Traversable**:

- **Preservation of structure**: It preserves the structure of the container it operates on. This means that traversing a container and then mapping over it should be equivalent to mapping over it and then traversing it. The order of traversal should not affect the resulting structure.

- **Composition of traversals**: `Traversable` supports the composition of traversals. This means that if you traverse a container with a composed function, it should be equivalent to traversing the container with each function individually and then composing the results. This property ensures that traversals can be combined and composed in a meaningful way.

- **Sequence preservation**: `Traversable` preserves the sequence of effects. This property ensures that the order in which effects are accumulated remains the same as the order of elements in the container. It guarantees that the traversal is performed in a predictable and consistent manner.

Laws

The following are the key laws of **Traversable**:

- **Naturality law**: The naturality law ensures that traverse preserves the structure of the container.

- **Identity law**: The identity law states that traversing a container with the identity applicative should return the same container.

- **Composition law**: The composition law ensures that composing two functions and then traversing a container is equivalent to traversing the container with the composed function.

In functional programming, **Traversable** is a type class that extends the capabilities of functor and foldable by providing a way to traverse a data structure while accumulating a result. The main idea behind **Traversable** is to provide a way to apply a function that returns an applicative effect to each element of a container and then accumulate the results into a single applicative value.

Overall, **Traversable** provides a powerful abstraction for generic traversal and accumulation of data structures in a functional and type-safe manner. It allows you to write code that is more reusable and modular by abstracting over the specific data structures and their traversal semantics.

Usage

Traversable is a powerful type class in functional programming that provides a uniform way to traverse and accumulate results from data structures. It allows you to perform operations on each element of a container and collect the results in a structured and controlled manner. The following are some common use cases and examples of using **Traversable** in functional programming:

- **Mapping over elements**: **Traversable** allows you to apply a function to each element of a container and collect the results. This is particularly useful when you have a container of values and want to transform each value independently, for example, you can use traverse to apply a parsing function to each element of a list and collect the parsed results.

- **Accumulating results**: `Traversable` enables you to accumulate results while traversing a container. This is helpful when you need to combine or accumulate values during the traversal process., for instance, you can use traverse to accumulate a sum or product of the elements in a list.

- **Effectful traversals**: `Traversable` allows you to perform effectful operations on each element of a container. This is useful when you have a container of values wrapped in some effect, such as Maybe or I/O, and you want to perform an effectful operation on each element, for example, you can use traverse to perform an I/O operation on each element of a list.

- **Sequence of effects**: `Traversable` provides the `sequenceA` function, which allows you to sequence a container of effects into a single effect that collects the results. This is useful when you have a container of effects, such as a list of Maybe values, and you want to collect the results while preserving the sequencing of effects.

- **Error handling and validation**: `Traversable` is often used for error handling and validation scenarios., for example, you can use traverse to apply a validation function to each element of a container and collect the validation results, or use `sequenceA` to sequence a container of either values and propagate the first encountered error.

- **Generic programming**: `Traversable` is a key building block for generic programming, allowing you to write code that works uniformly across a variety of data structures. By abstracting over the `Traversable` type class, you can write generic functions that traverse and operate on various containers, such as lists, trees, maps, etc.

`Traversable` is particularly useful when combined with other type classes, such as **Functor** and **Applicative**, as it provides a unified approach to traversing and accumulating results from data structures. It allows you to write code that is more modular, reusable, and abstract, by separating the traversal logic from the specific container types.

Monad

A monad is a monoid in the category of endofunctors.

In category theory, monads are a construct that generalizes the notion of monads in functional programming. They provide a way to describe computations or effects in a category theoretic setting. The concept of monads in category theory is more abstract and focuses on the relationships between objects and morphisms in a category.

In category theory, a monad consists of the following three components:

- **Endofunctor**: A monad is defined by an endofunctor (a functor from a category to itself) that maps objects and morphisms within the same category. This endofunctor represents the computational context or effect that the monad encapsulates.

- **Unit**: The unit, also known as the **return** or **pure**, is a natural transformation that assigns to each object in the category an arrow from the object to the image of the object under the endofunctor. It represents the capability to lift a value into the monadic context.

- **Multiplication**: The multiplication, also known as **bind** or **join**, is a natural transformation that takes the image of an object under the endofunctor and produces an arrow from the image to the image itself. It represents the ability to sequence and compose computations within the monadic context.

Monads in category theory provide a powerful tool for studying and analyzing computations and effects in a general categorical setting. They allow for the composition and manipulation of morphisms within a category while maintaining the necessary structure and coherence. The concept of monads in category theory has applications in areas such as functional programming, type theory, and denotational semantics, where it provides a formal and abstract framework for understanding and reasoning about computations.

Properties

The properties of a monad are as follows:

- **Associativity**: The bind operation often represented as **>>=** or **flatMap** in a monad is associative. This means that the order in which monadic operations are composed does not matter. This property ensures that the sequencing of monadic actions is consistent and independent of the specific order in which they are composed.

- **Identity**: Every monad has an identity element, which is typically represented as **return** or **pure**. Applying the identity element to a value and then using bind to compose it with a monadic action should be equivalent to simply applying the monadic action to the value.

Laws

The laws are as follows:

- **Left identity law**: Applying the identity element to a value and then binding it with a function f should be equivalent to just applying f to the value.

- **Right identity law**: Binding a monadic action *ma* with the identity element should be equivalent to the original monadic action *ma* itself.

- **Associativity law**: It ensures that the bind operation is associative.

These laws ensure that monadic operations behave consistently and compose in a predictable manner.

Usage

Monads are a central concept in functional programming, providing a way to sequence and compose computations that involve effects or context. They offer a powerful abstraction for working with effectful computations, such as handling state, handling errors, working with asynchronous operations, and more. The following are some common use cases and benefits of using monads in functional programming:

- **Effectful programming**: Monads provide a structured and composable approach to working with effectful computations. Whether it is handling I/O operations, managing state, dealing with exceptions, or performing asynchronous operations, monads allow you to encapsulate these effects and reason about them in a controlled manner.

- **Sequential composition**: Monads enable you to sequence computations in a predictable order. Each monadic operation represents a step in a computation, and by chaining these operations together, you can create a sequence of computations where the output of one step feeds into the input of the next. This sequential composition simplifies the management of dependencies and ordering.

- **Error handling and validation**: Monads facilitate error handling and validation by providing mechanisms for handling exceptions or alternative computations. For instance, the Maybe monad allows you to express computations that may produce a result or nothing. In contrast, the Either monad enables computations that can either produce a value or an error.

- **State management**: Monads can be used to manage state within computations. By carrying along a state value and threading it through a sequence of monadic operations, you can ensure that each operation has access to the current state and can modify it accordingly. This helps in maintaining data consistency and enables stateful computations.

- **Asynchronous and concurrent programming**: Monads are commonly used to handle asynchronous and concurrent operations. By utilizing monads like Future or Task, you can express computations that perform asynchronous operations, such as fetching data from a remote server or executing operations concurrently. Monads provide a structured way to manage the complexity of such computations.

- **Resource management**: Monads can be employed for managing resources that require acquisition and release, such as file handles, database connections, or network sockets. Monads like ResourceT or Bracket provide mechanisms for acquiring and releasing resources safely and automatically, even in the presence of exceptions.

- **Domain-specific languages**: Monads can be utilized to create **domain-specific languages (DSLs)** that abstract over specific computational patterns or workflows. By defining a monad instance for a custom data type, you can give it semantics that align with the desired DSL, allowing you to write expressive and concise code in a specific problem domain.

Reader monad

In functional programming, the reader monad is a common abstraction used to manage dependencies and provide a way to access values that are read or shared across multiple computations. It allows you to pass values as arguments implicitly, making the code more modular and decoupled from specific environments.

The reader monad represents a computation that depends on some environment or configuration. It wraps a function that takes an environment as input and produces a result. The primary benefit of using the reader monad is that it allows you to thread the environment implicitly through a chain of computations without manually passing it as an argument.

Usage

The following are some key aspects of the reader monad in functional programming:

- **Environment management**: The reader monad provides a mechanism for managing and accessing an environment within a computation. The environment typically contains values or configurations that are needed by various parts of the code.

- **Implicit dependency injection**: With the reader monad, you can inject dependencies implicitly, eliminating the need for explicit argument passing. Instead of explicitly passing the environment to each function, the reader monad takes care of passing the environment behind the scenes.

- **Modularity and separation of concerns**: The reader monad allows you to separate the concerns of obtaining values from the concerns of using those values. By encapsulating the environment in the reader monad, you can focus on the computation logic without worrying about how the values are obtained.

- **Dependency inversion**: The reader monad facilitates dependency inversion, where the control flow depends on abstract interfaces rather than concrete implementations. By using the reader monad, you can define an abstract interface (the reader) that represents the environment and provide different implementations for different contexts or environments.

- **Testability and reusability**: The reader monad promotes testability by decoupling the computation logic from the specific environment. You can create different instances of the reader monad with different environments for testing or reusing the computation in different contexts.

- **Composability and sequencing**: The reader monad can be easily composed with other monads or monadic operations, enabling the sequencing of computations that involve both dependency management and other effects. This composability allows you to build complex workflows from smaller, reusable components.

The reader monad is particularly useful in scenarios where you have a computation that requires access to a shared environment, such as accessing configuration settings, database connections, or other shared resources. By using the reader monad, you can manage these dependencies in a modular and flexible way, promoting code reuse and maintainability.

Writer monad

In functional programming, the writer monad is an abstraction that allows you to perform computations while also accumulating a log or a sequence of values alongside the computation. It provides a way to add a logging capability to computations in a composable and efficient manner. The writer monad is commonly used for scenarios where you need to collect and accumulate information or side effects during the computation.

Properties

The properties of writer monad are as follows:

- **Identity**: The identity property states that if you start with a pure value and perform a computation in the writer monad, the result should be the same as the original value, without any modifications to the accumulated log. Mathematically, it can be expressed, as follows:

$$runWriter(pure\ x) == (x, mempty)$$

This property ensures that pure computations do not affect the accumulated log.

- **Composition**: The composition property states that if you perform two sequential computations in the writer monad, the accumulated logs should be combined in the expected way.

  This property ensures that the order of computation and log accumulation is preserved when composing sequential computations.

- **Associativity**: The associativity property states that if you compose three sequential computations in the writer monad, the order of execution should not affect the accumulated logs.

  This property ensures that the grouping of computations and log accumulation does not affect the final result.

Usage

The following are some common use cases and benefits of using the writer monad in functional programming:

- **Logging**: The writer monad is often used for logging purposes. It allows you to perform computations while simultaneously appending log messages or values to a log. Each operation in the computation can contribute to the log, and the accumulated log can be extracted at the end of the computation.

- **Stateful computations**: The writer monad can be used for computations that maintain an additional state alongside the main result. The additional state can be updated and transformed throughout the computation, and the writer monad takes care of tracking and combining these states.

- **Debugging and tracing**: The writer monad is useful for adding debugging or tracing capabilities to computations. By logging intermediate values or execution steps, you can gain insights into the computation process and diagnose issues.

- **Performance monitoring**: The writer monad can be employed to collect performance metrics or statistical data during computations. By logging relevant information at different stages of the computation, you can analyze and optimize the performance of your code.

- **Audit trails and history tracking**: The writer monad allows you to build audit trails or track the history of computations. By appending relevant information or events to the log, you can later review and analyze the sequence of actions that led to a particular result.

- **Side effects encapsulation**: The writer monad provides a way to encapsulate side effects within a computation while maintaining purity. By performing the side effects such as logging within the context of the writer monad, you can isolate and manage the effects in a controlled manner.

- **Composability and sequencing**: The writer monad can be composed with other monads or monadic operations, enabling the sequencing of computations that involve logging or accumulating values. This composability allows you to build complex workflows from smaller, reusable components.

The writer monad is a powerful abstraction for computations that involve logging or value accumulation. It allows you to separate the concerns of performing the computation from the concerns of collecting and managing additional information or side effects. By using the writer monad, you can write code that is more modular, reusable, and maintainable, while still having the ability to track and analyze the progress of the computation.

State monad

In functional programming, the state monad is a powerful abstraction that allow to manage and manipulate state within computations. It provides a way to encapsulate stateful computations in a pure and composable manner. The state monad is commonly used in scenarios where you need to maintain and update state across multiple steps or computations.

The following are the main properties and laws associated with the state monad:

- **Identity**: The identity property states that if you start with a pure value and perform a computation in the state monad, the result should be the same as the original value, without any modifications to the state. This property ensures that pure computations do not affect the state.

- **Composition**: The composition property states that if you perform two sequential computations in the state monad, the resulting state should be the same as if you performed the individual computations and then combined the states manually. This property ensures that the order of computation and state transformation is preserved when composing sequential computations.

- **Associativity**: The associativity property states that if you compose three sequential computations in the state monad, the order of execution should not affect the resulting state. This property ensures that the grouping of computations and state transformation does not affect the final resulting state.

Usage

The following are some common use cases and benefits of using the state monad in functional programming:

- **Mutable state simulation**: It promotes immutability. Instead of using mutable variables, you define a stateful computation as a sequence of transformations on an immutable state. Each computation updates the state, and the state monad takes care of threading the updated state to subsequent computations.

- **Modularity and separation of concerns**: It separates the state management logic from the core computation. By encapsulating state within the state monad, you can focus on the computation itself without worrying about how the state is manipulated.

- **Dependency injection**: The state monad can be used for dependency injection, allowing you to pass state as an argument implicitly. The state monad handles the state propagation automatically, simplifying the code and reducing the need for explicit dependencies.

- **Stateful computations**: The state monad is useful for stateful transformations or operations. It provides a structured way to sequence and compose these operations, ensuring that each operation has access to the current state and can modify it accordingly without fear of accidently overriding of state.

- **Backtracking and exploration**: The state monad can be utilized for backtracking and exploration algorithms. By maintaining the state within the monad, you can easily backtrack to previous states or explore different paths, making it suitable for search algorithms, constraint solvers, or parsing applications.

- **Parsing and lexing**: The state monad is often used in parsing and lexing applications, where maintaining a parsing or lexing state is crucial. By using the state monad, you can keep track of the parsing or lexing state throughout the computation, making it easier to implement complex parsers or lexers.

- **Resource management**: The state monad can be employed for managing resources that require acquisition and release, such as file handles, database connections, or network sockets. By encapsulating the state of these resources within the state monad, you can ensure proper acquisition and release in a controlled manner.

The state monad provides a structured and composable approach to working with stateful computations in functional programming. It allows you to write code that is modular, reusable, and maintainable, while still maintaining the benefits of immutability and referential transparency. By leveraging the state monad, you can manage and manipulate state in a pure and controlled way, leading to more reliable and predictable code.

Optics

Optics refer to a set of abstractions and techniques used to manipulate and compose complex structures, such as data structures or immutable values. Optics provide a way to focus on specific parts of a structure and perform operations on them, while abstracting away the underlying details of the structure itself.

The fundamental idea behind optics is that they enable you to view a structure through a specific lens or perspective, allowing you to access, modify, or traverse its components in a precise and composable manner. Optics provide a way to zoom in on specific parts of a structure while maintaining referential transparency and immutability.

There are several types of optics commonly used in category theory, as follows:

- **Lenses**: Lenses allow you to access and modify a specific part of a larger structure, typically a record or a product type. They consist of two functions: A getter that extracts the focused part from the whole structure, and a setter that updates the focused part and returns a new structure with the modification.

- **Prisms**: Prisms are used to work with sum types or disjoint unions. They allow you to focus on specific alternative values within a sum type and handle them differently. Prisms provide functions to both check if a value matches a specific alternative and to construct the sum type with the desired alternative.

- **Traversals**: Traversals are used to traverse and modify multiple elements in a structure. They allow you to apply a function or an operation to every element within a container, such as a list or a tree, and collect the results in a new structure of the same shape.

- **Isomorphisms**: Isomorphisms represent a bidirectional relationship between two structures, allowing you to convert between them without any loss of information. They provide functions to convert from one structure to another and back, while ensuring the preservation of the underlying data.

Optics provide a powerful and composable way to manipulate and transform complex structures, promoting modularity and code reuse. They abstract away the specific details of the data structures and allow you to work with them in a uniform and generic manner.

Usage

The following are some common use cases and examples of optics usage in functional programming:

- **Accessing and modifying fields**: Optics, such as lenses, allow to access and modify individual fields within a data structure. This is useful when we want to update specific parts of a record or data type without affecting the rest. For example, using a lens, you can get or set the value of a specific field in a record or update a property in a nested data structure.

- **Traversing and transforming collections**: Traversals optics allow to apply a single modification to be applied to all collection. It iterates to all the object one by one and apply the modification to each object.

- **Handling optional values**: Prisms are useful for working with optional values or sum types. They allow to handle specific cases or alternatives within a sum type, such as dealing with a Just value in a Maybe type or accessing specific constructors in an algebraic data type. Prisms provide a way to focus on and manipulate these alternatives.

- **Composing optics**: These optics units can be combined using composition and hence could be used with more complex structure. It also enabled to work with nested fields with composed optics. Hence, it helps to reuse and existing optics to work in more sophisticated transformations.

- **Data validation and error handling**: Prisms with lenses provide a powerful mechanism for data validation and error handling. Prism focus on specific type in union type and lenses helps to modify or update any invalid values. It provides a mechanism to transform the data while ensuring correctness and maintain immutability.

By using optics, functional programmers can write code that is modular, reusable, and focused on specific aspects of the data structure. Optics libraries provide a unified and type-safe approach to manipulating complex data, allowing for concise and maintainable code. Popular optics libraries, like lens in Haskell or monocle in Scala, provide a rich set of abstractions and combinators for optics-based programming.

Conclusion

In this chapter, we covered the mathematical approach behind the functional programming which is category theory. We dug deeper into what category is, how it is made up of (objects and morphism), and important properties (identity, composability). We also looked at the different constructs and algebraic structure it provides, and how category theory help to study the structures and its relations ships.

We also leveraged how functional programming gets benefitted from all those concepts and how we can apply these mathematical concepts to solve real-world problem in a robust and easy reasoning manner. We also looked at how small component or structure works and how these structures, solve bigger problem with same ease as smaller problem.

In next chapter, we will apply our functional concepts and develop code using these concepts. We will use Scala language for developing functional modules. The choice of language is made based on its support for functional concepts which is anonymous functions, higher order functions, nested functions, currying, pattern-matching and its extended support for pure functions.

Join our Discord space

Join our Discord workspace for latest updates, offers, tech happenings around the world, new releases, and sessions with the authors:

https://discord.bpbonline.com

CHAPTER 3
Introduction to Scala

Introduction

This chapter provides a concise overview of the Scala programming language for readers who may not be familiar with its syntax and core constructs.

This chapter further talks about why Scala has been chosen for functional programming. All features that the language provides are aligned with a functional programming approach, which supports writing functional programs using the Scala language. Scala provides both object-oriented and functional programming.

Structure

In this chapter, we will cover the following topics:

- Scala
- Hands on Scala
- Scala for functional programming
- Function as first-class citizen
- Lambda function
- Closures
- Currying

- Partial applied function
- Functional implementation

Objectives

By the end of this chapter, readers will get a quick tour of Scala language. Further, reader will also go through what benefits Scala provides and how its technical constructs allow to write functional programming easily and how it is inclined to category theory which favors functional programming.

Scala

Scala is a modern multi-paradigm programming language designed to express common programming patterns in a concise, elegant, and type-safe way. It seamlessly integrates features of object-oriented and functional languages.[1]

It is **Java Virtual Machine (JVM)** based language. It means that it compiles to run on JVM (same as Java). It is my own opinion but Scala is an upgraded version of Java. It is static typed language. It uses the type metadata to provide many functionalities and ensures the program correctness. It supports object oriented and functional both programming paradigm. The best part is that it can use Java code in Scala programs (interoperable with Java) and hence it opens the gates for whole new world. As Java is so vastly used and it contains production ready for all sorts of libraries so reusing the same would minimize the effort without reinventing the wheel to create production ready application and it adds its updated functionalities on top of it.

Scala as object-oriented

Scala is an **object-oriented programming (OOP)** language. Every value in Scala is an object.

It also has OOP features, as follows:

- Inheritance
- Encapsulation
- Abstraction
- Polymorphism

Scala as functional

Scala treats every function as a value. It also supports all programming constructs which is required to write a functional program. It follows immutability and default data structure are immutable by default. It supports functions as first-class citizens, just like integers and strings. Moreover, higher order functions, pattern matching, lazy evaluation, pure functions

---

1. **https://scala-lang.org/**

(no side-effects and same output for same input always), and referential transparency, all these feature that helps to write a functional program easily and more efficiently.

Scala as statically typed

Strongly statically types meaning that each value or expression in language has its own types. These enforced types are very much useful to validate the correctness of code in compile time. For example, if there is a big expression where many manipulations are being done, if its types do not match with its resultant types then Scala type system used by **integrated development environment** (**IDE**) itself give error without at the same time instead of during running the program.

The following are other benefits for being a statically typed language:

- Enhanced tooling
- Performance optimization
- Documentation
- Readability, type itself
- Type-safety, able to catch error at compile time

Scala as extensible

Scala is known for its extensibility. It provides all the mechanisms and language tools that allow developers to extend the language itself for their own out-of-the-box domain requirements. This extensibility makes it language so powerful.

The following are the language tools for implementing extensibility:

- Implicit conversions and parameters
- Type classes
- Mixins and traits
- Macros (extension methods)

Scala interoperates with Java

Scala provides interoperability with Java language which ensures that Java code can be used in Scala programs which enables Scala to use all battle tested production ready libraries which reduces effort involved for creating those functionalities and allows to apply functional programming features on top of it. So, Scala enjoys best of both worlds.

Hands-on Scala

We discussed about Scala language and its features. Now, let us see how to setup Scala in our local and what other options are available for same to install Scala.

We will use macOS Ventura 13.4.1, but we will also update how it can be done in Microsoft Windows. So, let us get started.

Currently, the following are the two branches available for Scala version:

- Scala 2.13.xx
- Scala 3.x.x

Scala 2.13.xx is using updates for the Scala 2 branch, whereas there have been major rewrites or updates in the Scala 2 version, and the Scala 3 version has been created.

We will be using Scala 3.3.0 version across the book for any code.

The following are the differences between Scala 2 and Scala 3:

Feature	Scala 2	Scala 3
Syntax and language features	Traditional Scala syntax with some complexity	Simplified and more uniform syntax, reducing syntactic overhead
Type inference	Type inference can sometimes be limited and require explicit type annotations	Improved type inference, reducing the need for explicit type annotations
Enums	Enums are not available	Introduces enums as a language construct
Union types	Union types are not available	Introduces union types, allowing values of multiple types
Intersection types	Intersection types are not available	Introduces intersection types, combining multiple types
Implicit resolution	Implicit resolution can be complex and sometimes leads to unexpected behavior	Improved implicit resolution with more predictability
Macro system	Scala 2 has a macro system, which can be complex and sometimes difficult to use	Introduces a new macro system called inline meta, providing a simpler and more predictable metaprogramming mechanism
Java interoperability	Interoperability with Java requires some workarounds and can have limitations	Aims to improve interoperability with Java and align language constructs and APIs
Tooling and IDE support	Tooling and IDE support is well-established and mature	Enhancements made to the dotty compiler for faster compilation times and better error messages
Backward compatibility		Aims to maintain backward compatibility to ensure a smooth transition for existing codebases Backward compatibility with Scala 2 is maintained

Table 3.1: Scala 2 vs. Scala 3 features comparisons

Scala installation

The following are the ways to install Scala:

- **Mac installation using coursier cli**:

  Coursier (**https://get-coursier.io/**) is Scala artefact fetching tool. It is for Scala what **npm** is for Node. It easily allows to download all dependent libraries or any other Scala artefact (even Scala itself).

  First, we have to install **coursier** itself and will use **brew** to install the same. **brew** is package manager for mac. **https://brew.sh/**.

- **brew install coursier/formulas/coursier**:

This installs **coursier** on your system. Now, **coursier** is available with **cs** command in your Terminal. If you want the latest Scala 3, following is a simple way:

```
cs setup
```

Commands	Description
`scalac`	Scala compiler
`scala`	Scala REPL and script runner
`scala-cli`	Scala CLI, interactive toolkit for Scala
`sbt, sbtn`	The **sbt** build tool
`amm`	Ammonite is an enhanced REPL
`scalafmt`	Scalafmt is the Scala code formatter

Table 3.2: Scala Command tools

- If you want to install any other Scala version, it is also easy with **cs**, as follows:
  ```
  cs install scala:2.13.11 scalac:2.13.11
  ```

- **Windows installation**:
  - Coursier installer is available for windows which can be downloaded from the following:

    https://github.com/coursier/coursier/releases/latest/download/cs-x86_64 pc-win32.zip

  - **Now run**:
    ```
    cs setup
    ```

Scala IDE

Now, Scala is installed on your local system. It is time to run some Scala code to get our hand dirty. There are many better IDEs available for Scala development, as follows:

- **IntelliJ IDEA for Scala (https://www.jetbrains.com/idea/)**: IntelliJ IDEA has better support for Scala. Scala support is available as a plugin in IntelliJ IDEA. This is a commercialized IDE for the ultimate edition, so you have to pay the license. However, there is a community edition available, but there are some feature restrictions, so you would not get the full-fledged Scala IDE features and with the Scala plugin.

- **Visual Studio Code (https://code.visualstudio.com/)**: **Visual Studio Code** (VS Code) is free code editor from Microsoft. It is very light and easy to use. It also supports plugin structure and Scala is supported by metals (**https://scalameta.org/metals/docs/editors/vscode/**) VS Code plugin. It provides support for Scala 3 also. We will use this code editor for all code development in this book but you can use any of your choice.

In *Figure 3.1*, VS Code screen has been shared where Scala 3 is being run using metals plugin:

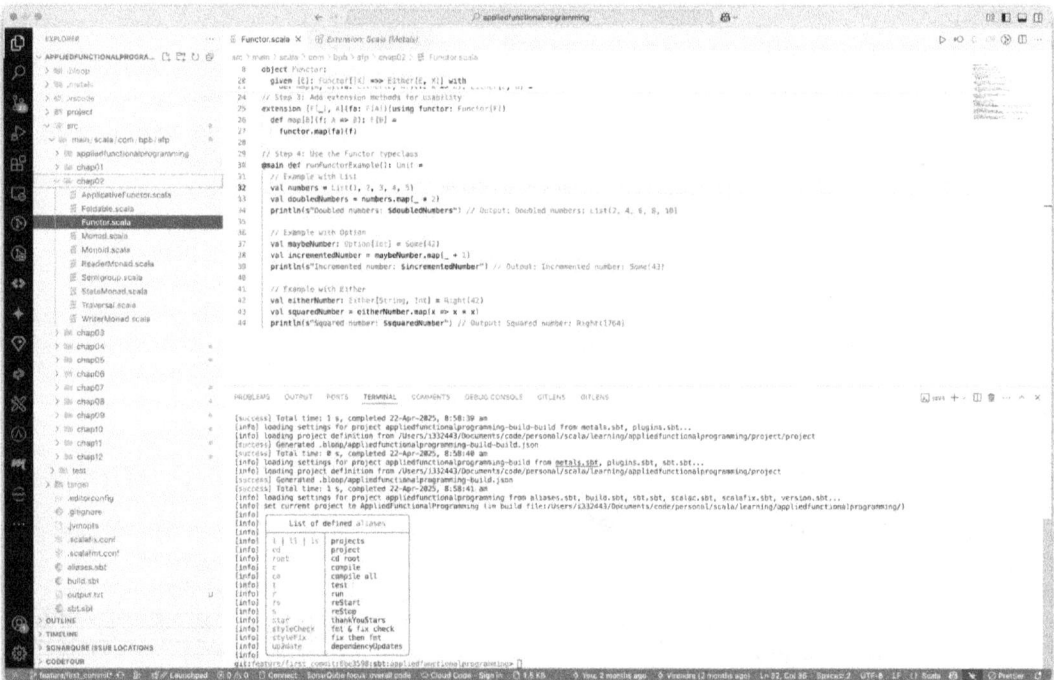

Figure 3.1: VS Code running metals plugin

Scala for functional programming

Scala is a programming language which supports functional programming as one of its core paradigms. It treats function as a value same as any other integer, character, or double in any other programming language. It allows functions to be treated as other values. For example, it could be saved in variable, passed to function as parameter and can be returned from any other function. As function represents a dynamic behavior (depends upon function implementation), it provides a lot of power and dynamicity to programming.

```
1. val operation1: (Int, Int) => Int = (a, b) => a + b
```

Above function type is **(Int, Int) => Int**, which represents that it takes two integer as input and one integer as output. Now, another higher order function could take this function type as input parameter **(Int, Int) => Int** and can used for its own implementation.

```
1. val implementer:(Int, Int, (Int, Int) => Int ) =>
   Int = (a, b, f) => f(a,b)
```

Note: **This function f can be implemented in many ways and implementer is used to apply that function.**

The following are other features that help a lot in Scala to be treated as functional programming:

- Higher order function
- Lambda function
- Closures
- Currying
- Partial applied function

Function as first-class values

We already discussed about what does function as first-class values in programming language mean. Let us explore it in greater depth to uncover its hidden strengths and understand why it is so essential.

If function is not available as first-class value, then each function will only accept values other than function, then function implementation would be very static as it can only accept integers, characters, string, double which does not contain any dynamic values, then function implementation would also be very static as those input parameters could only be used to implement available logic.

Now, function being a first-class citizen, it provides the ability to consume a function (dynamic behavior) as a function parameter, and it can also be stored in a data structure, just like other integers or strings. Function is represented by a function type.

The following is a dissect of the functional types and what information they describe about the function structure:

- Function with one integer input parameter and one integer output parameter, as follows:

  Int => Int

All parameters before `=>` are all input parameters and all parameters after `=>` are all output parameters.

- Function with two inputs and one string output:
  (Int, Int) => String

- Function with one integer, one string, and one string output parameter:
  (Int, String) => String

- Function with two integers, one string, and one string output parameter:
  (Int, Int, String) => String

The following are defined functional values template:

val <function name> : <function type> = <function implementation>

The following are the examples as per above function template:

```
1. val add : (Int, Int, Int ) => Int = (a, b, c) => a+b+c
2. val addStringOutput : (Int, Int) => String = (a, b) =>
   "output of addition is "+ (a+b)
```

Now, you saw that function itself can be created with **val**. Now, referencing function (a behavior) provides a lot of capability to move behavior around instead of only values integer, character string etc.

It is important to mention about methods in Scala. These two terms are used interchangeably where methods are also providing implementation of logic. It can be defined as follows:

```
1. def add(a: Int, b: Int) : Int = {
2. a+b
3. }
```

The following is the difference between methods and functions:

	Methods	Functions
Syntax and convocation	Defined within classes or objects and invoked on instances using dot notation	Standalone entities that are invoked directly by calling the function name
Closures and capturing	Have access to the internal state of the class or object they belong to	Can capture values from their surrounding lexical context
Currying and partial application	Do not inherently support currying or partial application	Can be curried and partially applied
Polymorphism and overloading	Can participate in polymorphism and overloading	Cannot participate in polymorphism or overloading directly

Table 3.3: Difference between method and function

Higher order function

Higher order function are the functions which uses function as input parameter or can return function as output. It is the fundamental concept in functional programming that uses functions as values and applies this to provide dynamic behavior, which is used within functions and, similarly, returns a function as output, creating dynamic behavior within the function and returning it to be used later.

It is essential for functional programming techniques that need a function as a parameter, like **map**, **filter**, **reduce**, or **compose**. It enables code reuse, modularity, and the ability to create higher abstractions. Scala's support for higher order functions allow you to write expressive and concise code and facilitates the construction of flexible and composable programs.

The following is an example of each variation:

- **Function as input parameter**: As discussed earlier, there are many functions that work upon another function to provide more abstract or general behavior out of it. Hence, it provides a more generalized function implementation, which inherently gets applied in many different scenarios, and less code for achieving the same functionality.

  Let us take an example of the **map** function, which is available for collections. It is actually a functor which provides a generalized implementation of converting all elements of type **A** to type **B**, if it provides conversion of single element type **A** to type **B,** as follows:

  ```
  1. def map[B] (f: (A) => B ) : List[B]
  2. def map[B] (f: (A) => B ) : Option[B]
  ```

  It applies this generic behavior to all elements in list but it needs to know how can it convert a single element **A** to element **B**. As type **A** and type **B** could be anything. So somehow this conversion behavior for single element needs to be passed to understand and apply the same across all elements of type **A** to type **B**. It would not be possible if function was not taken as input.

  There are many fundamental functions that provide the same generalization and need single behavior as an input, as follows:

  ```
  1. def filter (p: (A) => Boolean ) : List[A]
  2. def foldLeft [B] (z: B) (op: (B, A) => B ) : B
  ```

Function returned as output

There are other functions which are output functions too, instead of only being input function. Both the functions have different purpose for their own existence. When higher order function is applied as input, it would use it to apply to dynamic behavior, whereas the returning function as output provides creating that dynamic behavior.

The following is an example:

```
1. def createGreetingFunction(greeting: String): String => String = {
2.   (name: String) => s"$greeting, $name!"
3. }
```

The method **createGreetingFunction** is responsible for creating a function which accept **name** as parameter and provide the greeting to that person with the dynamic content provided to method.

The following are two functions that are generated with different greeting content. One is **Hello** whereas another is **Hi**.

```
1. val greetWithHello: String => String = createGreetingFunction("Hello")
2. val greetWithHi: String => String = createGreetingFunction("Hi")
```

These different functions are applied with a name that provide those specific greetings to that name, as follows:

```
1. val message1 = greetWithHello("Alice") // Result: "Hello, Alice!"
2. val message2 = greetWithHi("Bob")      // Result: "Hi, Bob!"
```

Lambda functions

Lambda functions are anonymous functions that are not assigned to any variable. These are small, concise, and more importantly, one-off functions that generally do not require further reference and are mainly used as a parameter for other higher order functions. We already discussed higher order functions, which focused on taking a function as a parameter (or returning a function as output).

Each higher order function call will require the function to be declared, which makes the code very clumsy, cluttered, and hard to maintain. Hence, Lambda functions are invented to provide those small functions as input to higher order functions without the need to declare them first.

Let us say we have a list of integers and we need to double them, so we can use of lambda syntax to define a double function inside the higher order function call, as follows:

```
1. val numbers: List[Int] = List (1,2,3,4,5,6)
2. numbers.map( (i: Int) => i * 2)
```

So, instead of creating new **doubler** function like **val doubler: Int => Int = n => n * 2**, we directly provided function inside the map function using lambda syntax which is as follows:

(<variable name> : <variable type>) => <function implementation>

Scala type inference already knows that each element provided to this lambda function is an **Int**. Hence, we can remove that and can be written, as follows:

```
1. numbers.map( (i) => i * 2)
```

As there is only one parameter, hence, even brackets can be removed in the parameter list, as follows:

```
1. numbers.map( i => i * 2)
```

Scala further helps to reduce the function description as the parameter is used only once. Hence, it can be replaced with _ (underscore) and the function can further be simplified, as follows:

```
1. numbers.map( _ * 2)
```

This is the power of lambda function which make code more concise and easier to understand.

Closures

Closure is the function whose result depends on one or more free variables.

Free variables are those variables that are not defined inside the function implementation, but the function is dependent upon their value for its execution.

Following is an example:

There is a function that calculates simple interest on a principal. We all know that it needs two variables, as follows:

- Principal amount
- Rate of interest

The following function is defined with only one input as principal amount and using rate of interest for calculating interest:

```
1. val calculateSimpleInterest : Double => Double =
   (principal : Double) => (principal * rate ) / 100
2. print(calculateSimpleInterest(100))
```

As you can see, the **rate** is not defined but is used to calculate interest. When you run it, the compiler will give an error. Place this definition where the parent scope defines **rate** is as follows:

```
1. val rate = 7;
2. val calculateSimpleInterest : Double => Double =
   (principal : Double) => (principal * rate ) / 100
3. print(calculateSimpleInterest(100))
```

This time it will not give an error and pass because of closure, and the variable rate defined here is a free variable.

When the compiler does not find any variable definition being used in a function, then it will try to search it in its nearest scope, and if it is defined, that variable is used.

The following is an example:

```
1.  var rate = 7
2.  val calculateSim pleInterest : Double => Double =
    (principal : Double) => (principal * rate ) / 100
3.  print(calculateSimpleInterest(100))
```

It will result in **7**.

The following will be the results:

```
1.  var rate = 7
2.  val calculateSimpleInterest: Double => Double =
    (principal : Double) => (principal * rate ) / 100
3.  println(calculateSimpleInterest(100))
4.  rate = 10
5.  println(calculateSimpleInterest(100))
```

It will give the following result:

7.0

10.0

Second time **rate** value gets changed. Hence, the latest value of free variable **rate** is **10**.

Closures are used in Scala for several reasons, as follows:

- **Encapsulation of state**: Closures allow functions to capture and retain references to variables from their enclosing lexical context. This enables the encapsulation of state within a function, allowing functions to maintain and access variables that are not in their immediate scope. Closures provide a way to package data and behavior together, creating self-contained and reusable units of functionality.

- **Preservation of context**: Closures preserve the context in which they were created, allowing them to access variables and values even when those variables are no longer in scope. This feature is particularly useful in scenarios where a function needs to access variables from its enclosing scope, such as callback functions or event handlers.

- **Functional composition**: Closures enable functional composition, allowing functions to be combined and chained together to create more complex behavior. By capturing variables from the surrounding context, closures can be used to create higher-level functions that encapsulate reusable logic and configuration.

- **Callback mechanisms**: Closures are commonly used in callback mechanisms, where a function is passed as an argument to another function and executed later.

The captured variables in the closure allow the callback function to access the necessary context or state when it is invoked. This is often used in asynchronous programming or event-driven systems.

- **Function factories**: Closures can be used to create specialized functions or function factories. By capturing variables during their creation, closures allow for the creation of functions with pre-configured behavior or customizable parameters. This promotes code reuse and allows for the creation of higher order functions tailored to specific use cases.

Overall, closures provide a powerful mechanism for maintaining state, preserving context, and creating reusable and modular code in Scala. They enable functional programming techniques and facilitate the construction of elegant and expressive programs.

Currying

Scala supports currying, where parameters of functions are decomposed into different groups, where each group is treated as a single argument. The benefit of this decomposed parameter group is that they can be partially applied by providing all parameter values of one group, whereas no parameter values need to be given from another group during function call, which returns a new function, fixes the provided parameter, and enables different parameters to be given against already fixed parameters. Hence, makes a function call as a partially applied function.

The following is an example of using the add method, which divides the parameters **x** and **y** into two groups of **x** and **y** individually:

```
1. def add(x: Int)(y: Int): Int = x + y
```

By providing values of the first group **x**, it returns another function that expects value of the remaining parameter **y** to be provided, as follows:

```
1. val addTen : Int => Int = add(10)
```

As you can see, the type of **addTen**, which says that it is a function that expects one **Int** parameter. Further, **result** could be calculated by providing new group to **addTen** function, as follows:

```
1. val result : Int = addTen(5) // result is 10+5 = 15
```

Hence, currying is very important for functional programming.

The following are the benefits of currying:

- **Partial application**: Curried functions allow you to create specialized functions by providing only a subset of their arguments. This can be useful when you want to create function variants with certain arguments pre-configured.

- **Function composition**: Currying facilitates function composition by breaking down functions with multiple arguments into a series of functions that can be easily composed together. This promotes code reuse and modularity.

- **Flexibility**: Currying provides flexibility in using and reusing functions by enabling partial application, allowing functions to be applied in different contexts with varying numbers of arguments.

Partial applied function

Currying actually enables a partial function to be applied. Partial applied function, as the name suggests, is the process to apply a particular function in a partial manner. It means that, providing partial arguments of function during function call actually fixes those parameters and resulting in a new function with remaining arguments left to be provided against fixed parameters.

The following is a contrived example of above **add**:

```
1. def add(x: Int)(y: Int)(z: Int) :Int = x + y + z
2. val addTwenty : (Int, Int) => Int = add(20)
```

Here, twenty is fixed for **z** parameter. Now, **addtwenty** is free to apply as many variation of partial function with different values of **x** and **y**, as follows:

```
1. val addThirty : (Int, Int) => Int = addTwenty (10)
   // 20 was already fixed. Adding 10 more to make it 30.
2. val addFourty : (Int, Int) => Int = addTwenty (20)
   // 20 was already fixed. Adding 20 more to make it 40.
3. val addFifty : (Int, Int) => Int = addTwenty (30)
   // 20 was already fixed. Adding 30 more to make it 50.
```

Three variations got created by fixing another variable **y** with different values that is how partial function works.

The following are the benefits of partial functions:

- **Customization and reusability**: Partially applied functions allow you to create specialized function variants by fixing some arguments. These specialized functions can be reused in different contexts, promoting code reuse and modularity.

- **Function composition**: Partial application facilitates function composition by allowing you to create new functions from existing ones. Partially applied functions can be combined with other functions using composition operators like and then or compose.

- **Deferred evaluation**: Partially applied functions delay the evaluation of the remaining arguments until they are provided. This can be useful when you need to defer the computation or when you want to apply the same function to different arguments later.

Function implementation

We talked about Scala features, its inclination towards functional programming and how these features help to write a functional program. The common between these structures that they represent some error possibility and define their specific instances which further bifurcate each possibility exhaustively. For example, option represent possibility of null values. So, there are only two possibilities either it has value or not. Same is represented by its instances, None[T] and Some[T]. Same way, Try and Either also behave which we will discuss further.

Based on above, the following are the behavior structures:

- **Composition and chaining**: They support functional composition and chaining through their combinators. Combinators defined inside allow you to transform and chain computations on these values; this promotes a functional style of programming, where operations on these values can be composed and combined effectively.

- **Pattern matching**: It integrates well with pattern matching in Scala. Pattern matching on option instances allows you to handle both some and none cases separately and extract values or perform different computations based on the presence or absence of a value. Pattern matching with them provides a concise and expressive way to handle these errors or scenario possibilities.

Option[T]

Option type provides tools to work with null values. It makes it easier to write robust code. It enables the management of optional values in the following ways:

- **Type-safety**: Parameterization of optional values is possible now. T type represents either null or a type T value.

- **Functionally aware**: A set of powerful functional capabilities.

The following are the two instances of Option[T]:

- **Some[T]**: Describe the notion of value present inside the option container.

- **None[T]**: Describes the value that is not present inside option.

The following are the benefits of option:

- **Avoiding null references**: Option provides a safe alternative to using null references. In many programming languages, null references can lead to runtime errors and unexpected behavior. By using option, you explicitly handle the absence of a value, making your code more robust and less prone to null-related errors.

- **Expressing absence**: Option explicitly represents the absence of a value. By wrapping a value in some when it is present or using none when it is absent, option allows you to handle optional values in a more explicit and readable way. This leads to code that clearly communicates the possibility of absence, improving code clarity.

- **Encouraging explicit handling**: The use of option encourages explicit handling of the presence or absence of a value. This helps to prevent null-related errors and forces you to handle the absence case explicitly. By using methods like **map**, **flatMap**, and **getOrElse**, you can safely perform computations on option values, even when they may be none.

- **Enhanced safety**: By using option, you can explicitly handle the possibility of absent values, reducing the chance of null-related errors and improving the safety of your code. The type system enforces the use of option for optional values, leading to more predictable and reliable code.

Try[T]

Try is inside **scala.util** package which provides the capability to do error handling in a functional way.

The following are the instances of Try:

- Success[T]
- Failure[T]

The following are the benefits of Try in functional programming:

- **Explicit error handling**: Try allows you to explicitly handle errors and failures in a functional and composable manner. Instead of relying on exceptions, which can be unpredictable and lead to control flow issues, Try provides a monadic container that represents both successful results (success) and failures (failure). This promotes explicit error handling, making it easier to reason about and compose error-prone computations.

- **Immutability**: Try enforces immutability by wrapping the result or exception in an immutable container. This aligns with functional programming principles, where immutability is favored for its benefits in reasoning, testing, and concurrent programming. By encapsulating error handling logic within Try instances can ensure that error handling remains pure and side-effect-free.

- **Error recovery**: Try provides a variety of methods for error recovery, such as **recover**, **recoverWith**, and **fallbackTo**. These methods allow you to define fallback behaviors or alternative computations to handle failures, providing flexibility in handling and recovering from errors. This is particularly useful in scenarios where you want to gracefully handle specific errors and provide fallback values or alternative computations.

Either [+A, +B]

It represents a union type that could represent one of two possible values. It can contain either an error of type A or a successful value of type B.

The following are the instances of Either:

- Left[T]
- Right[T]

Conventionally, Left represents the error value whereas, Right is for the success value.

The following are the benefits of Either in functional programming:

- **Discriminated union**: Either allows you to represent a discriminated union, where a value can be of either one type (Left) or another type (Right). This is particularly useful in scenarios where you explicitly want to handle both successful and failure cases.

- **Explicit error handling**: Either provides a clear and explicit way to handle errors and failures. By convention, Left type is typically used to represent failures or errors, while the Right type represents successful results. This makes the intent and flow of error-handling code more explicit and readable.

- **Error recovery**: Either provides methods like `getOrElse`, `orElse`, and `fold` that allow you to recover from errors or provide alternative values or computations. These methods provide flexibility in handling and recovering from errors, allowing you to define fallback behaviors or alternative computations based on the result of an Either value.

- **Error accumulation**: Either can be used to accumulate multiple errors in a functional way. By representing errors as Left values and successful results as Right values, you can use combinators like `map`, `flatMap`, and `orElse` to perform computations that accumulate errors and handle them collectively.

There are many functional constructs present in Scala type which helps for functional programming. The following are the other Scala functional constructs:

List [T]

The following are some of the types and functional implementations:

- **Map over (map)**: It provides capability to be mapped over with any provided function.

- **Composition (andThen, compose)**: Allows to do composition of two list items.

- **Catamorphism (fold, foldLeft, foldRight):** List item can be reduced to single value using catamorphism by `fold`, `foldLeft` and `foldRight` methods.

- **Notion of infinite list**: Represents that list could be created with infinite number of items and functional programming provide a way to work with them.

- **Pattern matching**: List can be matched overhead and cons.

- **Immutability**: By default, list is immutable which brings functional programming more closed as it is one of fundamental pillar.

Conclusion

In this chapter, we went through Scala language and its features. We also discussed the specific features which makes it easy to work with functional programming. We had taken thereafter a quick tour of Scala and understood how to start with Scala language in our local system and how to install and work with Scala and with some Scala code. Further, each functional features and Scala support for it was discussed. In last, we read different functional structure Scala provides like Option, Try and Either to work with error scenarios and working in functional and composable way.

In the next chapter, we will learn about Cats functional libraries which provide implementation of different functional constructs (functors, applicative functors, traversal, monads etc.) and how those could be used to implement real world scenarios and its unit-test frameworks to build confidence in implementation by validating all functional implementations.

Join our Discord space

Join our Discord workspace for latest updates, offers, tech happenings around the world, new releases, and sessions with the authors:

https://discord.bpbonline.com

CHAPTER 4

Understanding Cats

Introduction

This chapter focuses on implementation of the category theory concepts what we discussed in *Chapter 2, Implementation of Category Theory*. This chapter further talks about different tools in the Cats library that are designed to be modular, lightweight, and easy to use. It provides an easy way to ease functional programming with its type classes and data types. These help us to write safer code with having side effects and enhance our codebase for adopting reusability by helping us to write generic, more expressive, and concise code using these type classes. We will focus more on these categories and what benefits they provide.

Structure

In this chapter, we will cover the following topics:

- Understanding Cats
- Type classes
- Data types
- Transformers
- Free implementations
- Cats testing

Objectives

By the end of this chapter, readers will be able to see the implementation of category theory abstraction we discussed in *Chapter 2, Implementation of Category Theory*. Cats is the library as a first-level project in type level which implements these constructs in the Scala language. It is lightweight, modular, and extensible library. You will be able to use these functional abstractions in real world scenarios.

Understanding Cats

Cats is a library which provides abstractions for functional programming in the Scala programming language.[1]

Cats is an open-source library that provides abstractions and type classes for functional programming in Scala. It is similar in purpose to other functional programming libraries like Scala and is designed to help developers write more effective and maintainable code by leveraging functional programming concepts.

The following are some key features and concepts in Cats:

- **Type classes**: A type class is a concept used to define a set of operations that can be applied to a certain data type or a set of data types. Type classes enable ad-hoc polymorphism, allowing different data types to be used interchangeably in defined functions and operations over these type classes.

  In Cats library and in functional programming in general, type classes are implemented using traits in Scala. For example, the functor type class represents types that can be mapped over, monad represents types that support sequencing operations, monoid represents types that can be combined, and so on.

  The following are why type classes are essential and why you might want to use them:

  o **Polymorphism**: Type classes allow you to write polymorphic functions that can operate on a wide range of data types. This enables writing generic and reusable code.

  o **Separation of concerns**: Type classes help in separating the concerns of data and behavior. Data types do not need to be modified to make them instances of a type class, allowing you to add functionality to existing types without changing their code.

  o **Extensibility**: You can define new instances of type classes for custom data types, making it easy to integrate your own or third-party libraries into existing type class hierarchies.

---

1. **https://typelevel.org/cats/**

- o **Laws and reasoning**: Type classes come with laws that define the expected behavior of the operations. Adhering to these laws ensures consistency and correctness, making it easier to reason about the behavior of your code.

- o **Implicit resolution**: In Scala, implicit is used to resolve type class instances automatically. This allows the compiler to automatically find and use the appropriate instances without manual intervention, making the code concise and expressive.

- o **Functional composition**: Type classes enable functional composition. You can compose different functions and transformations that operate on type class instances, leading to a more modular and composable codebase.

- o **Abstraction**: Type classes provide a powerful way to abstract over different data types, allowing you to write algorithms and functions that are agnostic to the specific types they operate on.

- **Data types**: Data types are specialized structures that facilitate functional programming in Scala. Cats provides a wide range of data types that are designed to solve specific problems in functional programming. These data types are built on functional abstractions and offer improved composability, expressiveness, and safety over their counterparts in the standard Scala library.

Using data types from the Cats library offers several advantages in functional programming, as follows:

- o **Functional purity**: Cats data types encourage immutability and functional purity, ensuring that your programs are referentially transparent and easier to reason about. Immutable data types help avoid side effects, making your code more reliable and predictable.

- o **Safety and expressiveness**: Cats provides expressive and type-safe abstractions. By using Cats data types, you can encode more meaning into your types, reducing the possibility of runtime errors and improving the safety of your programs.

- o **Composability**: Cats data types are designed to be composable. You can easily combine different data types and operations, enabling you to build complex behaviors from simpler components. Composability fosters code reuse and maintainability.

- o **Functional abstractions**: Cats provides implementations of common functional programming abstractions such as functors, monads, applicative, etc. These abstractions allow you to write generic, polymorphic code that works across different data types, promoting modularity and abstraction.

- o **Error handling**: Cats provides data types like option and either which help in handling errors in a functional way. This eliminates the need for exceptions in your code, making error handling more predictable and manageable.

o **Concurrency and parallelism**: Cats provides abstractions like I/O for managing concurrency and parallelism. These abstractions allow you to write concurrent and parallel programs in a functional style, making it easier to reason about complex concurrency scenarios.

o **Laws and guarantees**: Cats data types come with laws and guarantees. Adhering to these laws ensures that your code behaves predictably and consistently. It helps in catching logical errors early during development.

o **Interoperability**: Cats is a widely used library in the Scala ecosystem. By using Cats data types, you ensure that your code can interoperate seamlessly with other libraries and codebases that also use Cats. This promotes ecosystem-wide consistency.

o **Community and documentation**: Cats has a vibrant community and extensive documentation. Leveraging Cats data types means that you can benefit from the collective knowledge and experience of the community. If you encounter issues, there are resources available to help you.

o **Functional transformation and composition**: Cats data types provide transformation and composition operations that enable you to build complex behavior from simpler parts. This is crucial for constructing complex programs from small, understandable, and testable pieces.

Cats data types provide transformation and composition operations that enable you to build complex behavior from simpler parts. This is crucial for constructing complex programs from small, understandable, and testable pieces.

We will discuss the above features and explore them with examples using Cats constructs to write functional programming. We will cover first all the type classes that Cats provide with their usage and try to write examples to understand it even better. Then, we will discuss all data types.

Type classes

Type classes are a powerful concept in functional programming languages like Scala and Haskell, where many object-oriented languages leverage subtyping for polymorphic code, functional programming tends towards a combination of parametric polymorphism (think type parameters, like Java generics) and ad-hoc polymorphism. They enable ad-hoc polymorphism, allowing you to define generic interfaces and implementations separately. This separation of concerns is essential for maintaining modularity and extensibility in your codebase.

It is a sort of interface that defines some behavior. If a type is part of a type class, it means that you can use functions that operate on that type. However, the type itself does not have to implement an interface explicitly; instead, instances for the type are defined separately.

The following is an example:

```scala
1.  trait Show[A] {
2.    def show(value: A): String
3.  }
4.
5.  object Show {
6.    // Typeclass instances for common types
7.    implicit val showInt: Show[Int] = (value: Int) => value.toString
8.    implicit val showString: Show[String] = (value: String) => value
9.
10.   // Syntax for convenient usage
11.   implicit class ShowOps[A](value: A) {
12.     def show(implicit instance: Show[A]): String = instance.show(value)
13.   }
14. }
15.
16. // Usage
17. import Show._
18.
19. val intValue: Int = 42
20. val stringValue: String = "hello"
21.
22. println(intValue.show)    // Output: 42
23. println(stringValue.show) // Output: hello
```

In this example, **Show** is a type class, and **showInt** and **showString** are instances of the **Show** type class for **Int** and **String** respectively. The **ShowOps** implicit class provides a convenient syntax for using the **show** method.

Figure 4.1 describes the relationship among the type classes:

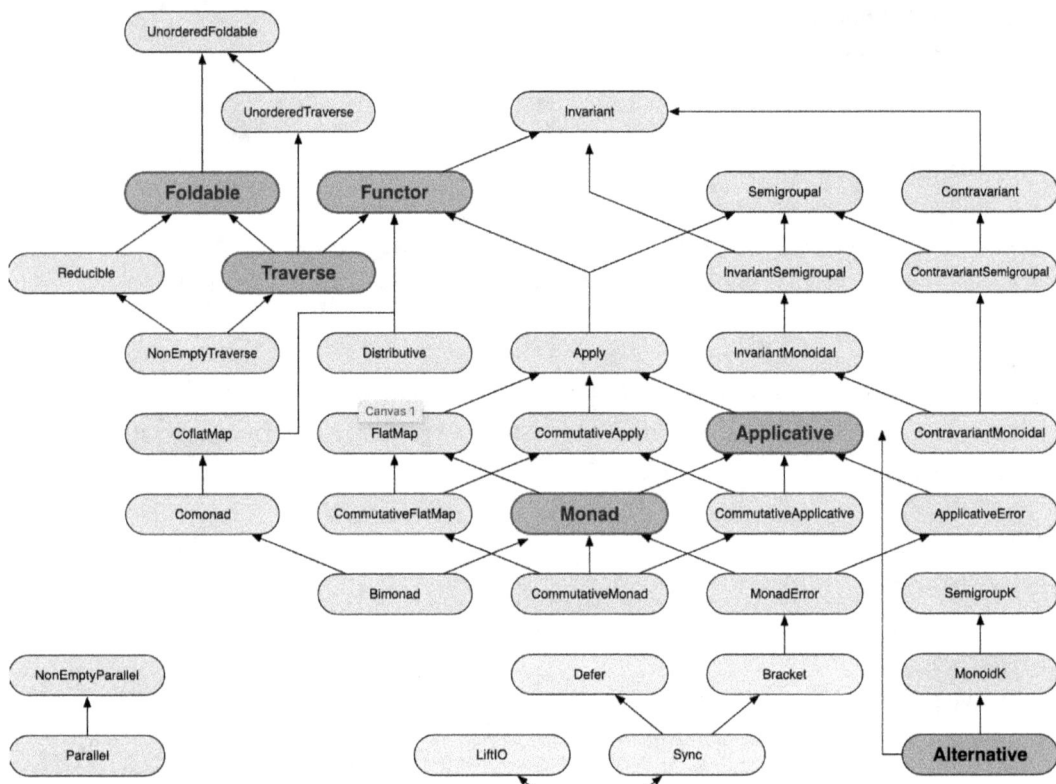

Figure 4.1: *Type class relationship*

Functor

A functor is a type class in functional programming that represents a container or context that can be mapped over. It provides a way to apply a function to the values inside the container while preserving the structure of the container. In other words, a functor allows you to transform the contents of a data structure without changing its shape.

The following are the uses of functor:

- **Abstraction**: Functors provide a high-level abstraction for working with different data types. They allow you to write generic functions that work with various types, promoting code reuse and modularity.

- **Functional composition**: Functors are composable. You can chain multiple mapping operations, creating complex transformations by combining simple functions. This composability is a fundamental principle in functional programming.

- **Preserving structure**: Functors maintain the structure of the container. When you **map** a function over a functor, the original shape of the data structure is preserved, ensuring that the transformed data is still within the same context.

- **Avoiding explicit looping**: In imperative programming, you often write explicit loops to apply a function to elements in a collection. With functors, you can achieve the same transformation in a more declarative and concise manner, avoiding the complexity of manual looping.

- **Functional purity**: Functors adhere to functional purity by not modifying the original data. Instead, they produce new transformed values, promoting immutability and making reasoning about code easier.

- **Laws and predictable behavior**: Functors obey specific laws (like identity and composition laws) that ensure their behavior is predictable and consistent. Understanding and adhering to these laws can lead to more reliable and maintainable code.

- **Interoperability**: Functors are widely used in functional programming libraries and frameworks. Understanding how to work with functors allows you to interact with various libraries and APIs in a functional and idiomatic way.

The following is an example of a functor in Scala:

```scala
1.  // Define a Functor type class
2.  trait Functor[F[_]] {
3.    def map[A, B](fa: F[A])(f: A => B): F[B]
4.  }
5.
6.  // Define a Functor instance for the Option data type
7.  implicit val optionFunctor: Functor[Option] = new Functor[Option] {
8.    def map[A, B](fa: Option[A])(f: A => B): Option[B] = fa.map(f)
9.  }
10.
11. // Usage of the Functor instance
12. val maybeValue: Option[Int] = Some(42)
13. val transformedMaybe: Option[String] = Functor[Option].map(maybeValue)
    (value => s"Value is $value")
14. println(transformedMaybe)  // Output: Some(Value is 42)
```

In this example, functor is used to **map** a function over an **Option**. The original **Option** structure is preserved, and the function is applied to the inner value, creating a new **Option** with the transformed result. Functors provide a consistent way to apply transformations across various data structures.

Invariant

An invariant is a type class that represents a data structure or a type constructor that is neither covariant nor contravariant. In other words, it does not change its behavior based on how its type parameters are transformed. Unlike covariant functors or contravariant functors, an invariant does not provide a way to map over or modify its content while preserving the structure. Invariants are rare in functional programming because many data structures naturally exhibit covariance or contravariance in their behavior. However, there are cases where invariance is desired or necessary.

Invariant usage

The following are the uses of invariant:

- **Semantic constraints**: Some data types have semantic constraints that cannot be preserved under mapping operations. For instance, **NonEmptyList** should always have at least one element. If you **map** a function over it and transform it to an empty list, the semantic constraint would be violated.

- **Data integrity**: Invariant data structures are useful when you need to ensure data integrity and enforce specific rules or constraints. For example, ensuring that a matrix always has a non-zero number of rows and columns.

- **Immutability**: Invariants can be helpful in enforcing immutability. If a data structure cannot be modified, invariant properties may need to be maintained through construction or transformation operations.

- **Safety**: Invariants can be used to create safe APIs by preventing certain transformations that could lead to runtime errors or invalid states.

- **Explicitness:** Invariant data structures make the code more explicit. When using an invariant data type, it is clear that certain operations are not allowed, providing a safety net against unintended manipulations.

- **Domain modelling**: Invariants are often used in domain modelling where certain rules and constraints need to be maintained across the application.

The following is a simplified example in Scala demonstrating a custom invariant type **NonEmptyString**, which represents a string that must not be empty:

```
1. case class NonEmptyString private (value: String) {
2.   require(value.nonEmpty, "NonEmptyString cannot be empty»)
3.
4.   override def toString: String = value
5. }
6.
7. object NonEmptyString {
```

```
8.   def apply(value: String): Option[NonEmptyString] =
9.     if (value.nonEmpty) Some(new NonEmptyString(value))
10.    else None
11. }
12.
13. val validString: Option[NonEmptyString] =
      NonEmptyString("Hello, World!")
14. val invalidString: Option[NonEmptyString] =
      NonEmptyString("")  // This will return None
15.
16. println(validString)   // Output: Some(Hello, World!)
17. println(invalidString) // Output: None
```

In this example, **NonEmptyString** is invariant. It ensures that a string is non-empty at the time of creation. If you attempt to create an empty **NonEmptyString**, it will not compile, enforcing the invariant property.

InvariantMonoidal

InvariantMonoidal combines invariant and semigroupal with the addition of a unit methods, defined in isolation the **InvariantMonoidal** type class could be defined, as follows:

```
1. trait InvariantMonoidal[F[_]] {
2.   def unit: F[Unit]
3.   def imap[A, B](fa: F[A])(f: A => B)(g: B => A): F[B]
4.   def product[A, B](fa: F[A], fb: F[B]): F[(A, B)]
5. }
```

Practical uses of **InvariantMonoidal** appear in the context of codecs, that is, interfaces to capture both serialization and deserialization for a given format. Another notable example is a semigroup.

It first shows how a semigroup is **InvariantMonoidal**, and how this can be used to create semigroup instances by combining other semigroup instances.

As explained in the invariant tutorial, a semigroup forms an invariant functor. Indeed, given a **Semigroup[A]** and two functions **A => B** and **B => A**, one can construct a **Semigroup[B]** by transforming two values from type **B** to type **A**, combining these using **the Semigroup[A]**, and transforming the result back to type **B**. Thus, to define an **InvariantMonoidal[Semigroup]**, we need implementations for unit and product.

Contravariant

Contravariant is a type class that represents types that can be used as input or consumed in some way. Unlike covariant types (which can be seen as the output of some process), contravariant types are used as inputs or arguments.

In Scala, contravariance is expressed using the symbol. **A** type class is contravariant if it can transform a type **A** into a type **B** whenever **B** can be transformed into **A**.

Contravariant usage

The following are the contravariant usage:

- **Function arguments**: **Contravariant** type classes are helpful when you need to work with functions that take certain types as arguments. For example, consider a type class for serializers. A **ContravariantSerializer** can serialize a supertype, which makes sense because it can also serialize any of its subtypes.

  Refer to the following code:

  ```
  1. trait ContravariantSerializer[-A] {
  2.   def serialize(value: A): String
  3. }
  ```

- **Dependency injection**: In the context of dependency injection, contravariant types allow you to inject dependencies that are more general than the required type, providing flexibility and enabling the reusability of components.

- **Predicate checks**: **Contravariant** type classes can be used to define predicates (functions that take an input and return a Boolean) that are contravariant. For example, a **Predicate[-A]** can accept a broader range of values to check, making it more flexible.

- **Functional composition**: **Contravariant** type classes can be composed with other contravariant or covariant type courses, allowing for functional composition of operations on input types.

Contravariant type classes allow you to model relationships between types where one type can be used where another is expected. By understanding and utilizing contravariance, you can create more flexible and reusable code.

The following code describes a **Contravariant** type class for input validation. We want to validate user input, but we are interested in functions that validate more general types:

```
1. import cats.Contravariant
2.
3. // Define a type class for input validation
4. trait Validator[-A] {
```

```
5.    def isValid(value: A): Boolean
6. }
7.
8. // Implement Contravariant instance for the Validator type class
9. implicit val validatorContravariant: Contravariant[Validator] =
   new Contravariant[Validator] {
10.   def contramap[A, B](fa: Validator[A])(f: B => A): Validator[B] =
   value => fa.isValid(f(value))
11. }
12.
13. // Example usage of the Validator type class
14. def validateLength(minLength: Int): Validator[String] = input
   => input.length >= minLength
15.
16. val lengthValidator: Validator[String] = validateLength(5)
17.
18. // Contravariant mapping allows us to transform a Validator[String]
   into a Validator[Any]
19. val anyValidator: Validator[Any] = Contravariant[Validator].
   contramap(lengthValidator)((any: Any) => any.toString)
20.
21. // Validation example
22. println(anyValidator.isValid("Hello, World!")) // Output: true
23. println(anyValidator.isValid("Hi")) // Output: false
```

In this example, we define a **Validator** trait representing input validation. We create a contravariant instance for the **Validator** type class, allowing us to transform a **Validator[String]** into a **Validator[Any]** using the **contramap** method. This demonstrates the **Contravariant** property: We can transform validators for specific types into validators for more general types (in this case, **String** to **Any**). **Contravariant** mapping allows us to focus on the input validation logic and reuse it for different input types.

Bifunctor

A bifunctor is a type class in functional programming that generalizes the concept of functors to structures that have two type parameters. While a regular functor operates on a single type within a context like **List[A]** or **Option[A]**, a bifunctor works on structures with two type parameters like **Either[A, B]** or **Tuple2[A, B]**.

A bifunctor provides two independent **map** like operations (**bimap** and **leftMap**/**second** in different conventions) that allow you to apply functions separately to each of the two types inside the bifunctor.

The following are the key components:

- **Bimap**: Applies a function to both type parameters of the bifunctor. For example, if you have `F[A, B]` and a function `A => C` and another function `B => D`, `bimap` transforms it into `F[C, D]`.

- **LeftMap (or first)**: Applies a function to the left component (the first type parameter) of the bifunctor. For example, if you have `F[A, B]` and a function `A => C`, `leftMap` transforms it into `F[C, B]`.

- **Second**: Applies a function to the right component, the second type parameter of the bifunctor. For example, if you have `F[A, B]` and a function `B => D`, the second transforms it into `F[A, D]`.

The following are the uses of bifunctor:

- **Flexible data transformations**: Bifunctors allow you to transform data structures that carry multiple types in a flexible and compositional way. You can apply different functions to each type of parameter independently.

- **Error handling**: Bifunctors are often used to represent computations that can fail, where the left component carries an error type and the right component carries the result. By using bifunctors, you can handle errors separately from successful results.

- **Product types**: Bifunctors can represent product types (like tuples) in a functional way. By mapping over both components, you can transform and manipulate tuples and other similar structures easily.

- **Sum types**: Bifunctors can represent sum types (like **Either**) in a functional way. You can apply different functions to the left (error) and right (success) components, making it useful for error handling and branching logic.

- **Functional composition**: Bifunctors play well with other functional abstractions. They can be composed with other type classes and higher order functions, allowing for expressive and concise code.

The following is a simple example of using a bifunctor (specifically, **Either**) in Scala:

```
1. val result: Either[String, Int] = Right(42)
   // Represents a successful result
2.
3. val transformedResult: Either[String, String] =
   result.leftMap(error => s"Error occurred: $error")
4.
5. println(transformedResult) // Output: Right(42)
   (unchanged because it is a Right value)
```

In this example, `leftMap` is used to apply a function to the left component of `Either`, leaving the right component unchanged. This kind of transformation is a typical use case for bifunctors, especially in error-handling scenarios.

Applicative

`Applicative` is a type class in functional programming that represents computations that can be sequenced and combined. It provides a way to apply a function in a context (wrapped in a functor) to a value also in a context. `Applicative` functors are more expressive than functors alone because they allow you to lift functions to operate on multiple values in a context, combining these computations.

The following are the key components:

- **pure (or point in some contexts)**: This function takes a pure value and lifts it into the functor context. It wraps a value in the applicative functor, allowing you to work with it in the context of that functor.

- **<*> (or ap in some contexts)**: This is the apply function. It allows you to apply a function wrapped in the applicative context to a value also wrapped in the same context. The result is a new value in the same context.

`Applicative` functors are particularly useful in scenarios where you have multiple computations in a context, and you want to apply a function to those computations, combining their results.

The following are the applicative usage:

- **Sequencing and parallelism**: `Applicative` functors allow you to sequence computations or perform them in parallel, when the applicative context supports parallelism. This is useful when you have multiple independent computations and you want to combine their results without any specific order.

- **Error handling**: `Applicative` functors can be used for error handling. If you have several computations that might fail, you can sequence them using applicative combinators and accumulate all the errors or the first encountered error, depending on your use case.

- **Combining multiple inputs**: When you have multiple inputs, possibly of different types and you want to apply a function to those inputs, you can use applicative functors to lift the function and the inputs into the same context, allowing for easy combination.

- **Readability and expressiveness**: `Applicative` code tends to be more readable and expressive, especially when working with complex data transformations. The combinators provided by applicative functors allow you to express operations in a clear and concise manner.

The following is a simple example in Scala using **cats**, a functional programming library for Scala, to illustrate the concept of **Applicative**:

```
1. import cats.Applicative
2. import cats.implicits._
3.
4. case class User(name: String, age: Int)
5.
6. val maybeName: Option[String] = Some("Alice")
7. val maybeAge: Option[Int] = Some(30)
8.
9. val user: Option[User] = Applicative[Option].map2(maybeName, maybeAge)
   (User)
10. // Result: Some(User("Alice", 30))
```

In this example, applicative is used to combine **maybeName** and **maybeAge** into a **User** case class. The **map2** function lifts the **User** constructor into the **Option** context and applies it to the **maybeName** and **maybeAge** values, resulting in an **Option[User]**.

Foldable

Foldable is a type class in functional programming that represents data structures that can be folded, meaning they can be reduced to a single value by sequentially applying an associative binary operation. In simpler terms, a foldable allows you to collapse a data structure into a summary value.

The following are the uses of **Foldable**:

- **Summarizing data**: **Foldable** enable you to summarize the contents of a data structure. For example, you can sum a list of numbers, find the maximum element, concatenate strings, or perform any operation that combines elements of the data structure into a single value.

- **Abstraction and generality**: **Foldable** provides a generic interface for working with different data structures like lists, trees, sets, etc., in a uniform way. This abstraction promotes code reuse and modularity. Algorithms written against the **Foldable** type class can work with various data types without modification.

- **Functional style**: In functional programming, looping constructs like for loops are replaced with higher order functions like **foldLeft**, **foldRight**, and **fold**. These functions abstract away the looping mechanism, making your code more declarative and functional.

- **Immutability**: Foldables can be used with immutable data structures. Since folding does not modify the original data, it fits well with the immutability principles of functional programming.

- **Expressive code**: Foldables allow you to write expressive, concise, and readable code. Operations like mapping, filtering, and reducing can often be expressed using folding, making your code more declarative and clearer.

- **Lazy evaluation**: In some functional programming libraries, folding operations can take advantage of lazy evaluation, allowing you to process large data structures without loading everything into memory.

- **Parallel processing**: In some scenarios, **Foldable** data structures can be processed in parallel, leveraging the power of multicore processors and optimizing performance for certain operations.

The following is an example of using **Foldable** in Scala with **cats**:

```
1. import cats.Foldable
2. import cats.instances.list._   // Import Foldable instances for List
3. import cats.instances.option._   // Import Foldable instances for Option
4.
5. val list = List(1, 2, 3, 4, 5)
6. val sum = Foldable[List].foldLeft(list, 0)(_ + _)
7. println(s"Sum of the list: $sum")   // Output: Sum of the list: 15
8.
9. val maybeValue: Option[Int] = Some(42)
10.val foldedMaybe = Foldable[Option].fold(maybeValue)
11.println(s"Folded Maybe: $foldedMaybe")   // Output: Folded Maybe: 42
```

In this example, **Foldable** is used to sum a list of integers and extract the value from an **Option**. By using **Foldable**, you can work with different data structures in a consistent and functional way.

Bifoldable

Bifoldable is a type class in functional programming that generalizes the concept of folding over two different types within a data structure. It is an extension of the **Foldable** type class, which allows folding over a single type within a data structure. In the case of **Bifoldable**, you can fold over two different types simultaneously.

The **Bifoldable** type class provides the **bifoldLeft** and **bifoldRight** functions, which enable folding over two different types within a data structure from left to right or right to left, respectively. These functions are similar to **foldLeft** and **foldRight** in **Foldable**, but they work for two different types instead of one.

```
1. //eagerly performs a left-associative bi-fold over `fab`
2.   def bifoldLeft[A, B, C](fab: F[A, B], c: C)(f: (C, A)
   => C, g: (C, B) => C): C
3.
4.   //lazily performs a right-associative bi-fold over `fab`
```

```
5.    def bifoldRight[A, B, C](fab: F[A, B], c: Eval[C])
      (f: (A, Eval[C]) => Eval[C], g: (B, Eval[C]) => Eval[C]): Eval[C]
```

The following are the parameter details used in **bifoldLeft** and **bifoldRight**:

- **fab:** bifoldable data structure containing elements of type **A** and **B**.
- **c:** initial accumulator value.
- **f:** function for folding over the left side of the **Bifoldable** structure (**A** type).
- **g:** function for folding over the right side of the **Bifoldable** structure (**B** type).

Bifoldable is useful when working with data structures that contain elements of two different types and you want to fold over both types simultaneously. It provides a unified interface for performing such operations, making your code more abstract and generic.

The following is a hypothetical example illustrating the use of **Bifoldable** with an **either** type:

```
1.  import cats.Bifoldable
2.  import cats.instances.either._
3.
4.  val either: Either[String, Int] = Right(42)
5.
6.  val result: String = Bifoldable[Either].bifoldMap(either)(
7.    error => s"Error occurred: $error",
8.    value => s"Result: $value"
9.  )
10.
11. println(result) // Output: Result: 42
```

In this example, **Bifoldable** is used to process both sides of an **Either**. It combines the left side (if it is a **Left**) and the right side (if it is a **Right**) using the **bifoldMap** function, allowing you to handle both cases in a unified way.

The following is an example for **Bifoldable**:

```
1.  import cats.Bifoldable
2.  import cats.instances.either._
3.
4.  object BifoldableExample extends App {
5.    // Define an Either with String on the Left and Int on the right
6.    val either: Either[String, Int] = Right(42)
7.
8.    // Define a custom function to combine Left and right sides
9.    def combineLeftAndRight(left: String, right: Int): String =
      s"Left: $left, Right: $right"
10.
11.    // Use Bifoldable to process both Left and right sides
12.    val result: String = Bifoldable[Either].bifoldMap(either)(
```

```
13.    left => s"Error occurred: $left",
   // Function for the left side (if it is Left)
14.    right => s"Result: $right"
   // Function for the right side (if it is Right)
15.  )
16.
17.  println(result) // Output: Result: 42
```

In this example, we use **Bifoldable[Either]** to handle both the **left** and **right** sides of an **Either** instance. The **bifoldMap** function is used to process both sides. If **either** is a left, the **left** function is applied; if it is a right, the right function is applied. Here, the **Bifoldable** type class abstracts over this process, allowing you to work with sum types in a unified manner.

Arrow

The **Arrow** type class is a fundamental concept in functional programming, especially in the context of arrows, which are a more general abstraction that captures computation in a functional manner. Arrows extend the concepts of categories and functions, providing a unified way to represent various computational structures. The **Arrow** type class captures these abstractions in Haskell and other functional programming languages.

The following are the key characteristics:

- **Composition**: Arrows can be composed, allowing you to combine multiple arrows into a new arrow. Composition in arrows is more general than function composition; it can represent computations with additional structure.

- **Identity arrow**: There exists an identity arrow that, when composed with any arrow, does not change the behavior of the arrow.

- **First and second arrows**: Arrows have operations first and second that allow you to transform the input or output of an arrow without changing the computation itself. For example, first applies an arrow to the first component of a pair, leaving the second component unchanged.

- **Arrows as functions**: Arrows generalize functions. In fact, any function can be seen as an arrow. However, arrows can represent more complex computations beyond simple functions, making them a versatile abstraction.

- **Parallel composition**: Arrows allow parallel composition of computations, providing a way to execute multiple computations concurrently and combine their results.

The following is an example for **Arrow** type class:

```
1. import cats.arrow.Arrow
2. import cats.syntax.arrow._
```

```
3.
4. object MyArrow extends Arrow[Function1] {
5.   def arr[A, B](f: A => B): A => B = f
6.
7.   def first[A, B, C](fa: A => B): ((A, C)) => (B, C) = {
8.     case (a, c) => (fa(a), c)
9.   }
10. }
```

In this example, we have created a custom **Arrow** instance for the **Function1** arrow type. We have defined the **arrow** method to lift a function into the arrow context and the **first** method to apply the arrow to the first element of a tuple, leaving the second element unchanged.

Now, you can create and compose arrows using your custom **Arrow** instance, as follows:

```
1. object ArrowExample extends App {
2.   // Create arrows
3.   val multiplyByTwoPlusOne: Int => Int = MyArrow.lift((x: Int)
     => x * 2 + 1)
4.   val square: Int => Int = MyArrow.lift((x: Int) => x * x)
5.
6.   // Compose arrows using `>>>` operator
7.   val composedArrow: Int => (Int, Int) = multiplyByTwoPlusOne
     &&& square
8.
9.   // Run the computation
10.  val input = 3
11.  val (result1, result2) = composedArrow(input)
12.  println(s"Result 1: $result1") // Output: Result 1: 7
13.  println(s"Result 2: $result2") // Output: Result 2: 9
14. }
```

In this example, **multiplyByTwoPlusOne** and **square** are arrows. The **>>>** operator is used to compose the arrows. The **&&&** operator is used to combine the arrows into a tuple.

This code demonstrates the basic usage of the **Arrow** type class in Cats for creating and composing arrows. Cats provides many more combinators and utilities for working with arrows, making it a powerful tool for functional programming in Scala.

Semigroup

A semigroup is an algebraic structure in mathematics and functional programming. It consists of a set and an associative binary operation defined on that set. The operation can be thought of as a way to combine two elements of the set, and associativity means that the way elements are grouped in the operation does not affect the result.

The following are the key components:

- **Set**: A set S of elements.

- **Operation**: An associative binary operation combines: $S \times S \rightarrow S$ that takes two elements and produces another element of the set.

- **Associativity property**: For all a, b, and c in S, the equation *(a combine b) combines c = a combine (b combine c)* holds.

The following is the semigroup usage:

- **Composing values**: Semigroups provide a way to compose or combine values. You can think of a semigroup as a rule or operation that allows you to merge two values of the same type into a single value, according to a specific rule.

- **Functional composition**: Semigroups enable functional composition. They allow you to combine functions in a pointwise manner. For example, if you have two functions *f: A => A* and *g: A => A*, a semigroup operation could combine them to create a new function *h: A => A* where *h(a) = f(a) combine g(a)*.

- **Error handling**: Semigroups are used in error accumulation. When dealing with computations that might fail, for example, parsing, validation, or data processing, semigroups can accumulate errors from multiple sources into a single error value.

- **Data reduction**: Semigroups can be used for data reduction or aggregation. For example, you can use a semigroup to aggregate a list of numeric values into their sum or product.

- **Parallelism**: Semigroups can be used in parallel processing. Associative operations allow parallel computations to be combined efficiently, improving performance in multicore systems.

- **Immutable data structures**: Semigroups can be used to build immutable data structures. When you add or append elements to a data structure, a semigroup operation can define how to merge the existing structure with the new element.

- **Mathematical abstraction**: Semigroups provide a mathematical abstraction for combining elements. This abstraction is used in various areas of mathematics and computer science, making it a powerful and widely applicable concept.

The following is an example of using a **Semigroup** in Scala:

```
1. import cats.Semigroup
2. import cats.implicits._
3.
4. // Define a Semigroup instance for Int (using addition as
   the combining operation)
5. implicit val intSemigroup: Semigroup[Int] = Semigroup[Int].combine
6.
```

```
7.  val result: Int = 1 |+| 2 |+| 3  // This uses the Semigroup
    instance to combine the numbers: 1 + 2 + 3 = 6
8.
9.  println(s"Result: $result")  // Output: Result: 6
```

In this example, the **|+|** operator is provided by **cats** to perform **Semigroup** combination. The implicit **intSemigroup** instance defines addition as the **Semigroup** operation for integers, allowing the numbers to be combined using addition.

SemigroupK

SemigroupK is a type class in Cats, a popular functional programming library in Scala. It represents a higher-level abstraction than a regular semigroup. While a semigroup combines two values of the same type into one, **SemigroupK** combines two type constructors into one, preserving their type structure.

In simpler terms, a **SemigroupK** allows you to combine two instances of type constructors (**F[_]** and **G[_]**) into a new type constructor **H[_]** while preserving the structure of **F** and **G**. It is particularly useful when working with higher-kind types, like **Option**, **List**, **Either** or **Any** other type constructor.

The following is how **SemigroupK** is defined in Cats:

```
1.  trait SemigroupK[F[_]] {
2.    def combineK[A](x: F[A], y: F[A]): F[A]
3.  }
```

F[_] is the type constructor for which **SemigroupK** is defined.

combineK is the method that takes two instances of **F[A]** and combines them into a new instance of **F[A]**.

The following are the uses of **SemigroupK**:

- **Combining higher-kinded types**: **SemigroupK** allows you to combine instances of different type constructors. This is particularly useful when you have different data structures and you want to combine their values without unwrapping them.

- **Functional composition**: It enables the composition of functions with different data structures. Functions that return type constructors (**F[_]**) can be composed using **SemigroupK**, providing a way to work with heterogeneous data structures in a composable manner.

- **Type-safety**: **SemigroupK** ensures type-safety when combining type constructors. It guarantees that you are combining instances of the same type constructor, preventing type errors in your code.

- **Modularity and reusability**: By using **SemigroupK**, you can create modular and reusable code that can work with a wide range of data structures. This promotes code modularity and makes your codebase more maintainable.

- **Conciseness and expressiveness**: **SemigroupK** operations often lead to more concise and expressive code. It abstracts away the details of combining data structures, allowing you to focus on the high-level logic of your program.

- **Library interoperability**: **SemigroupK** facilitates interoperability between different libraries. If different parts of your application use different type constructors, **SemigroupK** can be used to combine their results, promoting modular and loosely coupled designs.

The following is an example of using **SemigroupK** with the **Option** type constructor:

```
1. import cats.SemigroupK
2. import cats.implicits._
3.
4. // Define a SemigroupK instance for Option
5. implicit val optionSemigroupK: SemigroupK[Option] =
   new SemigroupK[Option] {
6.   def combineK[A](x: Option[A], y: Option[A]): Option[A] = x orElse y
7. }
8.
9. val result: Option[Int] = SemigroupK[Option].combineK(Some(42), None)
10.println(s"Result: $result")  // Output: Result: Some(42)
```

In this example, the **combineK** method for **Option** is defined to combine **Some** and **None** instances. The result is an **Option[Int]** that preserves the structure of the original **Option** values.

Monoid

A monoid is an algebraic structure in mathematics and functional programming. It consists of a set of values, an associative binary operation to combine those values, and an identity element with respect to that operation. The operation is typically denoted as **combine** or **+**, and the identity element is denoted as empty or zero.

The following are the key components:

- **Set**: A set M of values.

- **Operation**: An associative binary operation combines $M \times M \rightarrow M$ that takes two values and returns a value of the same type.

- **Identity element**: An identity element is an empty element M, for any element x in the set M.

  The equation holds the following:

$$combine(x, empty) = x$$

$$combine(empty, x) = x$$

The following are the uses of monoid:

- **Aggregation and summarization**: Monoids allow you to aggregate and summarize data efficiently. You can combine multiple values into a single result using the monoid operation, which is particularly useful in parallel or distributed computing.

- **Error handling**: Monoids can be used to handle errors in a functional and composable way. Instead of throwing exceptions, you can use a monoid to accumulate errors and handle them collectively.

- **Functional composition**: Monoids enable the composition of functions. If you have multiple functions that produce a result of the same type, you can combine them using the monoid operation to create a single function.

- **Immutable data structures**: Monoids can be used to build immutable data structures efficiently, for example, when you want to append elements to a list or concatenate strings immutably, a monoid operation can be employed.

- **Map-reduce paradigm**: Monoids play a central role in the map-reduce paradigm. The map step transforms data into a form that can be easily combined, and the reduce step, which is a monoid operation, combines the mapped data efficiently.

- **Formalization of computations**: In functional programming, monoids provide a formal way to express computations that can be combined and reduced. They offer a clear, mathematical structure for understanding and reasoning about data transformations.

The following is an example of a monoid for integers with addition as the operation and zero as the identity element:

```scala
1.  // Monoid type class
2.  trait Monoid[A] {
3.    def empty: A
4.    def combine(x: A, y: A): A
5.  }
6.
7.  // Monoid instance for integers with addition
8.  implicit val intMonoid: Monoid[Int] = new Monoid[Int] {
9.    def empty: Int = 0
10.   def combine(x: Int, y: Int): Int = x + y
11. }
12.
13. // Usage
14. val numbers = List(1, 2, 3, 4, 5)
15. val sum: Int = numbers.foldLeft(intMonoid.empty)(_ |+| _)
16. println(s"Sum of numbers: $sum")  // Output: Sum of numbers: 15
```

In this example, **Monoid** is used to compute the sum of a list of integers. The **combine** operation is used to add the elements, and **empty** is the identity element. Monoids offer a concise and composable way to perform aggregations and computations.

MonoidK

MonoidK is a type class in the Cats library, a popular functional programming library in Scala. **MonoidK** represents a higher-level concept than a simple **Monoid**. While a **Monoid** combines two values of the same type into one, **MonoidK** combines two higher-kind types into one, preserving their type structure.

The following are the uses of **MonoidK**:

- **Combining higher-kinded types**: **MonoidK** provides a way to combine values wrapped in different higher-kinded types. This is particularly useful in scenarios where you have polymorphic functions working with different data structures and want to combine their results without worrying about the specific type being used.

- **Functional composition**: Just like **Monoid** provides a way to compose functions that work on the same data type, **MonoidK** allows you to compose functions that work on different data types but have a similar higher-kind structure. This promotes functional composition and code reuse.

- **Type-safety**: By using **MonoidK**, you can ensure type-safety while working with different higher-kind types. It guarantees that you combine values of the same type structure, preventing type errors and enhancing code reliability.

- **Concise and readable code**: By abstracting over specific data types, **MonoidK** promotes concise and readable code. It allows you to write polymorphic functions that can handle a variety of data structures without having to write separate code for each type.

- **Library interoperability**: **MonoidK** facilitates interoperability between different libraries and components. If different parts of your application use different data types, **MonoidK** can be used to combine their results, promoting modular and loosely coupled designs.

The following is an example demonstrating the use of **MonoidK** with **cats** library:

```
1. import cats.MonoidK
2. import cats.instances.list._
3.
4. // Define a MonoidK instance for List
5. implicit val listMonoidK: MonoidK[List] = new MonoidK[List] {
6.   def empty[A]: List[A] = List.empty[A]
7.   def combineK[A](x: List[A], y: List[A]): List[A] = x ++ y
8. }
```

```
9.
10. val list1 = List(1, 2, 3)
11. val list2 = List(4, 5, 6)
12.
13. val combinedLists: List[Int] = MonoidK[List].combineK(list1, list2)
14. println(s"Combined Lists: $combinedLists")
    // Output: Combined Lists: List(1, 2, 3, 4, 5, 6)
```

In this example, **MonoidK** is used to combine two List instances. The **combineK** operation concatenates the lists. By providing a **MonoidK** instance for a specific data type, you enable the use of polymorphic functions and promote code modularity and reuse.

Traverse

Traverse is a fundamental concept in functional programming that allows you to transform and restructure data types in a type-safe and composable way. It combines two operations, that is, mapping (applying a function to each element) and sequencing (combining the results into a new structure). Traverse is particularly useful when you have a container-like data structure (such as a list, option, or future) and you want to apply a function that produces a container-like result, and then combine the results into a single container.

The following are the uses of traverse:

- **Combining mapping and sequencing**: Traverse allows you to map a function over the elements of a data structure and then sequence the results into a new structure. This operation is commonly used when dealing with effectful computations, like working with Option, Future, or any other monadic type.

- **Composability**: Traverse operations can be composed easily. You can perform multiple traversals sequentially, allowing complex transformations to be built from smaller, modular components.

- **Type-safety**: Traverse operations are type-safe. The types ensure that you cannot accidentally combine elements of different data structures, preventing type errors in your code.

- **Concurrency and parallelism**: In the context of effectful computations, traverse can be used for concurrent or parallel processing. Sequencing results does not necessarily mean sequential execution, as it can be performed concurrently or in parallel, depending on the effect type.

- **Error handling**: Traverse is useful for error handling. When you are dealing with multiple computations that can fail, traverse can accumulate errors and present them together, providing a clear view of all the failures.

- **Consistent data transformation**: Traverse provides a consistent way to transform data structures. Whether you are working with options, lists, futures, or other effect types, the traverse operation follows the same pattern, promoting consistency in your codebase.

- **Immutable data transformation**: Traverse operations can often be implemented in an immutable way. The original data structure remains unchanged, and the transformation produces a new structure.

- **Functional programming paradigm**: Traverse is an essential tool in functional programming. It allows you to apply functional transformations to data structures, promoting the functional paradigm's purity and composability.

The following is an example of using **traverse** in Scala with **Option**:

```
1. val numbers: List[Int] = List(1, 2, 3, 4, 5)
2.
3. // A function that can fail (returns an Option)
4. def safeDivide(n: Int): Option[Double] =
5.   if (n != 0) Some(10.0 / n) else None
6.
7. val result: Option[List[Double]] =
8.   numbers.traverse(safeDivide)
9.
10. println(result)  // Output: Some(List(10.0, 5.0,
    3.3333333333333335, 2.5, 2.0))
```

In this example, **traverse** is used to apply the **safeDivide** function to each element of the list numbers. The result is **an Option[List[Double]]**, where each element of the list is divided by **10.0**. The **traverse** operation combines the results into a single **Option**, ensuring that the overall result is **None** if any division fails.

Non-empty traverse

Non-empty traverse refers to the process of applying a function to the elements of a non empty data structure, such as a non-empty list or a non-empty tree and collecting the results while preserving the non-empty nature of the structure. The key distinction here is that the input data structure is guaranteed to be non-empty, meaning it contains at least one element.

In functional programming, traversing a non empty data structure is a common operation. It allows you to apply a function to each element of the structure and gather the results, typically within a context like **Option**, **Either**, or **Any** other type that represents computation with a possibility of failure or absence of a value.

The following is an example in Scala using the **cats** library demonstrating non-empty traverse on a non-empty list:

```
1. import cats.data.NonEmptyList
2. import cats.implicits._
```

```
3.
4. val nonEmptyList: NonEmptyList[Int] = NonEmptyList.of(1, 2, 3)
5.
6. def safeSquare(n: Int): Option[Int] =
7.   if (n != 0) Some(n * n) else None
8.
9. val result: Option[NonEmptyList[Int]] =
10.   nonEmptyList.traverse(safeSquare)
11.
12. println(result)  // Output: Some(NonEmptyList(1, 4, 9))
```

In this example, the function **safeSquare** squares a number but returns **None** if the input is **0**. By using **traverse**, you ensure that the resulting list is non-empty, even if some elements are transformed into **None**.

Alternative

The **Alternative** type class in functional programming provides a powerful abstraction for handling non-deterministic computations or computations with multiple possible outcomes. It extends **Applicative** with a **MonoidK**.

The following are the uses of **Alternative**:

- **Non-deterministic computations**: **Alternative** is particularly useful when dealing with computations where there can be multiple possible outcomes, and you want to explore all of them. This is common in parsing, validation, or scenarios where a function can be computed in multiple ways.

- **Combining alternative computations**: **Alternative** allows combining multiple computations and choosing the first one that succeeds. This can simplify complex decision-making processes where you must try different strategies or algorithms until one works.

- **Modularity and reusability**: By relying on type classes like **Alternative**, you can write polymorphic code that works with any data type that implements the **Alternative** behavior. This modularity allows you to reuse your code with different data types without modification.

- **Functional error handling**: **Alternative** can be used to represent computations that may fail and provide alternative strategies or fallback values in case of failure. This is a powerful way to handle errors in a functional, composable manner.

- **Expressiveness and readability**: Code that uses type classes like **Alternative** tends to be more expressive and readable. Functional combinators, such as '|' (**Alternative**), can often succinctly express complex branching and decision-making logic.

The following are the key components of **Alternative**:

- **Empty**: This operation represents a computation that fails or produces a zero value. It serves as the identity element for combining operation.

- **<|>** (or **orElse** in some languages) operation combines two computations. It takes two alternatives and produces a new alternative. It tries the left alternative first. If it succeeds, the result is used. If it fails (produces an empty or zero value), it tries the right alternative.

The following is an example:

```
1. import cats.Alternative
2. import cats.implicits._
3.
4. def parseNumber[A](input: String)(implicit A:
   Alternative[Option]): Option[A] =
5. A.orElse(A.parseInt(input), A.fromTry(scala.util.Try(input.toDouble)))
6.
7. val result: Option[Int] = parseNumber("42") // Some(42)
8. val result2: Option[Double] = parseNumber("3.14") // Some(3.14)
9. val result3: Option[Double] = parseNumber("not a number") // None
```

Monad

A monad is a design pattern in functional programming that represents a computation or a sequence of computations. It provides a way to structure computations that involve chaining operations together. Monads are a fundamental concept in functional programming and provide a solution to several common programming challenges.

A monad typically has three primary operations, as follows:

- **Unit (or return)**: It lifts a value into the monad, wrapping it in its context. In Scala, this operation is often represented as pure or unit.

- **Bind (or flatMap)**: It applies a function to the value inside the monad, returning a new monad. This operation allows chaining computations. In Scala, this operation is often represented as **flatMap**.

- **Associativity**: The order in which operations are performed does not matter. This property ensures that the sequence of computations does not affect the final result.

The following are the uses of a monad:

- **Sequencing computations**: Monads provide a way to sequence computations. When you have a series of operations that depend on the results of previous operations, monads allow you to chain these operations together clearly and concisely.

- **Effectful programming**: Monads represent computations with side effects, such as I/O, state changes, or exceptions. Monads provide a structured way to handle these effects while ensuring purity and immutability in the rest of the program.

- **Error handling**: Monads can be used to handle errors in a functional and composable way. For example, the **Option** monad represents computations that might fail, and the **Either** monad represents computations that can return either a value or an error.

- **Asynchronous programming**: Monads can be used to work with asynchronous or concurrent computations, allowing you to compose asynchronous tasks sequentially.

- **Dependency injection**: Monads can be used to represent computations with dependencies. By using a reader monad, for instance, you can pass dependencies implicitly without explicitly passing them as function arguments.

- **Composability**: Monads promote code composability. By chaining computations using monads, you can create complex behavior by combining simpler functions and monads.

- **Avoiding mutable state**: Monads allow you to perform computations in a way that avoids mutable state, promoting immutability and functional purity.

The following is an example of using the **Option** monad in Scala to handle potentially missing values:

```
1. val maybeName: Option[String] = Some("Alice")
2. val maybeLength: Option[Int] = maybeName.flatMap(name => Some(name.
   length))
3.
4. val lengthOrUnknown: String = maybeLength.
   map(length => s"Length: $length").getOrElse("Unknown")
5. println(lengthOrUnknown)  // Output: Length: 5
```

In this example, **Option** is used as a monad to handle the computation of the length of a name. If the name is present, the computation proceeds; otherwise, it returns **Unknown**. This demonstrates the sequential composition of computations using the **flatMap** operation, which is a characteristic of monads.

Comonad

A **Comonad** is a type class in functional programming that represents a dual concept to a monad. While monads allow you to embed values in a context and sequence computations, comonads provide a way to extract values from a context. Comonads are essential for modeling various contexts where you must focus on specific parts of a structure, such as zipper data structures, cellular automata, or signal processing in **functional reactive programming (FRP)**.

The following are the key characteristics of **Comonad**:

- **Extract operation (extract or copure)**: Comonads provide an operation to extract a value from the comonadic context. This operation allows you to focus on a specific element within the larger context.

- **Extend operation (extend or coflatMap)**: Comonads offer an extend operation that allows you to transform a comonadic context by applying a function to each element in the context. This operation is similar to map but maintains the comonadic structure.

Now, let us create the **StoreComonad** and demonstrate its usage using **cats**:

```scala
1.  import cats.Comonad //Define the Store data structure representing
    a value along with its context
2.  case class Store[A, S](current: A, context: S)
3.
4.  // Define Comonad instance for Store
5.  object StoreComonad {
6.    implicit def storeComonad[S]: Comonad[Store[?, S]] =
    new Comonad[Store[?, S]] {
7.      override def extract[A, S](x: Store[A, S]): A = x.current
8.      override def coflatMap[A, S, B](fa: Store[A, S])(f: Store[A, S]
    => B): Store[B, S] = {
9.        val newContext = fa.context
10.       val newCurrent = f(fa.copy()) // Pass a new Store to the
    function to preserve the original context
11.       Store(newCurrent, newContext)
12.     }
13.     override def map[A, B](fa: Store[A, S])(f: A => B): Store[B, S]
    = fa.copy(current = f(fa.current))
14.   }
15. }
16.
17. object ComonadExample extends App {
18.   // Import Comonad instance for Store
19.   import StoreComonad._
20.
21.   // Create a Store with an integer value and a list context
22.   val store: Store[Int, List[Int]] = Store(42, List(1, 2, 3, 4, 5))
23.
24.   // Extract the current value using extract function from Comonad
25.   val extractedValue: Int = Comonad[Store[?, List[Int]]].extract(store)
```

```
26.    println(s"Extracted value: $extractedValue") // Output:
       Extracted value: 42
27.
28.    // Apply a comonadic action (increment the current value) using
       coflatMap
29.    val incrementedStore: Store[Int, List[Int]] =
30.      Comonad[Store[?, List[Int]]].coflatMap(store)
       (s => s.copy(current = s.current + 1))
31.
32.    println(s"Incremented value: ${incrementedStore.current}")
       // Output: Incremented value: 43
33. }
```

In this example, we defined a store data structure, created a **Comonad** instance for **Store**, and then demonstrated the use of extract to extract the current value and **coflatMap** to apply a comonadic action (incrementing the current value) while preserving the context. The output demonstrates the extracted and incremented values.

The following are the uses of comonads:

- **Contextual focus**: Comonads are useful in situations where you need to focus on specific parts of a larger context, like analysing a particular element in a data structure or reacting to specific events in a stream of data.

- **FRP**: Comonads are employed in FRP libraries to model time-varying values and transformations on these values. Comonads help manage the flow of time-dependent data.

- **Stateful computations**: Comonads can be used to model stateful computations where the focus is on a specific part of the state. This allows you to perform computations based on the localized context, making it easier to manage stateful operations.

- **Data analysis and exploration**: Comonads can be applied in data analysis and exploration scenarios where you need to focus on specific data points or regions within a dataset.

- **Modularity and reusability**: Comonads can enhance the modularity of your code by allowing you to isolate and work with specific parts of your data structures. This can lead to more reusable and testable components.

While comonads might not be as commonly used as monads in everyday programming, they are valuable in specific contexts where you need to deal with localized computations or stateful operations within a larger context. Understanding comonads deepens your understanding of functional programming concepts and can be beneficial in certain problem domains.

Bimonad

A **Bimonad** is a type class in functional programming that combines the properties of both monads and comonads. To understand bimonads, it is essential to know what monads and comonads are first:

A bimonad is a structure that supports both the monadic sequencing (with **flatMap**) and the comonadic extraction (with extract). It combines the capabilities of monads and comonads, providing a unified interface for both sequential composition and value extraction.

```
1.  object BimonadExampleApp extends App {
2.    val bimonadValue = BimonadExample(42)
3.
4.    // Using monadic operations (flatMap in this case)
5.    val monadicResult: BimonadExample[Int] = bimonadValue.flatMap
      (x => BimonadExample(x * 2))
6.    println(s"Monadic Result: ${monadicResult.extract}")
      // Output: Monadic Result: 84
7.
8.    // Using comonadic operation (extract in this case)
9.    val comonadicResult: Int = BimonadExample.coflatMap(bimonadValue)
      (_.extract * 3).extract
10.   println(s"Comonadic Result: $comonadicResult")
      // Output: Comonadic Result: 126
11. }
```

In this example, **BimonadExample** is a custom data structure that combines both monadic and comonadic behaviors. It implements monad and comonad instances, providing implementations for **pure**, **flatMap**, **extract**, and **coflatMap**.

Eq

Eq is a type class that represents the concept of equality. It provides a way to test if two values of the same type are equal. The **Eq** type class defines the **eqv** method, which checks if two values are equal, and is commonly used for comparing values in a way that is consistent with their semantic meaning.

The following are the uses of **Eq**:

- **Correctness**: When you are working with complex data structures or writing algorithms, it is essential to ensure that your equality comparisons are correct. Using **Eq** helps you avoid simple mistakes in equality checks, ensuring that your programs behave as expected.

- **Abstraction**: **Eq** provides an abstract way to compare values. By relying on type classes, you can write generic functions and algorithms that work with any data type with an **Eq** instance. This abstraction promotes code reuse and modularity.

- **Consistency**: **Eq** enforces a consistent way of comparing values. This consistency is crucial for maintaining the correctness of your programs, especially in large and collaborative codebases.

- **Testing**: When writing unit tests, you can use **Eq** to compare the expected and actual values, ensuring that your functions and data structures produce the correct output.

- **Property testing**: In property-based testing, you can use **Eq** to define properties that must hold true for your functions. Property testing libraries can then generate a wide range of input values and check if these properties are satisfied, helping you discover edge cases and potential issues.

- **Functional abstractions**: In functional programming, equality is often a fundamental concept. Many functional programming libraries and techniques rely on equality for operations like filtering, grouping, and transforming data. Using **Eq** allows you to integrate your custom data types seamlessly with these functional abstractions.

The following is a simple example of how you might use **Eq** in Scala with the **cats** library:

```
1.  import cats.Eq
2.  import cats.instances.int._
3.  import cats.instances.string._
4.  import cats.syntax.eq._
5.
6.  // Define custom data type
7.  case class Person(name: String, age: Int)
8.
9.  // Define Eq instances for custom data type
10. implicit val personEq: Eq[Person] = Eq.instance[Person]
      { (person1, person2) =>
11.   person1.name === person2.name && person1.age === person2.age
12. }
13.
14. val person1 = Person("Alice", 30)
15. val person2 = Person("Alice", 30)
16.
17. println(person1 === person2) // Output: true
      (uses Eq instance for Person)
```

In this example, **Eq** is used to compare instances of the **Person** class, ensuring that two **Person** objects are considered equal if their **name** and **age** fields are equal. The **===** syntax is provided by **cats**, allowing for a more natural way to perform equality comparisons.

Show

Show refers to a type class that provides functionality for converting values into human-readable strings. It is similar to the concept of **toString** in Java and other programming languages, but Show is more powerful and composable.

The **Show** type class allows you to define custom string representations for your data types. By defining instances of **Show** for your custom types, you can control how those types are displayed as strings, providing more meaningful and context-specific representations.

The following is an example of how you might use **Show** in Scala using the **cats** library:

```
1. import cats.Show
2. import cats.implicits._
3.
4. // Define a custom data type
5. case class Person(name: String, age: Int)
6.
7. // Define a Show instance for the Person type
8. implicit val personShow: Show[Person] = Show.show(person => s"${person.name}, ${person.age} years old»)
9.
10. val person = Person("Alice", 30)
11.
12. // Print the person using the custom Show instance
13. println(person.show)  // Output: Alice, 30 years old
```

In this example, **Show** is used to provide a custom string representation for the **Person** type. The **show** method is provided by **cats** syntax enrichment, allowing you to convert the **Person** instance into a string using the custom **Show** instance. This provides a way to display **Person** objects in a way that is meaningful for the domain of your application.

The following are the uses of **Show**:

- **Custom string representations**: Show allows you to define custom string representations for your types. You can display data in a meaningful way for your domain, making debugging and logging more informative.

- **Separation of concerns**: By defining **Show** instances for your types, you separate the concerns of displaying data from the actual data types. This separation makes your code more modular and maintainable.

- **Readability**: Custom string representations can enhance the readability of your code. When you print or log values, having meaningful representations can make it easier to understand the state of your program.

- **Debugging**: When debugging, it is often helpful to see the state of your data structures. Custom **Show** instances can provide formatted output tailored to your debugging needs, making it easier to identify issues in your code.

- **Testing**: In unit tests, having custom string representations can make it easier to understand the differences between expected and actual values when tests fail. This can speed up the debugging process.

- **Logging and output**: When working with log files or user interfaces, having meaningful string representations can be invaluable for tracking application behavior and user interactions.

Parallel

A **Parallel** type class represents a higher-level abstraction for concurrent or parallel computations. It is designed to work in conjunction with the **Applicative** type class, providing a way to perform independent computations in parallel and then combine their results. The **Parallel** type class is particularly useful when you have computations that can be executed concurrently, allowing you to harness the power of multicore processors and improve the performance of your applications.

Cats, a popular functional programming library in Scala, provides a **Parallel** type class.

The following is a basic example of using **Parallel** to perform parallel computations:

```
1.  import cats.Parallel
2.  import cats.implicits._
3.
4.  // Example computations
5.  def computation1: Int = 42
6.  def computation2: String = "Hello, World!"
7.
8.  // Create a Parallel instance for Option
9.  implicit val optionParallel: Parallel[Option, List] =
10.   Parallel.apply(Option.apply, List.apply)
11.
12. // Use Parallel to perform computations in parallel
13. val result: Option[(Int, String)] =
14.   (Option.parallel(computation1), List.parallel(computation2)).
      parTupled
15.
16. println(result)  // Output: Some((42,Hello, World!))
```

In this example, **Parallel** is used to perform computations **computation1** and **computation2** in **Parallel**. The **parTupled** method combines their results into a tuple, allowing them to execute concurrently.

Reducible

A **Reducible** represents data structures that can be reduced to a single value by applying an associative binary operation. In simpler terms, a **Reducible** is a collection-like data structure that can be combined or folded into a single result.

The following is an example of using a **Reducible** type class in Scala:

```scala
1.  // Define a Reducible type class
2.  trait Reducible[F[_]] {
3.    def reduce[A](fa: F[A])(f: (A, A) => A): A
4.  }
5.
6.  // Define a Reducible instance for List
7.  implicit val listReducible: Reducible[List] = new Reducible[List] {
8.    def reduce[A](fa: List[A])(f: (A, A) => A): A = fa.reduceLeft(f)
9.  }
10.
11. // Usage of the Reducible instance
12. val numbers = List(1, 2, 3, 4, 5)
13. val sum = Reducible[List].reduce(numbers)(_ + _)
14. println(s"Sum of the list: $sum")  // Output: Sum of the list: 15
```

In this example, **Reducible** reduces a list of integers to their sum. The **reduce** method abstracts away the reduction logic, providing a uniform way to aggregate data in different types of structures.

The following are the uses of **Reducible**:

- **Uniform interface: Reducible** provides a uniform interface for reducing or aggregating data across different data structures. By adhering to the **Reducible** type class, various collection-like types can be manipulated in a consistent and predictable manner.

- **Abstraction and generality**: **Reducible** allows you to write generic functions that work with different data structures. Functions defined on reducible data structures can be reused across various collection types, promoting code modularity and reuse.

- **Functional composition**: The ability to reduce a data structure to a single value, enables functional composition. You can compose complex transformations by combining simpler reduction functions. This composability is a fundamental principle in functional programming.

- **Expressive code**: **Reducible** operations like folding, reducing, or aggregating can often be expressed using higher order functions like **foldLeft**, **foldRight**, and **reduce**, making your code more declarative and clearer.

- **Immutability**: `Reducible` operations can often be implemented in an immutable way, allowing you to work with immutable data structures. This aligns with the functional programming paradigm and promotes the use of immutable data.

- **Parallelism and concurrency**: Some reduction operations can be parallelized, allowing you to take advantage of multicore processors. `Reducible` data structures can be processed concurrently or in parallel, optimizing performance for certain operations.

- **Data aggregation**: `Reducible` structures are useful for aggregating data, whether it is a sum of numbers, concatenation of strings, or any other type of aggregation operation. This is valuable in various domains, including data processing, statistics, and analytics.

Data types

In the Cats library, there are several data types that are commonly used to implement functional programming patterns in Scala. These are kept generally in `cats.data` package.

The following are some of the key data types provided by Cats:

- **Validated (cats.data.Validated)**: Represents a value that can be either valid or invalid, along with a collection of `errors.Cats` provides the `Validated` data type for accumulating errors in data validation scenarios.

- **Writer (cats.data.Writer)**: Represents a computation that produces a log along with a result. Cats provides the `Writer` monad for performing computations with logging.

- **Reader (cats.data.Reader)**: Represents a computation that depends on some input. Cats provides the `Reader` monad for dependency injection.

- **State (cats.data.State)**: Represents a computation that carries some state along and produces a result. Cats provides the `State` monad for managing and passing state in functional programs.

- **Validated (cats.data.Validated)**: It is used for accumulating errors in a data validation process. Unlike `Either`, which short-circuits on the first error encountered, `Validated` allows you to accumulate all errors. This can be particularly useful in scenarios where you want to validate multiple conditions and collect all validation errors instead of stopping at the first failure.

- **Kleisli (cats.data.Kleisli)**: Represents a function `A => F[B]` where `F` is a monad. Cats provides the `Kleisli` arrow for composing functions that return monadic values.

- **Const (cats.data.Const)**: Represents a constant value associated with a type parameter. It is often used in the context of type classes to provide a constant implementation for certain type class methods.

- **Chain (cats. Data.Chain)**: Chain is an immutable sequence data structure that allows constant time prepending, appending and concatenation. This makes it especially efficient when used as a monoid, e.g. with **Validated** or **Writer**. As such it aims to be used where list and vector incur a performance penalty. Cats also includes type class implementations to support using **Chain** as a general-purpose collection type, including traverse, monad, and alternative.

These data types in Cats provide abstractions and monads for various functional programming patterns, enabling developers to write more expressive, composable, and type-safe code in Scala. By leveraging these data types, developers can build robust and maintainable functional applications.

Transformers

Transformers are part of Cats data types. The problem with monads is that they do not compose. In any expression, if there is more than one monad to combine, then it is very problematic to add those monads by using some artificial way to work together. Hence, Transformers are the way to provide composability easily. In Cats, monad transformers are a powerful tool for working with multiple monadic effects in a concise and composable way. They allow you to combine the features of different monads into a single monad, making it easier to work with complex computations that involve multiple effects. Monad transformers are particularly useful when you need to stack monadic computations, such as working with both **Option** (for possible absence of values) and **Either** (for error handling) within the same computation.

A monad transformer is essentially a wrapper around a monad that adds additional capabilities to it. Cats provides a variety of monad transformers, such as **OptionT**, **EitherT**, **WriterT**, **StateT**, etc., each tailored for specific use cases.

The following is an overview of some common monad transformers in Cats:

- **OptionT**: **OptionT[F[_], A]** is a monad transformer that combines the effects of **Option** and another monad **F[_]**. It allows you to work with computations that can return an **Option** within the context of a different monad **F**.

- **EitherT**: **EitherT[F[_], A, B]** combines the effects of **Either[A, B]** and another monad **F[_]**. It is used for computations that can return either a value of type **A** (left) or a value of type **B** (right) within the context of monad **F**.

- **WriterT**: **WriterT[F[_], W, A]** combines the effects of logging (**Writer[W, A]**) and another monad **F[_]**. It allows you to log values of type **W** alongside computations of type **A** within the context of **F**.

- **StateT**: **StateT[F[_], S, A]** combines the effects of state manipulation (**State[S, A]**) and another monad **F[_]**. It is used for computations that involve mutable state of type **S** within the context of **F**.

- **KleisliT: Kleisli[F[_], A, B]** represents a function **A => F[B]**, where **F[_]** is a monad. **Kleisli** is not exactly a monad transformer but is used to compose monadic functions in a convenient way.

Using these transformers, you can build complex monadic computations without having to deal with the nesting and unwrapping of monads manually. They provide a clean and elegant way to handle the composition of different monadic effects.

The following is an example using **OptionT**:

```
1.  import cats.data.OptionT
2.  import cats.implicits._
3.
4.  // Sample computations returning Option values
5.  val getUser: Option[User] = Some(User("Alice", 30))
6.  val getOrders: Option[List[Order]] = Some(List(Order(1), Order(2)))
7.
8.  // Combine Option effects with OptionT
9.  val result: OptionT[Option, Order] = for {
10.    user <- OptionT(getUser)
11.    orders <- OptionT(getOrders)
12.    order <- OptionT.fromOption[Option](orders.find(_.userId == user.id))
13. } yield order
14.
15. // Extract the result
16. val finalResult: Option[Order] = result.value
17.
18. println(finalResult)  // Output: Some(Order(1))
```

In this example, **OptionT** combines computations that return **Option** values (**getUser** and **getOrders**). The monad transformer allows you to compose these computations naturally, and you can extract the final result using the **value** method.

Free implementations

Free implementations are a part of Cats data type. The term free often refers to constructions that provide minimal capabilities or laws, allowing you to derive more complex structures for specific purposes. These constructions are referred to as free because they come with minimal constraints and provide maximal freedom to interpret and extend them according to your needs.

There are several free implementations in functional programming, and they are typically used to model specific abstractions in a more general and composable way.

The following are a few common examples:

- **Free monad**: A free monad is a construction that allows you to build monadic structures without specifying the concrete monad implementation. It is essentially a data structure representing a sequence of monadic operations (such as **flatMap** and **map**) that you can interpret later using different monads. Free monads are particularly useful when you want to separate the description of your program from its execution, enabling powerful techniques like program transformation, optimization, and interpretation.

- **Free applicative**: Similar to free monads, free applicatives provide a way to compose applicative functors in a generic way. They allow you to build complex applicative computations using a minimal set of operations (pure and ap), separating the structure of your computation from the specific applicative functor you want to use. Free applicatives are useful when you need to combine multiple independent computations using the applicative style.

- **Free arrow**: Free arrows generalize the concept of arrows in functional programming. Arrows provide a way to abstractly represent computations with input and output. Free arrows allow you to build arrow-like structures without committing to a specific arrow implementation, providing a way to compose and manipulate computations in a generic way.

- **Free monoid**: A free monoid is a monoid that is freely generated by a set. Given a set of elements, a free monoid constructs a monoid where elements are sequences of the original set's elements. The free monoid is free because it imposes no additional relations between elements other than those necessary for the monoid laws. It is a foundational concept in algebra and is used in various areas of computer science, including formal language theory.

- **Free semigroup**: Similar to free monoids, a free semigroup is a semigroup that is freely generated by a set. Semigroups are algebraic structures with an associative binary operation. Free semigroups are semigroups where elements are sequences generated from a set, and the operation is the concatenation of sequences. Free semigroups find applications in areas like formal languages and automata theory.

These free constructions provide a way to model abstract algebraic structures, compose computations, and reason about programs in a more general and modular manner. They are foundational concepts in functional programming and have applications in various domains, including compilers, interpreters, language theory, and formal verification.

Cats testing

Testing is an essential aspect of software development, and the Cats library in Scala provides support for testing your functional programs and abstractions. Cats offers several utilities and techniques to facilitate testing, including property-based testing, laws testing, and testing with type classes.

The following is an overview of some testing aspects in Cats:

- **Property-based testing**: Cats includes integration with property-based testing libraries like **scalacheck**. You can use **scalacheck** to define and run property-based tests for your type classes and data structures. Property-based tests allow you to check that the properties or invariants of your code hold for a wide range of inputs.

- **Laws testing**: Many type classes in Cats come with a set of laws that must hold for their instances. Laws are mathematical properties that your instances should satisfy to ensure correctness. Cats provides tools to help you test whether your type class instances adhere to these laws. For example, you can use the laws trait for specific type classes to generate and run tests that verify the laws are satisfied.

- **Discipline**: Discipline is a library used with Cats to specify and run laws testing for type classes. It provides a structured way to define and verify the consistency of type class instances. Discipline ensures that the same set of laws is tested for different data types, promoting consistency across different libraries and implementations.

- **Arbitrary instances**: In Cats, you can use the arbitrary type class from **scalacheck** to generate random instances of your data types. This is useful for property-based testing, where you want to test your code with a wide range of inputs. Cats provides instances for many common data types, and you can create custom arbitrary instances when needed.

- **Matchers and syntax sugar**: Cats provides matchers and syntax sugar for testing, for example, you can use Cats **Eq** type class to compare values for equality and Cats matchers to simplify testing assertions. Cats matchers provide a more idiomatic way to express expectations in your tests.

- **Testing with state transformers**: Cats provides state transformers, like **StateT**, which can be used for deterministic stateful computations. These transformers can be tested by running them with initial states and examining the resulting state and values.

- **Testing laws for custom type classes**: If you define custom type classes in your application, you can use Cats tools and techniques to specify and test the laws associated with those type classes. This ensures the correctness of your custom abstractions.

The following is an example of property-based testing in Cats using **scalacheck**:

```
1. import cats.Eq
2. import cats.implicits._
3. import org.scalacheck.Properties
4. import org.scalacheck.Prop.forAll
5.
```

```
 6.  object MyTypeClassProperties extends Properties("MyTypeClass") {
 7.    // Define a custom type class and its Laws
 8.    trait MyTypeClass[A] {
 9.      def combine(a: A, b: A): A
10.      def identity: A
11.    }
12.
13.    // Define a property-based test for the associativity law
14.    property("associativity") = forAll { (a: Int, b: Int, c: Int) =>
15.      val typeClassInstance = new MyTypeClass[Int] {
16.        def combine(a: Int, b: Int): Int = a + b
17.        def identity: Int = 0
18.      }
19.
20.      Eq[Int].eqv(
21.        typeClassInstance.combine(typeClassInstance.combine(a, b), c),
22.        typeClassInstance.combine(a, typeClassInstance.combine(b, c))
23.      )
24.    }
25. }
26.
27. object MyApp extends App {
28.    MyTypeClassProperties.check()
29. }
```

In this example, we defined a property-based test for the associativity law of a custom type class. We use **scalacheck** to generate random inputs and test whether the associativity law holds for the **combine** operation. The **Eq** type class from **cats** is used to compare values for equality. You can run this test by executing the **MyApp** object.

Conclusion

In this chapter, we discussed all the type classes Cats provides, their usage, and how to use them in real scenarios in examples. We also looked into Cats's data types' which also provides help in writing functional, composable, and modular code. We further explored the transformers and their usage and free implementation. In the end, we also tried to understand the different types of testing available to test our functional code.

In the next chapter, we will learn about ZIO, which is a powerful library for asynchronous and concurrent programming to handle complex effects in a purely functional way. It helps to build high-performance, scalable, and resilient applications. We will learn its concurrency management, resource management, and unit test framework to validate all our functional implementations.

Join our Discord space

Join our Discord workspace for latest updates, offers, tech happenings around the world, new releases, and sessions with the authors:

https://discord.bpbonline.com

CHAPTER 5

Understanding ZIO

Introduction

This chapter focuses on the implementation details of category concepts that we learned in *Chapter 2, Implementation of Category Theory,* using ZIO library. ZIO is a powerful, type-safe, and functional library for building asynchronous and concurrent applications in Scala. It provides a modern, high-performance, and purely functional programming framework designed to handle complex effects, resource management, and state in a concise and composable way.

In this chapter, we will discuss different tools that the ZIO library provides, to ease functional programming. We will also talk about, different ZIO constructs that help in writing modular and composable applications.

Structure

In this chapter, we will cover the following topics:

- Introduction to ZIO
- ZIO type aliases
- ZIO control flow
- ZIO error management

- ZIO layer
- ZIO concurrency
- ZIO resource management
- ZIO testing

Objectives

By the end of this chapter, readers will be able to see the implementation of category theory abstraction that we briefly discussed in *Chapter 2, Implementation of Category Theory*.

ZIO is a high-performance, purely functional Scala library for managing effects, concurrency, and resource safety. It is designed to help writing in functional programming, for example, handling side effects, managing state, and dealing with asynchronous operations in a composable and type-safe manner. Readers who are not well-versed with category concepts can also write functional code using ZIO. We will also go through samples using ZIO and its integrated libraries.

Introduction to ZIO

According to **https://zio.dev/**, *ZIO is type-safe, composable, asynchronous, concurrent high-performance functional programming for Scala.*

ZIO is a powerful, purely functional library for asynchronous and concurrent programming in Scala. It is designed to help developers build highly scalable, reliable, and maintainable applications by providing abstractions for managing asynchronous, concurrent, and effective computations. ZIO stands for zero-cost and asynchronous I/O, emphasizing its focus on performance and asynchronous programming. *John de'goes* and *Adam* who started the company *Ziverge*, focused on ZIO and its library integration with ZIO to enlarge its ecosystems to all other libraries; making it easier to work, due to its large support to other libraries.

The following are some of the key features of ZIO:

- **Purely functional**: ZIO encourages purely functional programming practices, enabling developers to write composable, referentially transparent, and side effect-free code.

- **Asynchronous and concurrent programming**: ZIO provides a powerful asynchronous and concurrent programming model, allowing developers to work with fibers (lightweight, non-blocking threads) to manage concurrent computations. Fibers in ZIO are designed to be extremely lightweight, making them efficient to work with concurrent tasks.

- **Error management**: ZIO offers a robust error management system, allowing developers to model and handle errors in a type-safe manner. Error types are explicitly defined, preventing the need for exceptions and promoting safe error handling practices.

- **Resource management**: ZIO helps manage resources efficiently by providing a built-in mechanism for acquiring, using, and releasing resources safely and concurrently. This is especially useful for managing resources like database connections, network sockets, or files.

- **Testability**: ZIO applications are easy to test, due to their purely functional nature. Effects can be easily tested in isolation, without the need for complex mocking frameworks. ZIO also provides a test environment that facilitates writing unit tests for ZIO programs.

- **Environment**: ZIO applications are built around the concept of an environment, which is a set of dependencies required for the application to run. ZIO's environment model allows for dependency injection and facilitates modular and testable code.

- **Composable and declarative**: ZIO encourages a declarative style of programming, where applications are constructed by composing small, pure, and reusable components. This composability simplifies the development and maintenance of complex applications.

- **Type-safety**: ZIO leverages Scala's powerful type system to provide strong guarantees about the correctness of your programs, at the time of compilation. Type annotations and type inference, help catch errors before runtime.

- **Integration and interoperability**: ZIO integrates seamlessly with other Scala libraries and frameworks, making it suitable for a wide range of applications. It also provides an interop with popular libraries for http, JSON, etc.

ZIO is often used in applications where high concurrency, fault tolerance, and ease of testing are essential requirements. It is widely adopted in the Scala community and continues to evolve, providing new features and improvements, to make functional programming in Scala more accessible and powerful.

ZIO type aliases

Now, let us discuss the ZIO type so that we can understand the need for its aliases.

ZIO is the fundamental type of ZIO functional library. This data type represents a functional effect and is the description of any computation or interaction. A functional library implements functional constructs that are executed by the runtime. ZIO is not any different; this basic building block functional description is executed by the ZIO runtime, which then results in a success or failure value, with a few exceptions. This data type is represented as `ZIO[R, E, A]` which is a generic type and further defined by its type parameter `R, E, A`.

This data type can be understood as a function, as follows:

```
R => Either[E, A]
```

This function requires **R** and produces a failure of type **E** or a success value of type **A**.

As per **https://zio.dev**, the meaning of these type parameters is as follows:

- **R environment type**: The environment type parameter represents the type of contextual data that is required by the effect before it can be executed, for example, some effects may require a connection to a database, some may require an HTTP request, and others might require a user session. If the environment type parameter is **Any**, then the effect has no requirements, which means that the effect can be executed without being provided with any specific context first.

- **E failure type**: This failure type parameter represents the type of error that the effect can fail with when it is executed. Although, exception or throwable are common failure types in ZIO applications, ZIO does not require the error type, and it is sometimes useful to define custom business or domain error types, for different parts of an application. If the error type parameter is nothing, it means the effect cannot fail.

- **A success type**: The success type parameter represents the type of success that the effect can succeed with when it is executed. If the success type parameter is unit, it means the effect produced no useful information like a void-returning method, whereas if it is nothing, it means the effect will run forever, unless it fails.

Let us understand it better by using examples, as follows:

- **ZIO[Any, IOException, Byte]** represents an effect that does not require an environment. The declaration is using its environment type **R** as **Any** (**scala.Any**), furthermore, it implies that this effect could fail, by generating an **IOException** (**E** failure type parameter) or succeed by producing a **Byte** (**S** success type parameter).

  In the same way, any database interaction can be coded, as follows:

  ○ **ZIO [Connection, SQL Exception, ResultSet]** which needs a **Connection** as the input (its **R** parameter), could generate the error as **SQLException** (its **E** parameter) or produce **ResultSet** (its **S** parameter) on success.

    A single type that represents all HTTP web interactions.

  ○ **ZIO[HttpRequest, HttpFailure, HttpSuccess]** where the client requests for **HttpRequest** as the input, could result in an error with **HttpFailure**, or success with **HttpSuccess**.

    Generally, we do not need these three parameters to define the interaction or effect. As it becomes cumbersome to use all parameters whenever it does not require any specific parameter, for example, environment or exception. Keeping all the parameters when it is not required in code also makes the code less maintainable and harder to grasp. So, ZIO provides its aliases for the combination of parameters required and its relevant functional behavior, by redefining the ZIO function in its companion object for that combination of parameters.

The type aliases are defined, as follows:

- **UIO[A]**: A type alias for `ZIO[Any, Nothing, A]`, representing an effect with no requirements, cannot fail, and can succeed with **A**.

- **URIO[R, A]**: A type alias for `ZIO[R, Nothing, A]`, representing an effect that requires an **R**, cannot fail, and can succeed with **A**.

- **Task[A]**: A type alias for `ZIO[Any, Throwable, A]`, representing an effect without requirements, may fail with a **Throwable** value, or succeed with **A**.

- **RIO[R, A]**: A type alias for `ZIO[R, Throwable, A]`, representing an effect that requires an **R**, may fail with a **Throwable** value, or succeed with **A**.

- **IO[E, A]**: A type alias for `ZIO[Any, E, A]`, representing an effect without requirements, may fail with an **E**, or succeed with **A**.

Let us discuss these type aliases in detail, as they will be used more in programming, due to their succinct description for the same behavior provided by their ZIO counterpart.

We will see how these aliases are defined in the core library.

UIO[A]

UIO[A] is a type alias, representing an effect that cannot fail (*U* stands for unexceptional or unfailing), and produces a value of type **A**.

The following is the full definition of **UIO**:

```
type UIO[+A] = ZIO[Any, Nothing, A]
```

In this type alias:

- **A** represents the type of successful value produced by the effect.

- **Nothing** indicates that the effect cannot fail with any specific error type.

- **Any** signifies that the effect does not require any specific environment; it can run in any environment.

So, **UIO[A]** represents a ZIO effect that will always succeed and produce a value of type **A**, without raising any exceptions or errors.

You might use **UIO** in situations where you have a computation that is guaranteed not to fail, such as a constant value, a pure computation, or a value obtained from a reliable data source. By using **UIO**, you convey to readers of your code that the effect is safe and will always produce a result without any failures.

For example, consider a simple ZIO program that returns the constant value **42**:

```
1. import zio._
2.
3. object Main extends App {
4.
5.   // A UIO effect that always succeeds and produces the value 42
6.   val constantValue: UIO[Int] = ZIO.succeed(42)
7.
8.   // Main program
9.   override def run(args: List[String]): ZIO[ZEnv, Nothing,
      ExitCode] = {
10.    constantValue.foldM(
11.      _ => putStrLn("Error occurred").as(ExitCode.failure),
12.      value => putStrLn(s"Result: $value").as(ExitCode.success)
13.    )
14.  }
15.}
```

In this example, **constantValue** is of type **UIO[Int]**, indicating that it is an effect that always succeeds and produces an integer value. The use of **UIO** communicates that the effect is guaranteed to be successful.

URIO[R, A]

URIO[A] is a type of alias, representing an effect that cannot fail (*U* stands for unexceptional or unfailing), and produces a value of type **A**.

The following is the full definition of **URIO**:

type URIO[-R, +A] = ZIO[R, Nothing, A]

In this type alias:

- **R** represents the type of environment required by the effect. It is a contravariant, meaning that if you have an **URIO[R1, A]**, you can use it as an **URIO[R2, A]** if **R2** is a supertype of **R1**. Contravariance allows you to widen the required environment type.

- **A** represents the type of successful value produced by the effect.

- **Nothing** indicates that the effect cannot fail with any specific error type.

URIO[A] represents a ZIO effect that will always succeed and produce a value of type **A**, without raising any exceptions or errors. The primary difference between **UIO[A]** and **URIO[A]** is the ability to specify a required environment **R** in **URIO**, allowing the effect to access services or resources within that environment while still being guaranteed not to fail.

You might use **URIO** in situations where, you need to access some environment (such as configuration, logging, or external services) to compute a result, but you are certain that the computation will never fail.

For example, consider a ZIO program that reads a configuration value from the environment and uses it to compute a result, as follows:

```
1. import zio._
2.
3. case class Config(apiKey: String)
4.
5. object Main extends App {
6.
7.   // An URIO effect that reads the API key from the environment
   and uses it to compute a result
8.   def computeResult: URIO[Config, String] =
9.     ZIO.accessM[Config](config => URIO.succeed(s"Result using API key:
   ${config.apiKey}"))
10.
11.   // Main program
12.   override def run(args: List[String]): ZIO[ZEnv,
   Nothing, ExitCode] = {
13.     val config = Config("my-api-key")
14.
15.     // Provide the configuration to the computeResult effect and
   handle the result
16.     computeResult.provide(config).foldM(
17.       _ => putStrLn("Error occurred").as(ExitCode.failure),
18.       result => putStrLn(s"Result: $result").as(ExitCode.success)
19.     )
20.   }
21. }
```

In this example, **computeResult** is of type **URIO[Config, String]**, indicating that it requires a **Config** environment and produces a **String** result. The **provide** operator is used to provide the necessary environment to the effect before running it. This way, the effect can access the required environment (**Config** in this case) to compute its result without the possibility of failure.

Task[A]

Task[A] is a type alias, representing an effect that can fail with an error of type **Throwable** or produce a value of type **A**.

The following is the full definition of **Task**:

```
type Task[+A] = ZIO[Any, Throwable, A]
```

In this type alias:

- **A** represents the type of successful value produced by the effect.

- **Throwable** indicates that the effect can fail with any throwable error.

Task[A] is a powerful data type in ZIO that represents asynchronous, potentially error-prone computations. You might use **Task** in situations where, you perform I/O operations, network requests, database queries, or any other asynchronous operations that can result in errors. It provides a structured and composable way to handle asynchronous and concurrent programming, ensuring that errors are properly managed and that your code remains resilient.

The following are a few reasons to use **Task[A]**:

- **Error handling**: **Task** provides a robust and concise way to handle errors in asynchronous operations. You can compose multiple **Task** operations and handle errors at specific points, ensuring that failures are managed in a controlled manner.

  The following code shares the template on how to handle asynchronous or erroneous operation using **Task[A]**:

  ```
  1. val task: Task[Int] = Task {
  2. // Perform asynchronous or error-prone operation here
  3. // ...
  4. // Return an integer result or throw an exception if an
        error occurs
  5. }
  ```

- **Concurrency and parallelism**: **Task** integrates seamlessly with ZIO's powerful concurrency primitives, allowing you to run multiple tasks concurrently and compose them to achieve parallelism. This makes it easier to write efficient, concurrent, and scalable applications.

  The following code explains how two tasks can be executed using for comprehension:

  ```
  1. val task1: Task[Int] = // ...
  2. val task2: Task[Int] = // ...
  3.
  4. val result: Task[Int] = for {
  5. value1 <- task1
  6. value2 <- task2
  7. } yield value1 + value2
  ```

- **Composition and transformation**: **Task** provides a rich set of combinators and operators to transform, compose, and sequence asynchronous computations. You can use methods like **map**, **flatMap**, **zip**, and **fold** to manipulate **Task** values, making it easy to express complex asynchronous workflows.

The following code describes how **task** transforms data with **processData** function using **flatMap:**

```
1.  val task: Task[String] = fetchDataFromAPI()
2.
3.  val processed Task: Task[String] = task.
    flatMap(data => processData(data))
```

- **Resource safety**: **Task** ensures resource safety, by providing dedicated combinators like **Bracket** and **Managed**, for acquiring, using, and releasing resources. This ensures that resources are properly managed, even in the presence of errors or early termination of computations.

The following code explains how resource safety is applied using **Managed. fromEffect:**

```
1.  val acquire: Task[Resource] = Task.effect(Resource.acquire())
2.
3.  val managedResource: Managed[Throwable, Resource] = Managed.
    fromEffect(acquire)
```

By using **Task[A]** in your ZIO applications, you can write robust, concurrent, and asynchronous code, that is both expressive and safe. Task-based programming in ZIO simplifies error handling, promotes composability, and provides a high level of concurrency control, making it a popular choice, for building scalable and reliable applications.

RIO[R, A]

RIO[R, A] is a type alias, representing an effect that requires an environment of type **R**, which may fail with an error, and produces a value of type **A**.

The following is the full definition of **RIO**:

```
type RIO[-R, +A] = ZIO[R, Throwable, A]
```

In this type alias:

- **R** represents the type of environment required by the effect. It is contravariant, meaning that if you have an **RIO[R1, A]**, you can use it as an **RIO[R2, A]** if R2 is a supertype of **R1**. Contravariance allows you to widen the required environment type.

- **A** represents the type of successful value produced by the effect.

- **Throwable** indicates that the effect can fail with any throwable error.

RIO[R, A] is a fundamental data type in ZIO that captures the essence of many functional programming patterns, including dependency injection and the reader monad. You might use RIO in situations where, your computation depends on some environment, such as configuration settings, database connections, or other services.

The following are a few reasons to use **RIO[R, A]**:

- **Dependency injection**: **RIO** promotes the dependency injection pattern by making the dependency on the environment explicit. By requiring an environment of type **R**, you ensure that the necessary dependencies are available when the effect is executed. This makes your code more modular and testable.

  Refer to the following code:

  ```
  1. case class DatabaseConfig(url: String)
  2.
  3. def fetchDataFromDatabase: RIO[DatabaseConfig, String] =
  4. ZIO.accessM[DatabaseConfig](config => {
  5. // Use the configuration to fetch data from the database
  6. // ...
  7. // Return the fetched data as a String
  8. })
  ```

- **Testability**: **RIO** makes dependencies explicit, so it makes it easy to test your effects in isolation. You can provide mock or test implementations of the required environment to test specific parts of your application logic without relying on external resources.

  Refer to the following code:

  ```
  1. val testConfig = DatabaseConfig("test-url")
  2. val testData = "test-data"
  3.
  4. val testEffect: UIO[String] =
  5. fetchDataFromDatabase.provide(testConfig).
     orDie // orDie converts Throwable to Nothing
  6.
  7. // Test the effect with a specific configuration
  8. assertRuntime(testEffect)(equalTo(testData))
  ```

- **Encapsulation**: **RIO** allows you to encapsulate the dependencies required by your effects. This encapsulation promotes the separation of concerns, clarifying which parts of your code rely on specific environments. It also allows you to compose effects that depend on different environments, ensuring that each effect has access to the dependencies it needs.

  Refer to the following code:

  ```
  1. def complexLogic: RIO[DatabaseConfig with LoggingConfig, String] =
  2. for {
  3. data <- fetchDataFromDatabase
  4. _     <- log(s"Fetched data: $data»)
  5. } yield data
  ```

- **Composition**: `RIO` effects are composable. You can combine and transform `RIO` values using various combinators, allowing you to create complex, multi-step workflows. composable effects enable you to build sophisticated applications from simple, reusable components.

  Refer to the following code:

  ```
  1. val result: RIO[DatabaseConfig with LoggingConfig, String] =
  2. complexLogic.flatMap(data => processData(data))
  ```

By using **RIO[R, A]** in your ZIO applications, you can build modular, testable, and maintainable code. It promotes separation of concerns, facilitates dependency injection, and enables powerful composition of effects, making it a valuable tool for functional programming in Scala.

IO[E, A]

IO[E, A] is a data type, representing an effective computation that may fail with an error of type E, or succeed with a value of type **A**.

The following is the full definition of **IO**:

`type IO[+E, +A] = ZIO[Any, E, A]`

In this type:

- **E** represents the type of error that the computation can fail with.

- **A** represents the type of successful value produced by the computation.

- **IO[E, A]** is one of the core data types in **ZIO** and is widely used for building robust, asynchronous, and concurrent applications.

The following are some reasons why you might want to use **IO[E, A]**:

- **Error handling**: **IO** provides a structured and composable way to handle errors. When you perform operations that can fail such as I/O operations, network requests, or database queries, wrapping them in **IO** allows you to handle errors in a functional and declarative manner. You can use combinators like **map**, **flatMap**, **fold**, **orElse**, and **catchAll** to handle different error scenarios.

  Refer to the following code:

  ```
  1. val result: IO[Error, String] = fetchDataFromDatabase()
  2.
  3. val processedResult: IO[Error, String] = result.
     flatMap(data => processData(data)).
     catchAll(error => handleError(error))
  ```

- **Composition**: **IO** values can be composed together using combinators to create complex and multi-step workflows. You can chain multiple **IO** computations sequentially, transforming the output of one computation and passing it to the next. This composability makes it easy to express complex business logic, concisely and with clarity.

Refer to the following code:

```
1. val result: IO[Error, String] = fetchDataFromDatabase().
   flatMap(data => processData(data))
```

- **Asynchronous and concurrent programming**: **IO** supports asynchronous and concurrent programming out of the box. You can create asynchronous effects using **ZIO.effectAsync** or **ZIO.effectAsyncInterrupt**, and you can run multiple **IO** computations concurrently using combinators **like ZIO.collectAll**, **ZIO.collectAllPar**, and **ZIO.fork**.

Refer to the following code:

```
1. val io1: IO[Error, String] = fetchDataFromDatabase()
2. val io2: IO[Error, String] = fetchDataFromNetwork()
3.
4. val result: IO[Error, (String, String)] =ZIO.
   collectAllPar(List(io1, io2))
```

- **Resource management**: **IO** is used for managing resources safely. **ZIO** provides combinators like **ZIO.bracket** and **ZManaged**, to acquire, use, and release resources, ensuring that resources are properly managed, even in the presence of failures.

```
1. val acquire: IO[Error, Resource] = openResource()
2.
3. val managedResource: ZManaged[Any, Error, Resource] = ZManaged.
   fromEffect(acquire)
```

By using **IO[E, A]** in your **ZIO** applications, you can write robust, composable, and concurrent code. It provides a principled and type-safe way to handle errors, manage resources, and express complex asynchronous workflows. ZIO's **IO** type helps you build scalable and reliable applications in a functional and declarative style.

Type aliases provide the following features:

- **Readability and expressiveness**: Type aliases can make code more readable and expressive, by providing meaningful names to complex or generic types. Instead of seeing a long, parameterized type signature, developers can use a concise alias that describes the purpose of the type.

- **Abstraction and encapsulation**: Type aliases allow you to abstract away implementation details. If the internal representation of a type changes, you can update the alias, without changing the entire codebase. This abstraction helps in encapsulating complexity.

- **Code maintenance and refactoring**: Type aliases make it easier to refactor code. If a particular type is used in multiple places and needs to be changed, you can update the alias in one place, making it less error-prone, rather than manually changing the type in multiple locations.

- **Documentation and intent**: Type aliases serve as a form of documentation. They convey the intent of the code to other developers, making it clear what a specific type represents without requiring them to understand the underlying complexity.

- **Code reusability**: By defining meaningful type aliases, you create reusable components. If a specific pattern of types and functionality is used in multiple places, defining a type alias for it allows for consistent use and behavior throughout the codebase.

ZIO control flow

ZIO functionally defines control flow. These control flow refers to how you structure and manage the execution of asynchronous and concurrent workflows, ensuring correct sequencing, error handling, and decision-making. ZIO provides many tools for controlling the flow of your program effectively while maintaining its functional nature. These controls contain conditional or loop control flow. It provides operators, to define these control flows and functionally execute them.

ZIO conditional flow

ZIO provides combinators for conditional logic, both with, or without effects. Generally, if it is without effect then, only combinators; otherwise, another variation of combinator, defined with the operator and **Zio** is added to it.

The following code is an example:

```
1. Zio.when(< Boolean condition>) (<logic to be executed for true case>)
2. Zio.whenZio(< Boolean condition>) (<effect logic to be executed
   for true case>)
```

When expression

As we have observed in the aforementioned example, **when** is used to execute the logic, the condition provided evaluates as true.

If logic contains effects to be executed then, its **Zio** variation would be used with the same parameters.

```
1. def validateWeightOption(weight: Double): ZIO[Any,
   Nothing, Option[Double]] =
2.   ZIO.when(weight > 0)(ZIO.succeed(weight))
```

```
3.
4.
5. def randomIntOption: ZIO[Any, Nothing, Option[Int]] =
6.    Random.nextInt.whenZIO(Random.nextBoolean)
```

Unless expression

This is another variation of conditional logic combinators, which is the opposite of **when**. It executes when the condition provided is evaluated as false instead of true (in case of **when**).

ifZIO expression

It is an effective logic execution in which the conditional logic evaluates to be true.

```
1. def flipTheCoin: ZIO[Any, IOException, Unit] =
2.    ZIO.ifZIO(Random.nextBoolean)(
3.       onTrue = Console.printLine("Head"),
4.       onFalse = Console.printLine("Tail")
5.    )
```

ZIO loop flow

ZIO provides loop combinators that execute (or replicate) the iterations of a bunch of code based on conditions. It is the same as the while and do-while operators, that you might have seen in Java or Scala programming languages.

Let us discuss what ZIO provides as loop operators.

Loop expression

It is used to iterate a bunch of code, a limited number of times in a functional way. It is defined in the **ZIO** object, as follows:

The following is the definition of **ZIO.loop**:

```
1. def loop[R, E, A, S](
2.       initial: => S
3.    )(cont: S => Boolean, inc: S => S)
      (body: S => ZIO[R, E, A]): ZIO[R, E, List[A]]
```

So, it provides three parameters. First, for the **initial** value. The second defines the **cont** condition that evaluates every next turn, and **inc** is the increment function for the **loop** variable, where the last parameter **body** is executed every time.

Iterate expression

The **iterate** function repeatedly executes the **body** function, passing the current state as an argument. It continues iterating as long as the **cont** predicate returns true. The function returns a **ZIO[R, E, S]** representing the final state after the iterations are complete.

The following is the definition of **ZIO.iterate**:

```
1. def iterate[R, E, S](
2.     initial: => S
3.   )(cont: S => Boolean)(body: S => ZIO[R, E, S]): ZIO[R, E, S]
```

Foreach expression

It is a combinator in the ZIO library that allows you to apply a function to each element of the collection and collect the results in a ZIO effect. The function takes a collection and a function, applies the function to each element of the collection, and returns a new effect that produces a collection of the results.

The following is the definition of **ZIO.foreach**:

```
1. def foreach[R, E, A, B](in: Iterable[A])
     (f: A => ZIO[R, E, B]): ZIO[R, E, List[B]]
```

The following are the details for input parameters of **foreach**:

- **in**: The collection of elements of type **A** to iterate over.

- **f**: The function to apply to each element of the collection. It takes an element of type **A** and produces a **ZIO** effect that may succeed with a value of type **B** or fail with an error of type **E**.

- **Returns**: A **ZIO** effect that, when executed, will iterate over the input collection, apply the function f to each element, and produce a list of the results of type **B**.

ZIO error management

Error management in ZIO is based on the concept of effect types, which allow you to express the possibility of errors explicitly. ZIO provides a rich set of combinators for handling errors in a functional, composable, and type-safe way. It is an essential aspect of writing robust, reliable, and maintainable applications.

ZIO describes errors in three broader categories, as follows:

- Failures are expected errors. We use **ZIO.fail** to model failures. As they are expected, we know how to handle them. We should handle these errors and prevent them from propagating throughout the call stack.

- Defects are unexpected errors. We use **ZIO.die** to model a defect. As they are not expected, we need to propagate them through the application stack, until in the upper layers one of the following situations happens:

  o In one of the upper layers, it makes sense to expect these errors. So, we will convert them to failure, and then they can be handled.

  o None of the upper layers will catch these errors, so it will finally crash the whole application.

- Fatals are catastrophic, unexpected errors. When they occur, we should kill the application immediately without propagating the error further. At most, we might need to log the error and print its call stack.

  Besides the IO type alias, ZIO has four different type aliases, which can be categorized into two different categories, as follows:

  o **Exceptional effect**: Task and RIO are two effects whose error parameter is fixed to Throwable, so we call them exceptional effects.

  o **Unexceptional effect**: UIO and URIO have error parameters that are fixed to Nothing, indicating that they are unexceptional effects. So, they cannot fail, and the compiler knows about it.

Error recovery

ZIO defined a very mature error recovery system. We can catch errors and handle the error accordingly. There is another way to provide fallback in case of errors. Further errors could be folded or retried with different functional variations. There are other variations of the time-out function.

The following are the functions provided by ZIO for error recovery:

- **Catch failures**:
  Zio#catchAll
  Zio#catchSome

- **Catch defects**:
  Zio#catchAllDefect
  Zio#catchSomeDefect

- **Catch causes**:
  Zio#catchAllCause
  Zio#catchSomeCause

- **Catch traces**:
  Zio#catchAllTrace
  Zio#catchSomeTrace

- Catch non-fatal:
  `Zio#catchNonFatalOrDie`

- Fallbacks:
  `Zio#orElse`
  `Zio#orElseEither`
  `Zio#orElseSucceed`
  `Zio#orElseFail`
  `Zio#orElseOptional`
  `Zio#firstSuccessOf`

- Folding errors:
  `Zio#fold / Zio#foldZIO`
  `Zio#ignore`
  `Zio#foldCause / Zio#foldCauseZIO`
  `Zio#foldTraceZIO`

- Retrying:
  `Zio#retry`
  `Zio#retryN`
  `Zio#retryOrElse`
  `Zio#retryOrElseEither`
  `Zio#retryUntil / Zio#retryUntilZIO`
  `Zio#retryUntilEqual`
  `Zio#retryWhile / Zio#retryWhileZIO`
  `Zio#retryWhileEquals`

- Timing out:
  `Zio#timeout`
  `Zio#timeoutTo`
  `Zio#timeoutFail / Zio#timeoutFailCause`

- Sandboxing:
  `Zio#sandbox`

Error accumulation

Error accumulation refers to the process of collecting errors that occur during the execution of multiple effects. ZIO provides ways to run multiple effects concurrently and collect all the errors they might produce. One of the most common methods for error accumulation in ZIO is using **ZIO.collectAllParN** or **ZIO.collectAllPar**.

Using ZIO.collectAllParN for error accumulation

ZIO.collectAllParN allows you to execute a collection of effects in parallel and accumulate all the errors that occur during their execution. You can specify the maximum number of concurrent executions using the *n* parameter.

You can use **ZIO.collectAllParN** for error accumulation, as follows:

```
1.  import zio._
2.
3.  val effects: List[ZIO[Any, MyError, String]] = List(
4.    fetchDataFromService1().mapError(Service1Error),
5.    fetchDataFromService2().mapError(Service2Error),
6.    fetchDataFromService3().mapError(Service3Error)
7.  )
8.
9.  val accumulatedErrors: ZIO[Any, NonEmptyList[MyError], List[String]] =
10.   ZIO.collectAllParN(3)(effects).mapError(errors => NonEmptyList.
      fromListUnsafe(errors))
```

In this example, **fetchDataFromService1()**, **fetchDataFromService2()**, and **fetchDataFromService3()** are effects that may fail with **errors** specific to each service. **ZIO.collectAllParN** runs these effects concurrently, accumulating all the errors into a **NonEmptyList** data structure, which ensures there is at least one error.

Using ZIO.collectAllPar for error accumulation

If you want to execute the effects concurrently without specifying the maximum number of concurrent executions, you can use **ZIO.collectAllPar**. This function behaves similarly to **ZIO.collectAllParN**, but it does not limit the number of parallel executions, as follows:

```
val accumulatedErrors: ZIO[Any, List[MyError], List[String]] =
  ZIO.collectAllPar(effects).mapError(_.toList)
```

In this case, all the effects in the effects list will run concurrently, and any errors that occur will be accumulated into a **List**.

By using these combinators, errors can be accumulated from multiple concurrent effects and handled in a structured way. It is advisable to adjust the number of concurrent executions based on the resources available and the requirements of your application to avoid overloading the system.

Error channel operators

Error channels are an essential part of managing errors in a functional and type-safe manner. ZIO provides various operators and combinators to work with error channels, allowing you to handle, transform, and compose errors in your applications.

The following are some of the key error channel operators and combinators in ZIO:

- **mapError**: This operator allows you to transform errors from one type to another. It takes a function that maps the input error type to the desired output error type.

  ```
  1. val updatedError: ZIO[Any, NewError, A] = originalErrorEffect.
     mapError(error => transformError(error))
  ```

- **catchAll**: This combinator is used to handle errors and produce a new effect regardless of the type of error that occurred.

  ```
  1. val result: ZIO[Any, NewError, A] = originalEffect.catchAll {
  2.    case specificError => handleSpecificError(specificError)
  3.    case otherError => handleOtherError(otherError)
  4. }
  ```

- **foldM**: This combinator allows you to handle both success and failure cases and produce a new effect based on the outcome.

  ```
  1. val result: ZIO[Any, NewError, String] = originalEffect.foldM(
  2. failure => handleFailure(failure),
  3. success => handleSuccess(success)
  ```

- **orElse**: This combinator is used for fallback behavior. It tries the first effect, and if it fails, it falls back to the second effect.

  ```
  1. val result: ZIO[Any, MyError, String] =
     firstEffect.orElse(secondEffect)
  ```

- **Alternative operator**: The **<>** operator is an alias for **orElse**. It allows you to specify an alternative effect to run if the first effect fails.

  ```
  1. val result: ZIO[Any, MyError, String] = firstEffect <> secondEffect
  ```

- **ensuring**: This combinator allows you to run a finalizer, regardless of whether the effect succeeds or fails. It is often used for **resource** cleanup.

  ```
  1. val result: ZIO[Any, MyError, String] = effectWithResource.
     ensuring(closeResource())
  ```

- **onError**: This combinator is used to execute an effect when the original effect fails.

  ```
  1. val result: ZIO[Any, NewError, A] = originalEffect.foldCauseM(
  2.    cval result: ZIO[Any, MyError, String] = originalEffect.
     onError(logError("Failed to execute effect"))ause =>
     handleCause(cause),
  3.    success => ZIO.succeed(success)
  4. )
  ```

- **foldCauseM**: This combinator allows you to handle different types of failures by pattern matching on the cause of the failure.

```
1. val result: ZIO[Any, NewError, A] = originalEffect.foldCauseM(
2.   cause => handleCause(cause),
3.   success => ZIO.succeed(success)
4. )
```

These operators and combinators enable you to manage errors effectively in ZIO applications. By leveraging these constructs, you can handle failures in a structured and composable way, making your code more robust and reliable.

ZIO layer

ZLayer is a fundamental abstraction for managing dependencies and their construction, composition, and disposal in a type-safe and composable manner. **ZLayer** allows you to encapsulate resources and services, making it easy to handle complex dependency graphs, isolate components, and write modular and testable applications.

Basics of ZLayer

A **ZLayer** is a data structure representing a layer of services that can be combined and transformed.

type ZLayer[-RIn, +E, +ROut] = ZManaged[RIn, E, ROut]

The type parameters are as follows:

- **RIn**: The input environment required by the layer.

- **E**: The potential errors that can occur while acquiring the resources.

- **ROut**: The output environment provided by the layer.

Construction

You can create **ZLayer** by defining how to acquire and release resources in the **ZManaged** construct.

```
1. val myLayer: ZLayer[Any, Nothing, MyService] =
2.   ZLayer.fromAcquireRelease(ZIO.succeed(new MyServiceImpl))
     (service => ZIO.effectTotal(service.close()))
```

In this example, **ZLayer.fromAcquireRelease** is used to create a layer that acquires an instance of **MyServiceImpl** and releases it properly when the layer is no longer needed.

Composition

You can compose **ZLayers** using various combinators to build complex dependency graphs.

```
1. val composedLayer: ZLayer[Any, Nothing, MyCombinedService] =
2.   myLayer1 ++ myLayer2 >>> MyCombinedService.combine
```

Here, **++** composes two layers, and **>>>** combines them into a new layer. **MyCombinedService.combine** is a function that combines the services provided by **myLayer1** and **myLayer2**.

Providing environment

You can use a **ZLayer** to provide a specific environment to a ZIO effect:

```
1. val myProgram: ZIO[MyService, Throwable, Unit] = ???
2. val finalResult: ZIO[Any, Throwable, Unit] =myLayer.build.use
   (myProgram.provide)
```

Here, **myLayer.build.use** transforms the effect to run in the environment provided by **myLayer**.

Using services

You can access services provided by a **ZLayer** using **ZIO.service**.

```
1. val myEffect: ZIO[MyService, Throwable, Unit] =
2.   ZIO.service[MyService].flatMap(service => service.doSomething())
```

Here, **ZIO.service[MyService]** accesses the **MyService** provided by the environment.

Lifecycle management

ZLayer automatically handles the acquisition and release of resources, ensuring proper resource management and cleanup, even in the presence of failures.

These are some fundamental aspects of **ZLayer** in ZIO. By using **ZLayer**, you can build modular, composable, and testable applications, managing your dependencies and resources in a purely functional way. It provides a powerful foundation for writing scalable and maintainable applications in ZIO.

ZIO concurrency

Concurrency in ZIO is achieved through fibers, which are lightweight, non-blocking threads of execution. ZIO provides powerful and composable abstractions for concurrent programming, allowing you to write highly scalable and efficient applications.

ZIO fibers

Fibers are lightweight, non-blocking threads of execution in ZIO. They are a fundamental concurrency primitive provided by the ZIO runtime. Fibers allow you to perform asynchronous and concurrent computations without the overhead of traditional operating system threads. ZIO's fiber model is inspired by the concept of green threads, enabling high levels of concurrency and parallelism in a memory-efficient manner.

The following are the key aspects of ZIO fibers:

- **Creation and execution**: You can create fibers using the **ZIO#fork** operator. **ZIO#fork** takes a ZIO effect and runs it concurrently in a new fiber.

  ```
  1. import zio._
  2.
  3. val fiber: UIO[Fiber[Nothing, Unit]] =
  4. ZIO.effectTotal(println("Hello, World!")).fork
  ```

  Fibers are executed by the ZIO runtime. The runtime automatically manages their execution, scheduling, and lifecycle, as follows:

- **Fiber composition**: Fibers can be composed and combined using various operators and combinators. For example, **zip, &&, forkAll**, etc., allow you to compose fibers in parallel or in sequence.

  ```
  1. val composedFiber: UIO[Fiber[Nothing, (Int, String)]] =
  2. (ZIO.succeed(42) <*> ZIO.succeed("Hello, World!")).fork
  ```

- **Supervision**: Fibers can be supervised, allowing you to handle their failures. You can use supervisors to specify how to handle errors and interruptions in fibers.

  ```
  1. val supervisedFiber: UIO[Fiber[Throwable, Unit]] =
     failingFiber.supervised
  ```

- **Interruption**: Fibers can be interrupted explicitly using the **interrupt** method. Interruption allows you to terminate a fiber prematurely, releasing resources and cleaning up.

  ```
  1. val interruptedFiber: UIO[Fiber[Nothing, Unit]] =
     runningFiber.interrupt
  ```

- **Fiber status**: You can query the status of a fiber, such as whether it is done, whether it succeeded, or whether it failed.

  ```
  1. val status: UIO[Fiber.Status] = runningFiber.status
  ```

- **Error handling**: Fibers can fail with errors. You can handle errors using combinators like **catchAll, foldM**, or **orElse**.

  ```
  1. val result: UIO[Either[MyError, Unit]] =
  2.   failingFiber.foldM(
  3.     error => ZIO.succeed(Left(error)),
  4.     _ => ZIO.succeed(Right(()))
  5.   )
  ```

- **Fiber locals**: Fibers can have thread-local variables called **fiber locals**. Fiber locals are used for thread-safe, fiber local mutable state.

  ```
  1. val local: UIO[FiberLocal[Int]] = FiberLocal.make(0)
  2. val result: UIO[Int] = local.flatMap(fiberLocal => fiberLocal.get)
  ```

ZIO's fiber model provides a powerful and flexible way to achieve concurrent and parallel execution in a type-safe, functional, and composable manner. Fibers are managed automatically by the ZIO runtime, allowing you to focus on writing correct and efficient concurrent code, without worrying about low-level thread management.

ZIO synchronization

In concurrent applications, proper synchronization is crucial to ensure that shared resources are accessed safely and without conflicts. ZIO provides several constructs for synchronization, allowing you to coordinate the execution of concurrent tasks and manage shared mutable state, as follows:

- **Ref**: It is a data structure provided by ZIO for managing shared, mutable state in a purely functional way. Ref is an atomic reference that can be read and modified atomically, providing thread-safe access to its content.

  Creation:

  ```
  1.  import zio._
  2.
  3.  val ref: UIO[Ref[Int]] = Ref.make(0)
  4.  Reading and Updating:
  5.
  6.  val result: ZIO[Ref[Int], Nothing, Int] =
  7.  for {
  8.  value <- ref.get
  9.  _      <- ref.set(value + 1)
  10. } yield value
  ```

- **Semaphore**: It is a synchronization primitive that allows controlling access to a resource with a limited number of permits. Semaphores are useful for managing access to a limited number of resources concurrently.

  Creation:

  ```
  1.  import zio._
  2.
  3.  val semaphore: UIO[Semaphore] = Semaphore.make(3)
  4.  Acquiring and Releasing Permits:
  5.
  6.  val acquire: ZIO[Semaphore, Nothing, Unit] = semaphore.acquire
  7.  val release: ZIO[Semaphore, Nothing, Unit] = semaphore.release
  ```

- **Promise**: It is a synchronization primitive for managing the result of a concurrent computation. It allows one fiber to complete a promise, and other fibers to wait for the result.

Creation and completion:

```
1. import zio._
2.
3. val promise: UIO[Promise[Throwable, String]] =
   Promise.make[Throwable, String]
4. val complete: ZIO[Promise[Throwable, String], Nothing, Unit] =
   promise.complete(ZIO.succeed("Result"))
5. Waiting for Completion:
6.
7. val result: ZIO[Promise[Throwable, String], Throwable, String]
   = promise.await
```

- **Queue**: It is a data structure for managing a stream of values between fibers. It allows fibers to enqueue and dequeue elements asynchronously, providing a way for fibers to communicate and coordinate.

Creation:

```
1. import zio._
2.
3. val queue: UIO[Queue[String]] = Queue.bounded[String](100)
4. Enqueuing and Dequeuing:
5.
6. val enqueue: ZIO[Queue[String], Nothing, Unit] = queue.
   offer("Value")
7. val dequeue: ZIO[Queue[String], Nothing, String] = queue.take
```

These synchronization primitives provide a foundation for building complex concurrent applications in ZIO. By leveraging these constructs, you can ensure safe and efficient coordination between concurrent tasks, allowing you to build scalable and reliable applications.

Note: **Remember to choose the appropriate synchronization primitive based on your specific use case and requirements.**

ZIO STM

Software transactional memory (STM) is a powerful concurrency primitive provided by ZIO for managing shared mutable state in a purely functional and composable way. STM allows you to work with mutable variables and perform transactions over those variables in a manner that ensures **atomicity, consistency, isolation, and durability (ACID)** properties without the need for locks.

The following are the key concepts related to STM:

- **TRef**: It is a transactional reference, like **Ref**, but specifically designed for STM transactions. **TRef** allows you to perform atomic transactions on mutable variables.

Creation:
```
1. import zio._
2.
3. val tref: UIO[TRef[Int]] = TRef.make(0)
4. Reading and Updating:
5.
6. val result: STM[Nothing, Int] =
7.   for {
8.     value <- tref.get
9.     _     <- tref.set(value + 1)
10.  } yield value
```

- **STM transactions**: Transactions are composable and atomic operations performed on shared, mutable state, for example, **TRef**, **TMap**, or **TSet**. It allows to manage state changes in a thread-safe and conflict-free manner without locks or manual synchronization. ZIO STM transactions ensure atomicity, consistency, and isolation.

Combining operations:
```
1. val combinedTransaction: STM[Nothing, (Int, String)] =
2.   for {
3.     intValue    <- tref1.get
4.     stringValue <- tref2.get
5.     _              <- tref1.set(intValue + 1)
6.     _              <- tref2.set(s"Value: $stringValue")
7.   } yield (intValue, stringValue)
```

- **Retrying and OrElse**: STM transactions can include retry points using **STM.retry** and be composed using the **orElse** operator, allowing for retries and fallbacks.
```
1. val transactionWithRetry: STM[Nothing, Int] =
2.   tref1.get.flatMap {
3.     case 0 => STM.retry
4.     case n => STM.succeed(n)
5.   }
6.
7. val combinedWithRetry: STM[Nothing, Int] =
8.   transactionWithRetry.orElse(tref2.get)
```

STM composition

STM transactions can be combined and composed using various combinators, such as **flatMap**, **map**, and **zip**.
```
1. val composedTransaction: STM[Nothing, (Int, String)] =
2.   tref1.get.flatMap(value1 => tref2.get.
   map(value2 => (value1, value2)))
```

```
3.
4. val zippedTransaction: STM[Nothing, (Int, String)] =
5.    tref1.get.zip(tref2.get)
```

Fiber-scoped transactions

STM transactions can be executed within fibers using the **STM#commit** operator, ensuring that the transactional effects are run atomically.

```
1. val fiberScopedTransaction: ZIO[Any, Throwable, (Int, String)] =
2.    STM.atomically(for {
3.      value1 <- tref1.get
4.      value2 <- tref2.get
5.    } yield (value1, value2)).commit
```

STM in ZIO provides a powerful and composable way to handle shared mutable state in a concurrent environment without the complexity and pitfalls of traditional locking mechanisms. By leveraging STM transactions, you can write concurrent applications that are both safe and efficient, ensuring consistency and correctness in a purely functional manner.

ZIO resource management

ZIO provides robust and composable abstractions for resource management, allowing you to acquire, use, and release resources in a safe and resource leak-free manner. Proper resource management is crucial for building reliable and scalable applications.

ZIO offers main constructs for managing resources, that is, **ZIO.bracket** and **ZManaged, ZIO.fromAutoCloseable**, as follows:

- **Using ZIO.bracket for resource management:**

  ZIO.bracket is a high order function that ensures the acquisition and release of a resource, even if an error occurs during the computation. It follows the pattern of, acquire, use, and release.

  The following is the general syntax:

  ```
  1. def myResource: ZIO[Environment, Throwable, ResourceType] = ???
  2.
  3. val result: ZIO[Environment, Throwable, ResultType] =
  4.    ZIO.bracket(myResource)(
  5.      resource => ZIO.succeed(resource.operation()),
  6.      resource => ZIO.effectTotal(resource.close())
  7.    )
  ```

  In this example, **myResource** is the effect of acquiring the resource.

The second argument to **ZIO.bracket** is the use function, which takes the acquired resource and produces a new effect.

The third argument is the **release** function, which takes the acquired resource and releases it, typically closing the resource.

If an error occurs during the acquisition or the use phase, the **release** function is guaranteed to be executed.

- **Using ZManaged for resource management**:

ZManaged is a data type in ZIO specifically designed for managing resources. It provides a more ergonomic and concise way to handle resources compared to **ZIO.bracket**.

The following is how you can use **ZManaged**:

```
1. val managedResource: ZManaged[Environment, Throwable,
   ResourceType] = ???
2.
3. val result: ZIO[Environment, Throwable, ResultType] =
4.   managedResource.use(resource => ZIO.
   succeed(resource.operation()))
```

In this example, **managedResource** is of type **ZManaged**, representing the managed resource.

The **use** method of **ZManaged** takes a function that uses the acquired resource and produces a new effect. The resource is automatically acquired and released by the **ZManaged** instance.

ZManaged also provides combinators for working with multiple resources, composing managed resources, and acquiring resources lazily or eagerly.

- **Using ZIO.fromAutoCloseable for auto-closing resources**:

For resources that implement the **AutoCloseable** interface, **ZIO** provides a convenient function called **ZIO.fromAutoCloseable** for automatic resource management:

```
1. val autoCloseableResource: AutoCloseable = ???
2.
3. val result: ZIO[Environment, Throwable, ResultType] =
4.   ZIO.fromAutoCloseable(ZIO.effect
   (autoCloseableResource.operation()))
5. ZIO.fromAutoCloseable automatically handles the closing of
   the AutoCloseable resource.
```

By using these constructs, you can ensure that your resources are properly managed, even in the presence of failures or early termination of computations. Proper resource management in ZIO helps prevent resource leaks and ensures the correct handling of resources, making your applications more robust and reliable.

ZIO testing

Testing in ZIO is a crucial aspect of building reliable and maintainable applications. ZIO provides a powerful testing framework that allows you to write tests for your ZIO applications in a purely functional and deterministic manner. ZIO's testing facilities are built around the concept of environments, which allow you to isolate the dependencies of your application, making it easier to write unit and integration tests.

Test environments

In ZIO testing, a test environment contains all the required dependencies for your test. These dependencies are typically provided as ZIO services. By isolating the test environment, you can test your application components in isolation, mocking external services or dependencies:

```
1. import zio._
2.
3. trait Database {
4.   def getData: Task[String]
5. }
6.
7. val testEnvironment: ULayer[Has[Database]] = ZLayer.
   succeed(new Database {
8.   override def getData: Task[String] = ZIO.succeed("test data")
9. })
```

In this example, **Database** is a service with a **getData** method. The **testEnvironment** provides a mock implementation of the **Database** service for testing purposes.

Using zio.test package

zio.test package is a part of the ZIO ecosystem designed to provide a powerful, type-safe, and composable framework for testing ZIO-based applications. It offers various features to make writing, organizing, and running tests easy and flexible, supporting both functional and effective code.

It includes various modules for writing tests, assertions, and test runners.

The following are foundational concepts that organize and execute tests in a structured and efficient way. Let us explore how they work and how you can use them effectively:

- **Specs**: You can define test specifications using the **zio.test.specs** module. Specs allow you to structure your tests hierarchically and compose them using combinators.

```
1.  import zio.test._
2.
3.  val testData: Spec[Has[Database], TestFailure[Nothing],
    TestSuccess] =
4.    suite("Database Service")(
5.      testM("get data from the database") {
6.        for {
7.          data <- ZIO.service[Database].flatMap(_.getData)
8.        } yield assert(data)(equalTo("test data"))
9.      }
10.  )
```

- **Test runners**: ZIO includes test runners for running tests and reporting the results. You can run tests using the **DefaultRunnableSpec** runner or other specialized runners like **TestRunner** and **JunitRunnableSpec**.

Running tests

To run tests, you will create a **RunnableSpec** that describes the tests to run and the test environment to use. Then, you can use a test runner to execute the tests:

```
1.  import zio.test._
2.
3.  object MyTestSuite extends DefaultRunnableSpec {
4.    def spec: Spec[Environment, TestFailure[Nothing], TestSuccess] =
5.      suite("My Test Suite")(/* ... your tests ... */)
6.  }
7.
8.  object Main extends zio.App {
9.    def run(args: List[String]): ZIO[zio.ZEnv, Nothing, Int] =
10.     MyTestSuite.run().map(_.fold(_ => 1, _ => 0))
11. }
```

In this example, **MyTestSuite** is a **RunnableSpec** object representing your test suite. The **run** method of **DefaultRunnableSpec** executes the tests and produces test results.

Asynchronous testing

ZIO tests can handle asynchronous effects and assertions. You can use **assertM** for asynchronous assertions, and you can wrap asynchronous effects in **ZIO.succeed** or **ZIO.effect** for assertions.

Mocking dependencies

ZIO provides facilities for mocking dependencies and services, allowing you to isolate components for unit testing. You can use **ZIO.mock** and **Mock** to define and compose mock services.

These are some of the key aspects of testing in ZIO. By leveraging ZIO's testing capabilities, you can write robust, isolated, and deterministic tests for your applications, ensuring the correctness of your code and enabling fast feedback during development.

Conclusion

In this chapter, we discussed the intent of ZIO library and how it helps us to write composable, concurrent, type-safe, and testable code easily in a functional way. The best part of ZIO is that you do not have to understand all the criticalities of functional programming or category theory. It takes care of all difficult tasks and provides an easy-to-use **application programming interface (API)** based interface, which you can directly use, without worrying about the intricacies of category concepts.

We also discussed ZIO type aliases, its error management, concurrency, and how we can write test cases, using ZIO testing. ZIO is easy and has a vast eco-system that allows the user to do functional programming.

In the next chapter, we will investigate the functional effects, and how Cats and ZIO provide constructs, to work with effects.

Join our Discord space

Join our Discord workspace for latest updates, offers, tech happenings around the world, new releases, and sessions with the authors:

https://discord.bpbonline.com

CHAPTER 6
Effects Implementation in Pure Way

Introduction

This chapter focuses on implementation details about effects and their role in functional programming. It discusses writing programs using effects, and it is impossible to write any real-world scenario without using effects. We will also learn about side effects and how to avoid them to make programs more reasonable. We will also look into the functional library to support effects systems.

Structure

In this chapter, we will cover the following topics:

- Effects and side effects
- Handling side effects
- Functional exception handling
- I/O as side effects
- Functional I/O implementations
- Cats Effects
- ZIO effects

Objectives

By the end of this chapter, readers will be able to understand the effects and side effects in functional programming and why side effects should be avoided during functional programming by examples and their impact. We will also learn how to avoid these side effects by using Cats and ZIO library. They provide quite robust support to handle effects, as it is impossible to write code without side effects.

Effects and side effects

In functional programming, effects and side effects are two distinct concepts that are crucial to understanding and designing pure functions.

Effects refer to the overall outcome or transformation that a function produces, encompassing both its return value and any additional changes it makes to the program or its environment. Effects are the intended consequences of a function's execution, representing the desired impact on the program's state or external world.

In functional programming, the concepts of effects and side effects revolve around how functions interact with their environment and data, as follows:

- **Pure functions**: These are functions that consistently return the same output for the same input, without causing any observable side effects. They rely solely on their input parameters to produce a result, without modifying any external state or relying on global variables. Pure functions help write code that is easier to reason about, test, and parallelize.

- **Referential transparency**: This property ensures that an expression can be replaced with its value without changing the program's behavior. It is a consequence of using pure functions and immutability, enabling predictability and simplifying reasoning about code.

On the other hand, side effects are unintended or extraneous changes that a function introduces, going beyond its primary purpose of returning a value. These side effects can manifest in various forms, such as modifying global variables, performing **input/output (I/O)** operations, or altering shared data structures, as follows:

- **State changes**: Side effects occur when a function modifies or relies on mutable state, such as modifying a global variable, changing the internal state of an object, or altering data structures in place.

- **I/O operations**: Any input or output operation, like reading from or writing to a file, fetching data over the network, or interacting with the user through the console, introduces side effects. These operations involve interactions beyond the function's scope and can have unpredictable results.

- **Concurrency and mutability**: In a concurrent environment, a shared mutable state can lead to side effects when multiple functions or threads simultaneously access and modify the same data.

The distinction between effects and side effects lies in their control and predictability. Effects are deliberately incorporated into a function's design, ensuring that the function's impact is transparent and manageable. Side effects, on the other hand, introduce hidden dependencies and unexpected behavior, making it difficult to reason about the program's overall state.

In functional programming, the emphasis is on minimizing side effects, promoting the use of pure functions. Pure functions are functions that produce consistent output for the same input, without causing any side effects. This purity enhances code predictability, simplifies testing, and facilitates modularity.

However, eliminating side effects entirely is not always feasible or practical. Certain operations, such as I/O or interfacing with external systems, inherently involve side effects. To manage these unavoidable side effects, functional programming employs techniques like monads, which encapsulate impure operations and provide a structured way to compose them with pure functions.

By understanding the distinction between effects and side effects, programmers can strive to write more predictable, testable, and maintainable functional code, leading to more robust and reliable software.

Side effects as blocker

Side effects can be considered blockers for achieving pure functional implementation because they introduce unpredictability and make reasoning about code more complex.

The following is how side effects can impede pure functional programming:

- **Complexity and debugging**: Side effects make code harder to understand and debug because they introduce hidden dependencies and behavior that might not be immediately apparent. Functions with side effects can have unexpected consequences, making it challenging to track down issues.

- **Testability**: Pure functions are inherently testable as they rely solely on their inputs and produce deterministic outputs. However, functions with side effects are harder to test because their behavior might vary depending on the state of the external environment, making it difficult to create reliable and consistent tests.

- **Concurrency and parallelism**: Side effects can lead to issues in concurrent or parallel environments where multiple functions are interacting with shared mutable state. This can result in race conditions or unexpected behavior due to concurrent modifications of state.

- **Predictability**: Pure functions have referential transparency, meaning they can be replaced by their values without changing the program's behavior. However, functions with side effects lack this property, making code less predictable and harder to reason about.

- **Functional composition**: Functional programming emphasizes composing small, reusable functions to create larger systems. Side effects hinder composition because they introduce hidden dependencies and make it harder to combine functions without unintended consequences.

To mitigate the impact of side effects, functional programming encourages techniques, as follows:

- **Immutability**: Using immutable data structures reduces the need for mutable state and minimizes side effects.

- **Monads and functors**: These abstractions help encapsulate side effects, allowing for better management and control over impure operations.

- **Pure functions**: Writing functions that minimize or eliminate side effects, focusing on returning values based solely on their inputs.

Functional programming languages and paradigms offer tools and patterns to isolate and manage side effects, but achieving a completely side effect-free codebase in real-world applications might not always be feasible due to the need for I/O operations or interaction with the external environment. However, functional programming aims to minimize side effects where possible to create more reliable, predictable, and maintainable code.

Pure functions are the cornerstone of functional programming, and side effects can make it difficult to achieve purity.

The following are some specific examples of how side effects can block functional implementation:

- **Mutable variables**:
    ```
    1. var counter = 0
    2.
    3. def incrementCounter(): Unit = {
    4.    counter += 1
    5. }
    ```

    The **incrementCounter** function modifies the **counter** variable, causing a side effect by altering external state.

- **I/O operations**:
    ```
    1. import scala.io.Source
    2.
    3. def readFromFile(filename: String): List[String] = {
    4.    val source = Source.fromFile(filename)
    ```

```
5.    val lines = source.getLines().toList
6.    source.close()
7.    lines
8. }
```

The **readFromFile** function performs I/O operations by reading lines from a file, interacting with the external file system.

- **Printing to console**:
    ```
    1. def greet(name: String): Unit = {
    2.    println(s"Hello, $name!")
    3. }
    ```

    The **greet** function causes a side effect by printing to the console.

- **Mutable collections**:
    ```
    1. var numbers = List(1, 2, 3)
    2.
    3. def addNumberToList(num: Int): Unit = {
    4.    numbers = numbers :+ num
    5. }
    ```

    The **addNumberToList** function modifies the numbers list, introducing a side effect by changing external state.

The following code shows the external API calls:

```
1. import scalaj.http.Http
2.
3. def fetchDataFromAPI(endpoint: String): String = {
4.    val response = Http(endpoint).asString
5.    response.body
6. }
```

The **fetchDataFromAPI** function performs an HTTP request, interacting with an external API and causing a side effect.

In some cases, it is possible to work around side effects and still implement a functional solution. For example, you can use monads to encapsulate impure operations and provide a way to compose them with pure functions. However, in other cases, side effects may be unavoidable. For example, if you need to interact with a legacy system that is not designed for functional programming, you may need to use side effects.

Handling side effects

In functional programming, managing side effects is crucial for writing predictable, testable, and maintainable code. Scala, being a language that supports both functional and imperative styles, offers ways to handle side effects in a functional manner.

The following are some strategies:

- **Using pure functions**: Scala encourages writing pure functions that do not produce side effects. These functions depend only on their inputs and do not modify external state, as follows:

  ```
  1.  def add(a: Int, b: Int): Int = a + b
  ```

- **Immutability**: Immutable data structures help prevent side effects by ensuring that data does not change after creation, as follows:

  ```
  1. val immutableList = List(1, 2, 3)
  2. val updatedList = immutableList :+ 4 // This creates a new list
  ```

- **Monads and effects**: Scala provides abstractions like **Option**, **Either**, and libraries such as Cats or ZIO, which use monads or monad-like structures to manage effects in a functional way. These constructs allow you to encapsulate side effects and compose them in a controlled manner.

  For instance, using **Option** to handle the potential absence of a value, as follows:

  ```
  1. val maybeValue: Option[Int] = Some(10)
  2.
  3. val result = maybeValue.map(_ * 2) // Perform computation
     only if value is present
  ```

- **Functional effects using Cats or ZIO**: Libraries like Cats or ZIO offer a wide range of abstractions to manage effects in a purely functional manner.

  For instance, in Cats, IO represents a description of a computation that might have side effects but is executed in a referentially transparent way, as mentioned in the following code:

  ```
  1.  import cats.effect.IO
  2.
  3.  val readFromConsole: IO[String] = IO {
  4.    scala.io.StdIn.readLine()
  5.  }
  6.
  7.  val program: IO[Unit] = for {
  8.    _ <- IO(println("Enter your name:"))
  9.    input <- readFromConsole
  10.   _ <- IO(println(s"Hello, $input!"))
  11. } yield ()
  12.
  13. // Execute the IO program
  14. program.unsafeRunSync()
  ```

These approaches promote a functional way of handling side effects, allowing you to write more predictable and testable code while still dealing with the necessary interactions with the external environment. They enable you to isolate and control side effects within your codebase, enhancing its maintainability and reasoning.

Exceptions as side effects

Exceptions in programming can be seen as side effects because they represent unexpected behavior that occurs outside the normal flow of a program.

The following is why exceptions can be considered as side effects:

- **Altering program flow**: Exceptions disrupt the normal flow of execution when unexpected conditions occur. They divert the program from its regular path, affecting the expected behavior of the code.

- **Modifying state**: When an exception occurs, it can potentially leave the program in an inconsistent state. Resources might not be released appropriately, data structures might be partially updated, etc.

- **Interacting with the environment**: Exceptions often involve interactions with the external environment, like I/O operations, network connections, or accessing external resources. For instance, a file reading operation throwing an exception due to a missing file is interacting with the file system.

- **Non-local control flow**: Exceptions allow for non-local control flow, which means they can jump across multiple levels of the call stack, making it harder to reason about the program's execution.

In functional programming paradigms, managing exceptions as side effects involves encapsulating and controlling their impact on the program's flow and state. Functional languages and libraries provide mechanisms to handle errors in a more controlled and composable way, often using data types like **Option**, **Either**, or monadic structures to represent computations that might fail without resorting to exceptions.

For instance, using **Either** in Scala to handle errors explicitly without relying on exceptions, as follows:

```
1. def divide(a: Int, b: Int): Either[String, Int] =
2.   if (b == 0) Left("Cannot divide by zero!")
3.   else Right(a / b)
4.
5. val result: Either[String, Int] = divide(10, 0)
6. // Instead of throwing an exception, handle the failure case explicitly
```

Functional approaches aim to mitigate the negative impact of exceptions by providing mechanisms that allow errors to be managed in a more controlled, predictable, and composable manner, which aligns well with the principles of functional programming.

Functional exception handling

Functional programming emphasizes handling errors without relying on exceptions.

The following are some common functional approaches to managing errors in Scala:

- **Using option and some or none**: `Option` represents the presence or absence of a value. It is a functional way to handle scenarios where a value might be missing, as follows:

```
1. val maybeValue: Option[Int] = Some(10) // Some value
2. val missingValue: Option[Int] = None // Absence of value
3.
4. val result: Option[Int] = maybeValue.map(_ * 2)
   // Operate on the value if present
```

- **Either for explicit error handling**: `Either` allows handling errors or values in a functional way. **Left** represents an error, and **Right** represents a successful computation, as follows:

```
1. def divide(a: Int, b: Int): Either[String, Int] =
2.   if (b == 0) Left("Cannot divide by zero!")
3.   else Right(a / b)
4.
5. val result: Either[String, Int] = divide(10, 0)
6. // Pattern match or use other functional constructs to
   handle the Either result
```

- **Functional error handling libraries, Cats or ZIO**: Libraries like Cats or ZIO offer more sophisticated constructs for error handling in a functional way. For instance, in Cats, **Validated** can handle multiple errors while accumulating them, as follows:

```
1. import cats.data.Validated
2. import cats.syntax.validated._
3.
4. def validateAge(age: Int): Validated[String, Int] =
5.   if (age >= 18) age.valid else "Must be 18 or older".invalid
6.
7. val result: Validated[String, Int] = validateAge(20)
8. // Use functional constructs to work with the Validated result
```

- **Functional effects with I/O**: Cats Effect's I/O can represent computations that may produce side effects or errors. It enables managing effects in a pure and functional way, as follows:

```
1. import cats.effect._
2.
3. def readInput: IO[String] = IO(scala.io.StdIn.readLine())
4.
5. def processInput(input: String): IO[Unit] =
6.   IO(println(s"Received input: $input"))
7.
8. val program: IO[Unit] = readInput.flatMap(processInput)
9. // Compose IO operations to manage effects in a functional manner
```

These approaches focus on using functional constructs and data types to handle errors explicitly without resorting to exceptions. They encourage composing computations, providing a more predictable and controlled way of dealing with errors while aligning with the principles of functional programming.

I/O as side effects

I/O operations can be considered side effects in functional programming. I/O operations are typically performed by impure functions, which are functions that have side effects. This is because I/O operations involve interacting with the external world, such as reading from or writing to a file, or sending data over a network. These interactions can have unintended consequences, such as changing the state of a file or causing a network error.

As a result, I/O operations can make it difficult to reason about the behavior of functional programs. This is because the behavior of a program that performs I/O can depend on the state of the external world, which is not always under the control of the program.

In addition, I/O operations can make it difficult to test functional programs. This is because it can be difficult to create a test harness that accurately simulates the external world. As a result, it can be difficult to ensure that a program that performs I/O will behave correctly in all situations. Despite these challenges, there are a few techniques that can be used to manage I/O operations in functional programming.

One technique is to use monads, which are a way of encapsulating impure operations. Monads can be used to sequence I/O operations and to handle errors. Another technique is to use dependency injection, which is a way of providing dependencies to functions at runtime. Dependency injection can be used to provide I/O dependencies to functions, which can make it easier to test those functions.

Finally, it is important to use pure functions whenever possible. Pure functions are functions that do not have side effects and that always return the same output for the same input. Pure functions are easier to reason about and to test than impure functions. By using these techniques, it is possible to write functional programs that perform I/O operations in a way that is safe and predictable. However, it is important to be aware of the challenges that I/O operations pose for functional programming.

Functional I/O implementations

The following are the functional I/O implementations:

- **Encapsulation and immutability**: Functional programming emphasizes encapsulating I/O operations within functional constructs. Immutability ensures that I/O functions do not mutate data but instead produce new values.

- **Pure Functions with effects**: Functional languages often use constructs like monads or monad-like structures, for example, I/O in Cats Effect to manage I/O operations. These abstractions encapsulate side effects and allow composing I/O actions in a controlled and pure manner.

- **Separation of concerns**: Separating pure logic from I/O operations allows the functional core of the application to remain free from side effects. I/O operations are confined to specific parts, making it easier to reason about and test the pure functions.

- **Referential transparency**: Functional programming encourages writing functions that are referentially transparent, meaning they produce the same output for the same input and have no side effects. While I/O inherently has side effects, functional constructs allow controlling these effects while maintaining composability.

The following is an example for using **IO** in Cats Effect (Scala):

```
1. import cats.effect._
2.
3. object IOMonadExample extends IOApp {
4.   def readAndPrintInput: IO[Unit] = for {
5.     _ <- IO(println("Enter your name:"))
6.     input <- IO(scala.io.StdIn.readLine())
7.     _ <- IO(println(s"Hello, $input!"))
8.   } yield ()
9.
10.  def run(args: List[String]): IO[ExitCode] = {
11.    readAndPrintInput.as(ExitCode.Success)
12.  }
13. }
```

In this example, the **IO** monad encapsulates the I/O operations of getting user input and printing output. It allows composing these actions in a referentially transparent and controlled manner, managing I/O as a side effect within a purely functional context. This approach enables reasoning about and handling I/O operations while maintaining functional purity and composability. Functional I/O implementations in Scala utilize various techniques to handle side effects and maintain the purity of functional programming principles.

The following are some common approaches:

- **Monads**: Monads provide a structured way to encapsulate impure operations like I/O and integrate them with pure functions. The Cats Effect library is a popular implementation of monads in Scala, offering various monadic types and utilities for managing I/O operations.

- **Effect handlers**: Effect handlers allow for more fine-grained control over side effects by defining callbacks for handling specific effects. ZIO library is a notable example of effect handlers in Scala, providing a powerful abstraction for managing side effects and composing effects.

- **Pure functional I/O**: Pure functional I/O aims to eliminate side effects entirely by representing I/O operations as values within the functional paradigm. The fs2 library is an example of pure functional I/O in Scala, offering a stream-based approach to I/O operations.

- **Algebraic data types**: **Algebraic data types** (**ADTs**) can be used to represent different states of an I/O operation, such as success, failure, or pending. This allows for more explicit handling of I/O outcomes and error conditions.

- **Callback-based I/O**: While not strictly functional, callback-based I/O can be used in a functional style by avoiding side effects within the callback functions and relying on higher order functions to compose I/O operations.

Each approach has its advantages and disadvantages, and the choice depends on the specific requirements of the application and the desired level of abstraction. Monads and effect handlers provide a more structured and composable approach, while pure functional I/O offers greater purity but may require more upfront design effort. ADTs can be a good choice for representing different I/O states, and callback-based I/O can be useful for integrating with existing libraries or frameworks.

In summary, functional I/O implementations in Scala provide various techniques to manage side effects and maintain the purity of functional programming. The choice of approach depends on the specific requirements and preferences of the project.

Cats Effects

Cats Effect is a library in Scala that provides abstractions for handling and managing side effects in a purely functional way. It is built on top of Cats, a library for functional programming in Scala. Cats Effect aims to provide concurrency, resource safety, and effect control in a composable and declarative manner, adhering to functional programming principles.

The following figure depicts the relationship among the Cats Effect types:

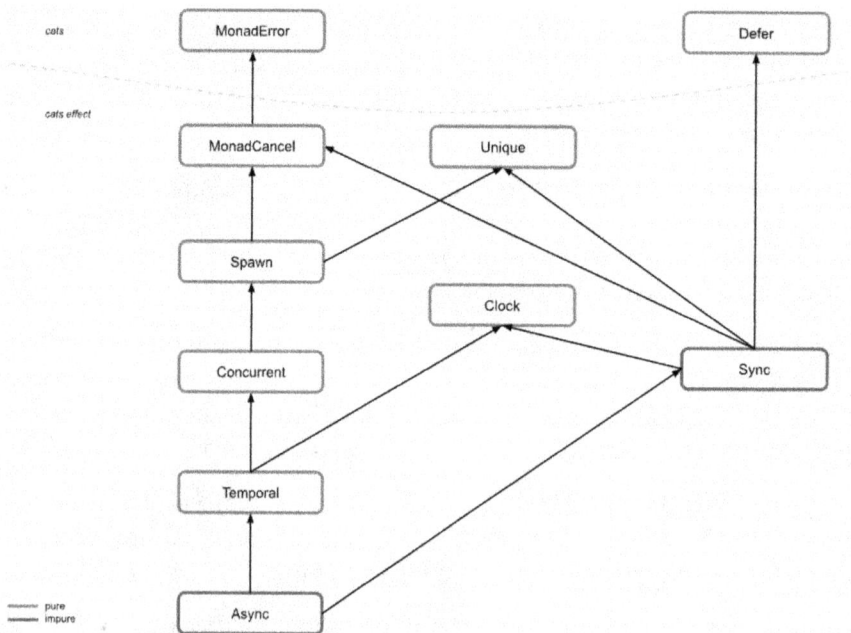

Figure 6.1: *Cats Effect 3 type class hierarchy*

The following are the key features and abstractions in Cats Effect:

- **IO monad**:
  - The cornerstone of Cats Effect is the **IO** data type, which represents a description of a side effectful computation.
  - **IO** is referentially transparent and allows composing, mapping, and chaining operations in a purely functional way.

- **Concurrency and parallelism**: Cats Effect provides abstractions for managing concurrent and parallel computations, enabling safe and efficient concurrency using constructs like **cats.effect.concurrent.Ref**, **Fiber**, **Semaphore**, etc.

- **Resource safety and error handling**:
  - Cats Effect helps manage resources safely, ensuring proper acquisition and release of resources via resource and bracket constructs.
  - It provides tools for handling errors in a functional way, such as EitherT, OptionT, or validated for error accumulation.

- **Effect control and asynchronous operations**: It offers utilities for controlling and managing various effects, including timer, async, concurrent, etc., allowing for managing asynchronous computations and timeouts.

- **Type classes and laws**: Cats Effect leverages type classes and laws to define abstractions and ensure consistency and lawful behavior across different implementations.

The following is an example using **IO** in Cats Effect:

```
1.  import cats.effect._
2.
3.  object CatsEffectExample extends IOApp {
4.    def readAndPrintInput: IO[Unit] = for {
5.      _ <- IO(println("Enter your name:"))
6.      input <- IO(scala.io.StdIn.readLine())
7.      _ <- IO(println(s"Hello, $input!"))
8.    } yield ()
9.
10.   def run(args: List[String]): IO[ExitCode] = {
11.     readAndPrintInput.as(ExitCode.Success)
12.   }
13. }
```

In this example, **IO** is used to encapsulate I/O operations (reading user input and printing output) in a purely functional manner. Cats Effect's **IO** allows composing these actions in a referentially transparent way, managing side effects while providing a safe and composable abstraction for handling effects. This promotes functional programming practices and ensures better control and reasoning about side effectful computations.

ZIO effects

Functional effects refer to the changes or modifications in the state of a program or system as a result of executing a specific function. These effects can include updating variables, creating or destroying objects, modifying data structures, or triggering external events such as sending messages or making HTTP requests. They are an important aspect of functional programming, as they allow developers to write code that is more predictable, composable, and testable. The use of functional effects in programming helps to promote a separation of concerns, making it easier to understand and manage the behavior of complex systems.

The following are the functional effects in ZIO:

- Functional effects in ZIO refer to the ability to model side effects in a functional and composable manner. In ZIO, effects are represented by the ZIO data type, which is a type that describes a side effectful computation.

- Functional effects allow for the creation of complex and asynchronous applications in a way that is easy to reason about and maintain. By using functional effects, developers can model side effects as first-class values, which can be composed, transformed, and manipulated in a type-safe and composable manner.

- In ZIO, functional effects are achieved through a combination of the ZIO data type, and the methods provided by the library for creating, composing, and transforming effects. This allows for the creation of effects that represent a wide range of side effects, such as I/O operations, database access, and system interactions, and that can be combined and composed in a manner that is similar to how functions can be composed in functional programming.

- Functional effects in ZIO also provide a way to handle failures and errors in a composable manner, by allowing effects to fail with an error, and by providing methods for handling and recovering from failures. This makes it easier to build reliable and resilient applications, as failures can be handled in a controlled and predictable manner.

In summary, functional effects in ZIO provide a way to model side effects in a functional and composable manner, making it easier to build scalable and reliable applications in Scala.

ZIO effects

ZIO effects are a key concept in the ZIO library, which is a functional library for Scala that provides a type-safe and composable way to build asynchronous, concurrent, and resilient applications. ZIO effects are an abstraction over side effects, which are actions that have an impact outside of a program, such as I/O operations, database access, or system interactions.

In functional programming, side effects are typically seen as a challenge to manage, as they make it difficult to reason about the behavior of a program and can lead to bugs and unexpected behavior. ZIO effects provide a way to manage and structure side effects in a type-safe and composable manner, making it easier to build reliable and scalable applications.

The basic building block of ZIO effects is the ZIO type, which is a data type that describes a side-effectful computation. A ZIO computation can be thought of as a description of a computation that will eventually produce a result of type A, along with any side effects that need to occur in order to produce that result. The ZIO type takes two type parameters: R and A. The R-type parameter describes the environment that the computation requires in order to run, such as a database connection, a configuration, or a logging system. The A-type parameter defines the type of result that the computation will produce.

The following are the different ways to create effects in ZIO:

- **ZIO.succeed**: This method creates an effect that immediately succeeds with a specified value. It can be used to create an effect that represents a constant value or a known result.

- **ZIO.fail**: This method creates an effect that immediately fails with a specified error. It can be used to create an effect that represents a known failure.

- **ZIO.effect**: This method creates an effect from an impure function that produces a side effect. The side effect is wrapped in a ZIO context, which allows for error handling, composition, and other benefits provided by ZIO.

- **ZIO.effectTotal**: This method is similar to **ZIO.effect**, but it creates an effect from a total function, meaning a function that cannot throw an exception. It can be used to create an effect from a function that is guaranteed to succeed, such as reading from a constant or pure function.

- **ZIO.effectAsync**: This method creates an effect from an asynchronous function, allowing for non-blocking and asynchronous execution of the side effect.

- **ZIO.effectSuspend**: This method creates an effect from a ZIO that is suspended, meaning that it is executed lazily and only when the effect is run. It can be used to delay the execution of an effect or to create an effect that depends on the result of another effect.

These methods provide different ways to create ZIO effects, and the choice of method will depend on the specific requirements of the application. By using these methods, developers can create effects that represent a wide range of side effects and can be combined and composed in a type-safe and composable manner.

The following is the user management system using ZIO effects:

```
1.  import zio._
2.
3.  case class User(id: Long, name: String, email: String)
4.
5.  trait UserRepository {
6.    def getUser(id: Long): ZIO[Any, Throwable, User]
7.    def updateUser(user: User): ZIO[Any, Throwable, Unit]
8.  }
9.
10. class UserService(userRepository: UserRepository) {
11.
12.   def updateUserName(id: Long, name: String): ZIO[Any,
      Throwable, User] =
13.     for {
14.       user <- userRepository.getUser(id)
15.            <- userRepository.updateUser(user.copy(name = name))
16.     } yield user
17. }
18.
19. object UserApp extends ZIOAppDefault {
20.
21.   val userRepository = new UserRepository {
22.
```

```
23.    def getUser(id: Long): ZIO[Any, Throwable, User] =
   ZIO.succeed(User(id, "Amit", "user@example.com"))
24.    def updateUser(user: User): ZIO[Any, Throwable, Unit] = ZIO.
   succeed(println(s"Updating user: $user"))
25.
26.  }
27.
28.  val userService = new UserService(userRepository)
29.
30.    override def run: ZIO[Any with ZIOAppArgs with Scope, Any, Any] =
31.
32. userService.updateUserName(1, "Rituraj").foldZIO(
33.    error => ZIO.succeed(println(s"Error: $error")).as(1),
34.    user => ZIO.succeed(println(s"Updated user: $user")).as(0)
35.  )
36.
37. }
```

The code defines a simple user management system with a **UserRepository** trait and a **UserService** class that depends on it. The **UserRepository** trait defines two methods: **getUser** and **updateUser**. The **getUser** method returns a ZIO effect that retrieves a user with a given **id**. The **updateUser** method returns a ZIO effect that updates a user in the repository.

The **UserService** class provides a method **updateUserName** that takes an **id** and a **name** as parameters and updates the **name** of a user with the given **id**. This method uses a for-comprehension to compose the **getUser** and **updateUser** effects from the repository to achieve the desired behavior of updating a user's name.

The **UserApp** object extends the app trait from ZIO and overrides the run method to execute the **updateUserName** effect. The **run** method uses the **foldZIO** method to handle errors that may occur during the execution of the effect and return a status code.

The code example demonstrates how to create, compose, and execute ZIO effects to build a functional, composable, and resilient application.

Conclusion

In this chapter, we looked into the effects and the side effects and their differences. We acknowledged the impact of side effects and how it impacts the reasoning of the code. We discussed how I/O produces side effects and exceptions as well. We also understand with examples how to handle side effects with effect systems provided by already learned functional libraries, Cats, and ZIO.

In the next chapter, we will look into the functional patterns to write programs using this functional construct.

CHAPTER 7
Functional Pattern Implementation

Introduction

This chapter focus on implementation details about the effects and its role in functional programming. It delves deep to write programs using effects and it is not possible to write any real-world scenario without using effects. This chapter focuses on a structure or design patterns that provides a standard way to solve a common characteristics problem and helps to extend easily when there is a change in requirement. These functional patterns provide a way how to solve a problem in functional structure and it also provide all benefits of requirement extension. We will also learn about the side effects and how to avoid side effects using implementing these functional patterns to make program more reasonable. Also, look into the functional library to support effects systems.

Structure

In this chapter, we will cover the following topics:

- Domain-specific language
- Using DSL to solve problem statement
- Tagless final
- Free implementations

- Free functor
- ZIO layer

Objectives

By the end of this chapter, readers will able to understand how to follow a functional pattern to write a problem solution in a functional way with all the functional constructs we understood in earlier chapters. We will look more into these patterns and how to combine them so we can reap out the benefits of all functional programming.

Domain-specific language

Domain-specific language (**DSL**) is a design pattern to focus on specific (domain) problem and creating a specific (programming) language to solve the domain-specific problem. It creates one higher level on top of a general-purpose programming language to execute the DSL. Now, it also helps to understand what is (generic) programming language and how can we create a new programming language as DSL focusses on same pattern to design a focused language.

The following are the benefits of DSL:

- **Improved readability**: DSLs are designed to be domain-specific, making the code more readable and understandable by domain experts. This leads to code that more closely resembles the problem domain, improving communication between technical and non-technical stakeholders.

- **Increased productivity**: DSLs allow developers to express complex concepts in a concise and intuitive manner. Writing code in DSL often requires fewer lines and reduces boilerplate, leading to faster development and maintenance.

- **Domain alignment**: DSLs are tailored to specific problem domains, aligning closely with the concepts and terminology used within that domain. This facilitates clearer communication and understanding of the codebase among team members familiar with the domain.

- **Reduced error-prone code**: By providing a higher level of abstraction and using domain-specific terms, DSLs can help reduce errors and bugs in the code. Developers can work at a higher level of abstraction, reducing the chances of misunderstanding or misrepresenting domain logic.

- **Separation of concerns**: DSLs can help separate different concerns within a system. By isolating domain-specific logic in a DSL, it becomes easier to maintain, test, and modify that logic without impacting the rest of the system.

- **Customization and flexibility**: DSLs can be customized to fit specific requirements within a domain. They offer flexibility by allowing developers to define syntax and operations tailored to the problem at hand.

- **Tooling support**: Creating a DSL often involves defining parsers, interpreters, or other tools to work with the language. Once these are established, they can provide powerful support for analysis, validation, and automated processing of DSL code.

Using DSL to solve problem statement

DSL provides a tool to implement a problem by encoding domains into types and its operators about how these domains interact with each other and solved all the problems created using the domain types.

There are three specific components in implementing DSL, as follows:

- **Types**: Encode problem domains into types
- **Constructors**: Define how to create domain objects
- **Operators or interpreters**: Details out the interaction of domain types

The following is an example of a popular expression problem: The expression problem is about solving a mathematical expressions that contain digits and operators, which generally employs BODMAS rules to solve the expression, which defines the priority of operators that would be evaluated first within the expression, and solving the expression step by step using this priority rule.

- $1 + 5$
- $3 + 5 + 6$
- $(2 + 5) - 6$
- $(4 - 2) * 8 / 4 + 3$
- $4 + 2 * 8 - 4 / 2$

Currently, we are defining our new problem into a different language DSL which will be mapped or translated further into source language and then get evaluated.

Now, the problem ahead is how can we encode our new expression domain language into source Scala language.

Initial encoding

Earlier or initially, it was thought of using **algebraic data types** (**ADT**) where types are created from the domain and then composite expression are generated using these types. It is also known as **initial encoding**.

Domain types for our expression problem are as follows:

- Literals (**Lit**)
- Additions (**Add**)

- Negations (**Neg**)
- Multiplication (**Mul**)
- Divisions (**Div**)

```
1. sealed trait Expr
2.
3. final case class Lit(data: Int) extends Expr
4. final case class Add(lhs: Expr, rhs:Expr) extends Expr
5. final case class Neg(lhs: Expr, rhs:Expr) extends Expr
6. final case class Mul(lhs: Expr, rhs:Expr) extends Expr
7. final case class Div(lhs: Expr, rhs:Expr) extends Expr
```

These domains are sufficient to translate any expression to our domain types. The following is an example:

- $3 + 5 + 6 = Add\ (Add(Lit(3),\ Lit(5)),\ Lit(6))$
- $(4 - 2) * 8 / 4 + 3 = Add(Mul(Neg(Lit(4),\ Lit(2)),\ Div(8,4)),\ Lit(3))$
- $4 + 2 * 8 - 4 / 2 = Neg(Add(Lit(4),\ Mul(Lit(2),\ Lit(8))),\ Div(Lit(4),\ Lit(2)))$

This is how each expression can be translated to a new domain.

We managed to translate a problem into a new domain. Now, the question comes how to solve this expression for which we need to create an interpreter that translates our DSL or ADT into the host language by pattern matching, where it could be evaluated further.

```
1. def interpreter(expr : Expr) : Int =
2.     expr match
3.         case Lit(data) =>  data
4.         case Add(lhs, rhs) => interpreter(lhs) + interpreter(rhs)
5.         case Neg(lhs, rhs) => interpreter(lhs) - interpreter(rhs)
6.         case Mul(lhs, rhs) => interpreter(lhs) * interpreter(rhs)
7.         case Div(lhs, rhs) => interpreter(lhs) / interpreter(rhs)
```

Encoding our DSL, as a straightforward ADT, is known as an **initial encoding**. Tagged part comes into discussion, where there is more than one type involved or for **generalized ADT (GADT)**.

The problem with initial encoding is as follows:

- **Performance**: Every time a problem statement needs to be encoded in domain language and then it gets deconstructed in interpreter which make performance hit for large number for types.

- **Extending the language**: If this domain language needs to be extended to a new ADT and then need to write new interpreters and further these new ADT must be composable with existing ADT to create valid programs.

Tagless final

As we saw, there are issues with Initial encoding of performance due to twice encoding and decoding of every statement in the new DSL. So, there are other techniques which evolved to overcome the same. It is tagless final or tagless final encoding. It is a technique used in functional programming, particularly in languages like Scala, to implement embedded DSL in a modular and composable way.

In tagless final, the idea is to represent operations in the DSL, as follows:

- Methods in a type class

- The interpreters for these operations are implemented as instances of that type class

There are no intermediate data structures (tags) to represent the operations; instead, the operations are directly encoded in the types. Hence, it is not causing performance hit as we got earlier with initial encoding. This approach feels very similar to **object-oriented programming** (**OOP**) interface base programming. Let us see further how it fixes issue and allows to implement multiple meanings (interpreters) for our newly created DSL.

The following is an overview of how tagless final works:

- **Define a type class**: Create a type class that represents the operations of your **embedded-DSL** (**EDSL**). Each method in the type class corresponds to an operation in the language, as follows:

```
1. trait MyDSL[F[_]] {
2.   def op1: F[Result1]
3.   def op2(arg: ArgType): F[Result2]
4.   // ...
5. }
```

- **Write interpreters**: Implement interpreters for your EDSL by providing instances of the type class for different data types (**F**). These interpreters can be for different contexts, such as testing, logging, or actually executing the operations, as follows:

```
1. class MyInterpreter extends MyDSL[IO] {
2.   def op1: IO[Result1] = // implementation
3.   def op2(arg: ArgType): IO[Result2] = // implementation
4. }
```

- **Programs are functions**: Instead of constructing a data structure that represents a program, you express programs as functions that take an interpreter as an argument, as follows:

```
1. def myProgram[F[_]](dsl: MyDSL[F]): F[Result] = {
2.   import dsl._
3.   for {
```

```
4.      res1 <- operation1
5.      res2 <- operation2(someArg)
6.      // ...
7.    } yield finalResult
8.  }
```

- **Dependency injection**: The interpreter (**MyInterpreter** in this case) is injected into the program when it is run. This allows you to swap interpreters for different contexts without changing the program logic, as follows:

```
1.  val result: IO[Result] = myProgram(new MyInterpreter)
```

Tagless final provides a way to build EDSL that are type-safe, modular, and easy to extend. It avoids the need for intermediate data structures (tags) used in other approaches like initial algebras, making the code more concise and expressive.

Assume that you have a simple tagless final DSL representing arithmetic operations, as follows:

```
1.  trait MathDSL[F[_]] {
2.    def add(a: Int, b: Int): F[Int]
3.    def multiply(a: Int, b: Int): F[Int]
4.  }
5.
6.  object MathDSL {
7.    def apply[F[_]](implicit mathDSL: MathDSL[F]): MathDSL[F] = mathDSL
8.  }
```

Now, you can write a program using this DSL, as follows:

```
1.  import cats.effect.IO
2.
3.  def mathProgram[F[_]: MathDSL]
      (implicit mathDSL: MathDSL[F]): F[Int] = {
4.    import MathDSL.ops._
5.    for {
6.      result1 <- add(3, 4)
7.      result2 <- multiply(result1, 2)
8.    } yield result2
9.  }
```

In this example, **MathDSL.ops._** provides syntax enrichment for more convenient usage.

Now, let us define interpreters for this DSL. You can create different interpreters for various contexts, such as a real interpreter using **IO** for execution or a test interpreter:

```
1.  object ProdInterpreter extends MathDSL[IO] {
2.    def add(a: Int, b: Int): IO[Int] = IO(a + b)
```

```
3.    def multiply(a: Int, b: Int): IO[Int] = IO(a * b)
4.  }
5.
6.  object TestInterpreter extends MathDSL[Option] {
7.    def add(a: Int, b: Int): Option[Int] = Some(a + b)
8.    def multiply(a: Int, b: Int): Option[Int] = Some(a * b)
9.  }
10.
```

With dependency injection, you can then run your program with different interpreters, as follows:

```
1.  val resultIO: IO[Int] = mathProgram[IO]( ProdInterpreter)
2.  val resultOption: Option[Int] = mathProgram[Option]
    ( TestInterpreter)
```

By using type class instances (interpreters) as implicit parameters, you achieve dependency injection. This allows you to swap out different implementations of your DSL for different contexts without modifying your core program logic, making your code more flexible and easier to test.

Free implementations

In functional programming, the term free implementation often refers to free monads, free functors, or other free structures that provide a way to separate the definition of a computation's structure from its interpretation. This is particularly useful for building modular and composable programs.

Free in this context does not mean no cost but rather unconstrained by interpretation. A free structure is the most generic or minimal implementation of a concept that satisfies a given set of laws or constraints. It helps you to define a behavior abstractly without committing to a specific interpretation.

Free functor

A free functor is a concept in category theory and functional programming. It provides a minimal or most generic way to lift objects from one category to another while satisfying the requirements of a functor. In practical terms, a free functor is often used to construct functorial structures where you represent computations or data transformations abstractly, without enforcing any specific implementation or interpretation.

Free functors abstractly describe computations or transformations without committing to a specific implementation. It is a minimal structure that satisfy the laws of a functor and are a building block for constructing free monads and other free structures in functional programming.

Applications

The following are the use cases for free functor:

- **Abstract syntax trees (ASTs):** Represent the operations of a DSL in a functorial way.

- **Modular interpretation:** Allow multiple interpretations of the same computation logic.

- **Code transformation:** Enable generic transformations of code or data structures that are functorial.

Free monad

A free monad is a concept in functional programming that allows you to build a DSL by separating the description of a computation from its execution. It is a way to represent a sequence of computations as a data structure without actually executing them immediately.

In essence, A free monad enables you to define a set of instructions or operations in a monadic structure without specifying how these operations are executed. Later, you can interpret or execute these instructions in different ways based on your requirements.

For instance, let us say you have DSL for a simple calculator with operations like addition, subtraction, and multiplication. You could define a free monad to represent these operations and then interpret it differently based on whether you want to execute the calculations immediately, optimize them, or even translate them into another language.

Free monad in category theory

A free monad can be a powerful tool for building composable and reusable abstractions in functional programming languages, allowing for separation of concerns between describing the computation and actually performing it.

In category theory, a free monad is a construct that arises in the context of monads, which is a way of modelling computational effects in a mathematical and abstract manner.

Given a functor F in a category C, a free monad construction produces a monad. This monad is characterized by a universal property: For any other monad M and a natural transformation from F to the underlying functor of M, there exists a unique monad morphism from free monad generated by F to M.

In simpler terms, a free monad is the initial object in the category of monads that are built from a given functor F. It captures the essence of the computational effects described by the functor F in the most general way.

A free monad construction is foundational in understanding how monads can be generated from functors, providing a theoretical framework to model computational effects in category theory. It helps establish connections between purely mathematical concepts in category theory and their computational interpretations in functional programming.

A free monad has several benefits and use cases in functional programming, as follows:

- **Separation of concerns**: It separates the description of computations from their execution. This helps in writing code that focuses on what needs to be done rather than how it is done. The program logic can be built using the free monad and then interpreted or executed in various ways.

- **DSL creation**: It facilitates the creation of DSLs by defining a set of operations using the free monad, you can create a specialized language tailored to your problem domain. This DSL can be more expressive and intuitive for solving specific tasks.

- **Composability and reusability**: A free monad allow for composability of operations. You can build complex computations by combining simpler operations. Additionally, these operations can be reused across different contexts or interpreted differently without changing the core logic.

- **Interpretation flexibility**: A free monad allows for different interpretations of the same computation. You can interpret the program for different purposes such as testing, optimization, parallelization, or even translation into other languages or systems.

- **Easier testing**: Since a free monad separates the description of computations, testing becomes easier. You can interpret free monad with a different interpreter specifically designed for testing, allowing for easy verification of program logic.

- **Lazy evaluation**: A free monad inherently support lazy evaluation. Computations described in free monad is not evaluated until interpreted. This lazy nature can be advantageous for efficiency, especially in scenarios where not all parts of the computation are needed.

- **Abstraction and modularity**: A free monad allow for a high level of abstraction and modularity. They provide a clean separation between the structure of the program and the specific implementations or side effects, promoting a more maintainable and understandable codebase.

Overall, a free monad is a powerful tool in functional programming, enabling the creation of modular, reusable, and expressive code by abstracting the description of computations from their execution and allowing for flexible interpretation and manipulation of these computations.

Free applicative

The free applicative is a construct in functional programming that extends the idea of the free monad to applicative functors. Applicative functors provide a way to sequence computations while allowing for parallelism and independence between these computations.

The free applicative is a data structure that allows you to build a sequence of independent computations without actually executing them. Similar to the free monad, it separates the description of computations from their execution.

In essence, it represents a sequence of applicative computations as a data structure. Each computation is wrapped in a functor context, allowing for potential parallelism and independent execution. This structure maintains the order of operations but does not immediately execute them.

Free applicative in category theory

In category theory, the concept of free applicative is closely related to the concept of free functor or free construction. It is a way to construct a free structure (in this case, an applicative functor) over a given set of objects.

Given a category C and a set of objects, the free applicative construction generates an applicative functor that is freely generated from these objects. This construction follows the notion of adjunctions and free constructions prevalent in category theory.

Similar to other free constructions in category theory, the free applicative functor has a universal property. Specifically, it is an initial object in the category of applicative functors generated by a given set of objects. This means that any other applicative functor that can be formed from the same set of objects will have a unique morphism to the free applicative functor.

This property signifies that the free applicative functor is the most general applicative functor that can be constructed from the given set of objects. It captures the essence of the applicative structure generated by these objects in a way that is agnostic of any particular interpretation or implementation.

In summary, in category theory, the free applicative construction follows the general paradigm of free constructions by providing a universal object (the free applicative functor) that characterizes the most general structure of an applicative functor generated from a given set of objects in a category.

Free applicative provides benefits similar to the free monad, as follows:

- **Separation of concerns**: It separates the description of applicative computations from their execution, allowing you to define the sequence of operations independently of how they are executed.

- **Interpretation flexibility**: Just like with free monads, free applicative structures can be interpreted in different ways. You can execute or interpret these sequences of computations differently based on your requirements, enabling optimizations or alternative execution strategies.

- **Composability and reusability**: Free applicative structures enable the composition of independent computations. These computations can be combined, reused, or modified without altering their structure, promoting code reusability.

- **Lazy evaluation**: The free applicative, similar to free monads, allows for lazy evaluation. Computations described within it are not evaluated until they are interpreted or executed.

- **Testing and abstraction**: Free applicative structures provide a way to separate the description of computations, allowing for easier testing and promoting abstraction, modularity, and maintainability in the codebase.

Overall, the free applicative is a powerful tool in functional programming for representing sequences of independent applicative computations in a composable and abstract manner, separating the description of these computations from their actual execution.

ZIO layer

ZIO layer (**ZLayer**) is a fundamental abstraction used for dependency management and resource acquisition. It is a powerful tool for managing the dependencies of your application in a purely functional way. **ZLayer** is part of ZIO's layer cake architecture, which helps in building modular, composable, and testable applications.

ZLayer represents a layer of services or dependencies that your application depends on. It is immutable and composable, allowing you to combine different layers to form a full application environment, as follows:

```
1. type ZLayer[-RIn, +E, +ROut] = RIn => async Either[E, ROut]
```

For example, a **ZLayer[Socket and Persistence, Throwable, Database]** can be thought of as a function that map **Socket** and **Persistence** services into **Database** service, as follows:

```
1. (Socket, Persistence) => Database
```

ZLayer provides the capability to compose dependencies both horizontally and vertically, referring to different ways of combining layers to build your application's environment, as follows:

- **Horizontal composition (++)**: Horizontal composition involves combining layers that provide services or capabilities at the same level, essentially merging them side by side. When you horizontally compose layers using the **++** operator, you are combining layers that offer different services independently.

  The following code is an example:
  ```
  1. val layerA: ZLayer[Any, Nothing, ServiceA] = ???
  2. val layerB: ZLayer[Any, Nothing, ServiceB] = ???
  3.
  4. val combinedLayer: ZLayer[Any, Nothing, ServiceA with
     ServiceB] = layerA ++ layerB
  ```

Here, **layerA** and **layerB** offer distinct services (**ServiceA** and **ServiceB** respectively). By using **++**, you combine them to create a single layer that offers both services.

- **Vertical composition (>>>)**: Vertical composition, on the other hand, involves stacking layers on top of each other, forming a dependency chain where the output of one-layer feeds into the input of the next. This chaining of dependencies forms a sequence or pipeline.

  The following code is an example:

  ```
  1. val layerC: ZLayer[ServiceA, Nothing, ServiceC] = ???
  2. val layerD: ZLayer[ServiceB with ServiceC, Nothing,
     ServiceD] = ???
  3.
  4. val composedLayer: ZLayer[Any, Nothing, ServiceD] = layerC >>>
       layerD
  ```

Here, **layerC** depends on **ServiceA**, and **layerD** depends on both **ServiceB** and **ServiceC**. Using **>>>**, you compose **layerC** and **layerD** into a single layer that provides **ServiceD**, with **ServiceA**, **ServiceB**, and **ServiceC** forming the underlying dependencies.

Horizontal composition (**++**) is used for combining services or capabilities at the same level, allowing for a combination of independent services into a single layer. Vertical composition (**>>>**) is used for building a dependency chain, where the output of one-layer feeds into the input of the next, forming a sequence of dependencies.

Both horizontal and vertical compositions are crucial for constructing complex environments in ZIO applications, enabling modular, composable, and testable designs by managing dependencies in a functional and expressive manner.

ZLayers are as follows:

- **Recipes for creating services**: They describe how to create services from given dependencies. For example, the **ZLayer[Socket & Database, Throwable, UserRepo]** is a recipe for building a service that requires **Socket** and **Database** service, and it produces a **UserRepo** service.

- **An alternative to constructors**: We can think of **ZLayer** as a more powerful version of a constructor, it is an alternative way to represent a constructor. Like a constructor, it allows us to build the **ROut** service in terms of its dependencies (**RIn**).

- **Composable**: Layers are an idiomatic way in ZIO to create services that depend on other services because of their excellent composition properties. We can define layers that are relying on each other.

- **Effectful and resourceful**: The construction of ZLayers can be effectful and resourceful. They can be acquired in an effectful way and safely released when the services are done being utilized or even in case of failure, interruption, or defects in the application.

For example, to create a recipe for a **Database** service, we should describe how the database will be initialized using an acquisition action. In addition, it may contain information about how the database releases its connection pools.

- **Asynchronous**: Unlike class constructors which are blocking, **ZLayer** is fully asynchronous and non-blocking.

  > Note: **In non-blocking applications we typically want to avoid creating something that is blocking inside its constructor.**

  For example, when we are constructing some sort of Kafka streaming service, we might want to connect to the Kafka cluster in the constructor of our service, which takes some time. So, it would not be a good idea to block inside the constructor. There are some workarounds for fixing this issue, but they are not as perfect as the ZIO solution which allows for asynchronous, non-blocking constructors.

- **Parallelism**: ZLayers can be acquired in parallel, unlike class constructors, which do not support parallelism. When we compose multiple layers and then acquire them, the construction of each layer will occur in parallel. This will reduce the initialization time of ZIO applications with a large number of dependencies.

- **Resilient**: Layer construction can be resilient. So, if the acquiring phase fails, we can have a schedule to retry the acquiring stage. This helps us write applications that are error-proof and respond appropriately to failures.

The following are some key aspects and benefits of **ZLayer**:

- **Dependency management**: **ZLayer** allows you to model your application's dependencies as immutable values. This ensures a clear and controlled way to manage dependencies throughout your application.

- **Modularity and composition**: Layers can be composed together using functional combinators (**+++**, **++**, **flatMap**, etc.) to build a complete application environment. This modularity makes it easy to reason about and test different parts of your application independently.

- **Resource management**: **ZLayer** facilitates resource management by allowing you to acquire and release resources safely. It provides a way to acquire resources lazily and ensures proper resource cleanup using ZIO's managed data type.

- **Testability**: The layer-based approach makes it straightforward to replace parts of your application with test implementations or mocks. This makes testing pure functions and effectful code much easier.

- **Encapsulation of complexity**: Layers encapsulate complexity and provide a clear separation between different concerns of your application. This separation leads to a more maintainable and understandable codebase.

- **Efficient runtime wiring**: **ZLayer** supports efficient and lazy dependency wiring. Dependencies are only built when needed, allowing for better resource utilization and reducing unnecessary resource allocation.

A typical usage of **ZLayer** involves defining layers for various parts of your application (such as database access, configuration, services, etc.) and combining these layers to form the full environment required by your application.

The following code is an example:

```
1. val databaseLayer: ZLayer[Any, Throwable, Database] = ???
2. val configLayer: ZLayer[Any, Throwable, Config] = ???
3. val serviceLayer: ZLayer[Database with Config, Throwable, Service] = ???
4.
5. val fullAppLayer: ZLayer[Any, Throwable, Service] = databaseLayer
   ++ configLayer >>> serviceLayer
```

The following is a detailed example:

```
1. import zio._
2.
3. // This is configuration class which defines configuration for Database
4. case class AppConfig(databaseUrl: String, username: String,
   password: String)
5.
6. //Configuration layer is defined based on above AppConfig
7. val configLayer: ZLayer[Any, Nothing, AppConfig] =
8.   ZLayer.succeed(AppConfig(
9.     databaseUrl = ??? // define the your local db like
   "jdbc:postgresql://localhost:5432/mydb",
10.    username = ??? // example username is "admin"
11.    password = ??? // example username is "password"
12.  ))
13.
14. // Database Service
15. trait Database {
16.   def query(sql: String): Task[String]
17. }
18.
19. case class DatabaseLive(url: String, username: String, password:
    String) extends Database {
20.   override def query(sql: String): Task[String] =
21.     ZIO.succeed(s"Executed: $sql on $url with user $username")
22. }
23.
```

```scala
24. val dbLayer: ZLayer[AppConfig, Nothing, Database] = ZLayer {
25.   for {
26.     config <- ZIO.service[AppConfig]
27.   } yield DatabaseLive(config.databaseUrl, config.username,
      config.password)
28. }
29.
30. // This is service to use the database to get the users based on
      user's id
31. trait UserService {
32.   def getUser(id: Int): Task[String]
33. }
34.
35. case class UserServiceLive(database: Database) extends UserService {
36.   override def getUser(id: Int): Task[String] =
37.     database.query(s"SELECT * FROM users WHERE id = $id")
38. }
39.
40. val serviceLayer: ZLayer[Database, Nothing, UserService] = ZLayer {
41.   for {
42.     db <- ZIO.service[Database]
43.   } yield UserServiceLive(db)
44. }
45.
46. // Composing all layers defined above just like as lego blocks
47. val fullAppLayer: ZLayer[Any, Nothing, UserService] =
48.   configLayer >>> dbLayer >>> serviceLayer
49.
50. // ZIO Program
51. val program: ZIO[UserService, Throwable, String] =
52.   UserService(_.getUser(1))
53.
54. //providing the final fullappLayer which is constructed layer-by-layer
55. val result: ZIO[Any, Throwable, String] =
56.   program.provideLayer(fullAppLayer)
57.
58. // Run the Program
59. object ZLayerExample extends ZIOAppDefault {
60.   override def run: ZIO[Any, Throwable, String] =
      result.tap(output => ZIO.debug(s"Result: $output"))
61. }
```

This code snippet demonstrates the creation of different layers for database access, configuration, and a service, and then combines them into a **fullAppLayer** representing the complete environment needed for the service to run.

Conclusion

In this chapter, we looked into the effects and the side effects. We acknowledged the impact of side effect and how it impacts the reasoning of the code. We saw how I/O produces side effects and exceptions as well. We also understand with examples how to handle side effects with effects systems provided by already learned functional libraries Cats and ZIO.

In the next chapter, we will look into the functional tools which provide solutions that is common during functional programming like getting and setting attributes (optics), asynchronous calls, JSON reading and writing, functional streams and functional collections etc.

Join our Discord space

Join our Discord workspace for latest updates, offers, tech happenings around the world, new releases, and sessions with the authors:

https://discord.bpbonline.com

Chapter 8
Functional Tools

Introduction

We learnt many fundamental designs and constructs to write our program to reap all benefits of functional programming. There are many common utilities which is required when working with real-world scenario, for example, functional way to update and get attributes from business objects (optics), asynchronous calls to optimize the CPU time, reading and writing JSON for the request or response, data collections to store and read form collections of values and data stream for unbounded data processing.

These are the common cross cutting concerns which you employ for any business service during its implementations. There are lots of functional tools available which we could rely on. There are utility libraries available which help to implement and optimize these common tasks. In this chapter, we will learn all these important tools which gets used in day-to-day tasks.

Structure

In this chapter, we will cover the following topics:

- Monocle for optics
- Monix for asynchrony
- Caliban

- Circe
- ZIO scheduling
- PureConfig
- Functional Streams for Scala
- Cats collections
- Cats retry

Objectives

By the end of this chapter, readers will be able to understand all important functional tools and how to use it. It not only shortens the implementation time but also provide standard and battle tested solution to its own specific problem. It increases efficiency and helps to produce less error-prone solutions.

Monocle for optics

Monocle[1] is an optics library for Scala to do optics operations in a functional way, but the question is what optics means and how it helps in problem-solving. Optics is a composable abstractions that allow the manipulation and querying of complex data structures in an immutable and composable manner. Immutability is a core theme for functional programming and getting and setting or updating in deep attributes of data structure:

The following is the relationship among the classes in the optics library:

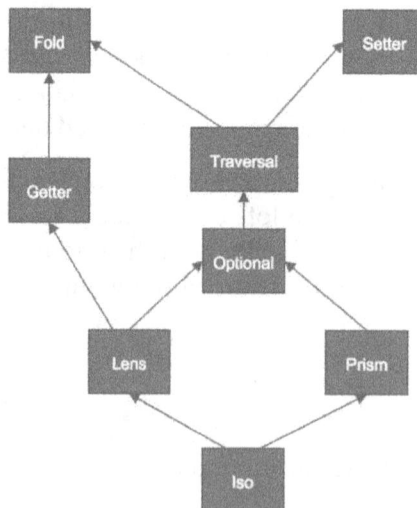

Figure 8.1: Optics constructs defined in monocle with their relationship

---

1. https://www.optics.dev/Monocle/

Each optics construct defined in monocle provides specific help in manipulation of data structures.

The following are the core concepts defined in monocle:

- **Iso**: An iso represents an isomorphism between two types, allowing for lossless conversion back and forth. This can be useful for converting between different representations of the same data.

- **Lens**: A lens is used to focus on a single element within a product type for example, a case class in Scala. It can be thought of as a getter and a setter combined into one abstraction. Lenses are useful for manipulating a specific field within a larger structure without modifying the rest of the structure.

- **Prism**: A prism is similar to a lens but is used for sum types (a co-product type for example, sealed trait hierarchies in Scala). It allows you to focus on a specific subtype of a sum type, enabling safe down casting and construction.

- **Optional**: An optional is a generalization of a lens that can focus on an optional element of a structure, making it useful for operations that might not always succeed, such as, looking up a key in a map.

- **Traversal**: A traversal generalizes the optional concept further to focusing on multiple elements at once, allowing for operations on collections of items within a structure.

The following table describes optics composability, an important theme of functional programming. It shows how these optics compose with other optics and what is the resultant optics of this composition. For example, when a lens is composed with prism then its resultant optics is optional.

	Fold	Getter	Setter	Traversal	Optional	Prism	Lens	Iso
Fold	Fold	Fold	Fold	Fold	Fold	Fold	Fold	Fold
Getter	Fold	Getter		Fold	Fold	Fold	Getter	Getter
Setter			Setter	Setter	Setter	Setter	Setter	Setter
Traversal	Fold	Fold	Setter	Traversal	Traversal	Traversal	Traversal	Traversal
Optional	Fold	Fold	Setter	Traversal	Optional	Optional	Optional	Optional
Prism	Fold	Fold	Setter	Traversal	Optional	Prism	Optional	Prism
Lens	Fold	Getter	Setter	Traversal	Optional	Optional	Lens	Lens
Iso	Fold	Getter	Setter	Traversal	Optional	Prism	Lens	Iso

Table 8.1: Composability of different optics

The following are the benefits that monocle provide:

- **Simplification of immutable data manipulation**: Monocle simplifies the manipulation of immutable data structures. In functional programming, immutability is a core principle that leads to safer and more predictable code. However, updating deeply nested immutable structures can be verbose and error-prone. Monocle provides a cleaner, more expressive way to handle such updates.

- **Composability**: Optics in monocle, such as lenses, prisms and optional, are highly composable. This means you can easily chain operations to focus deeply into a data structure with minimal boilerplate. This composability also enhances code reuse and modularity.

- **Type-safety**: Monocle enhances type-safety in your code. By using optics, you can perform many operations that would typically require potentially unsafe operations, like casting in a completely type-safe manner. This reduces runtime errors and makes the code more robust.

- **Readability and maintainability**: Code that uses monocle optics is often more readable and maintainable than traditional imperative code for manipulating complex data structures. Operations on data are expressed in a declarative style, making it clearer what the code is doing and easier to refactor or extend in the future.

- **Boilerplate reduction**: Monocle can significantly reduce boilerplate code, especially when dealing with updates to nested structures. Scala macros and implicit conversions in monocle help in generating much of the necessary boilerplate code automatically, keeping your codebase cleaner and more focused on business logic.

- **Interoperability**: Monocle is designed to work seamlessly with Scala's standard library and commonly used data structures. This makes it easy to integrate into existing Scala projects without needing to refactor your entire codebase around the library.

- **Enhanced functional programming experience**: By providing powerful abstractions and tools for immutable data manipulation, Monocle enhances the functional programming experience in Scala. It allows developers to more fully embrace functional principles, leading to code that is more expressive and aligned with functional programming paradigms.

- **Community and ecosystem**: Monocle benefits from a strong Scala community and ecosystem. There is active development and support, which means the library continues to evolve and improve. Moreover, there is a wealth of resources, examples, and documentation available to help developers get the most out of the library.

The example describes the monocle magic working with nested immutable data and simplifies fetch or update scenarios in nested structured data by composing different available lenses.

Setting up dependencies

First, ensure you have the necessary dependencies in your **build.sbt** file. You might need to adjust the versions depending on the latest releases, as follows:

```
1. libraryDependencies += "dev.optics" %% "monocle-core" % "3.2.0"
2. libraryDependencies += "dev.optics" %% "monocle-macro" % "3.2.0"
   // Optional, for macros
```

The following example creates a nested case class **company** and create an instance which does not have the manager (which is also an employee) defined. It creates **managerPrism** and updates the immutable instance with manager:

```
1. import monocle.Prism
2. import monocle.macros.GenPrism
3.
4. // Update Company to include an optional manager
5. case class Company(name: String, employees: List[Employee],
   manager: Option[Employee])
6.
7. val updatedCompany = Company(
8.   name = "Awesome Corp",
9.   employees = List(
10.     Employee(
11.       name = "Alice",
12.       address = Address(street = "123 Main St", city = "Metropolis",
   zipCode = "12345")
13.     ),
14.     Employee(
15.       name = "Bob",
16.       address = Address(street = "456 Elm St", city = "Gotham",
   zipCode = "67890")
17.     )
18.   ),
19.   manager = None
20. )
21.
22. // Prism for Option[Employee]
23. val managerPrism: Prism[Company, Employee] = GenPrism[Company,
   Option[Employee]].composePrism(Prism.some[Employee])
24.
25. // Set the manager
26. val companyWithManager: Company = managerPrism.set(
27.   Employee(name = "Charlie", address = Address(street =
   "789 Oak St", city = "Star City", zipCode = "11223"))
```

```
28. )(updatedCompany)
29.
30. println(s"Company with manager: $companyWithManager")
```

Monix for asynchrony

Monix[2] is a high-performance Scala or Scala.js library for composing asynchronous and event-based programs. It builds upon the foundational reactive streams paradigm and integrates seamlessly with Scala's future and the broader ecosystem of reactive programming in the **Java virtual machine (JVM)** environment. Monix is designed to enable fine-grained control over asynchronous execution and provides tools for building resilient, responsive and scalable applications.

The following are the key features of Monix:

- **Observable**: At the heart of Monix is the observable type, an asynchronous data stream that supports back-pressure. Observables goes beyond the capabilities of the standard Scala future by allowing the representation of multiple asynchronous events over time, making it ideal for handling streams of data for example, messages from a message queue or user events in a UI.

- **Task**: Monix introduces the task type, a lazy, composable abstraction over asynchronous computations. Task can be seen as an enhancement over Scala's future, providing better control over evaluation strategies and execution context. It supports lazy evaluation, making it possible to build complex asynchronous pipelines that are only executed when needed.

- **Scheduler**: Monix provides powerful scheduling capabilities that allow fine-grained control over the execution context of asynchronous operations. This is particularly useful for tasks that require precise timing or need to be executed repeatedly at specified intervals.

- **Cats integration**: Monix is integrated with the Cats library, a cornerstone of the Scala functional programming ecosystem. This integration ensures that Monix works well with the abstractions provided by Cats, such as monad, functor, and effect, making it a natural fit for applications built on functional programming principles.

- **Back-pressure**: Both observable and task support back-pressure, a mechanism that prevents overwhelming consumers of data streams or computation results. Back-pressure ensures that producers of data or events do not flood consumers, allowing for stable and efficient processing even in the face of high volumes of data.

---

2. **https://monix.io/**

- **Reactive and asynchronous programming**: Monix facilitates reactive and asynchronous programming by providing tools to compose, transform, and consume asynchronous data streams and computations. Its design encourages writing non-blocking code that is both efficient and easy to reason about.

Sub projects

There are many sub projects created which provide a problem specific implementation using Monix.

The following are the sub projects:

- **Monix-executions**: It provides low level utilities to work with concurrency using `scala.concurrent`.

- **Monix catnap**: It provides generic and purely functional utilities for concurrency built on top of Cats Effect.

- **Monix eval**: It creates `Task` and `Coeval` data types for working with purely functional effects in principled way.

- **Monix reactive**: It provides `Observable` data type with other utilities and a high-performance streaming abstraction for implementation of Reactive Manifesto in Scala.

- **Monix tail**: It provides iterant, a generic, purely functional, principled pull based streaming data type.

The following are the use cases:

- **Concurrent web services**: Monix is well-suited for building high-concurrency web services and APIs, where efficient handling of asynchronous I/O is crucial.

- **Stream processing:** Applications that need to process streams of data in real-time can leverage Monix `Observable` for efficient, back-pressured stream processing.

- **Asynchronous task pipelines**: Monix `Task` can be used to construct complex asynchronous workflows, allowing for dependency management and error handling in a composable way.

- **Time-based operations**: The scheduling capabilities in Monix make it ideal for tasks that require precise timing or periodic execution.

Monix stands out for its focus on performance, flexibility and providing a rich set of primitives for asynchronous and event-based programming in Scala. Its integration with the broader Scala ecosystem, including interoperability with reactive streams and functional programming libraries like Cats, makes it a powerful choice for developers building reactive applications on JVM.

Setting up dependencies

First, ensure you have the necessary dependencies in your **build.sbt** file. You might need to adjust the versions depending on the latest releases, as follows:

```
1. libraryDependencies += "io.Monix" %% "Monix" % "3.4.1"
```

Task (Async computations):

```scala
1. import Monix.eval.Task
2. import Monix.execution.Scheduler.Implicits.global
3. import scala.concurrent.duration._
4.
5. // Simulate a remote service call
6. def fetchUser(userId: Int): Task[String] = Task {
7.   // Simulate a delay of 5 seconds
8.   Thread.sleep(5000)
9.   s"User data for $userId"
10. }.delayExecution(1.second) // Add an additional delay
11.
12. // Combine multiple Tasks
13. val program: Task[String] = for {
14.   user1 <- fetchUser(1)
15.   user2 <- fetchUser(2)
16. } yield s"$user1 and $user2"
17.
18. // Run the program
19. val result = program.runToFuture
20.
21. // Print the result
22. result.foreach(println) // Output: User details for user 1 and user 2
```

Observable (Reactive Streams):

```scala
1. import Monix.reactive.Observable
2. import Monix.execution.Scheduler.Implicits.global
3.
4. // Create an Observable that emits numbers 1 to 50
5. val numberStream: Observable[Int] = Observable.range(1, 51)
6.
7. // Process the stream: filter even numbers and map to strings
8. val processedStream: Observable[String] = numberStream
9.   .filter(_ % 2 == 0) // Keep only even numbers
10.   .map(n => s"Even number: $n") // Map to strings
11.
12. // Subscribe to the stream and print each item
13. processedStream.foreach(println).runToFuture
```

```
14.
15. // Output:
16. // Even number: 2
17. // Even number: 4
18. // Even number: 6
19. // Even number: 8
20. // Even number: 10
21. //... up to 50
```

Caliban

Caliban[3] is a Scala library designed to make it easy to work with GraphQL. It aims to simplify the development of GraphQL servers and clients, emphasizing type-safety and minimal boilerplate. Caliban leverages Scala's advanced features, such as macros and implicits, to automatically derive GraphQL schemas directly from Scala case classes, reducing the need for manual schema definition and ensuring that the GraphQL schema stays in sync with the underlying Scala data models.

The following are the key features of Caliban:

- **Type-safety**: Caliban ensures that the GraphQL schema is always consistent with the Scala data types it represents. This reduces the risk of runtime errors and makes the codebase easier to refactor and maintain.

- **Schema derivation**: Caliban can automatically derive GraphQL schemas from Scala case classes. This feature minimizes boilerplate and helps keep the GraphQL schema and the Scala data model in alignment.

- **GraphQL subscriptions**: Caliban supports GraphQL subscriptions, allowing clients to subscribe to real-time updates. This is essential for building interactive, dynamic web and mobile applications.

- **Interoperability**: Caliban is designed to work well within the Scala ecosystem, offering integrations with popular Scala libraries and frameworks such as ZIO, Akka, Play, and http4s. This makes it a versatile choice for Scala developers working in various contexts.

- **Client and server support**: While Caliban focuses on building GraphQL servers, it also provides tools for generating Scala clients for GraphQL APIs. This means you can use Caliban not only to create your GraphQL backend but also to interact with other GraphQL services.

- **Customizability**: Caliban offers hooks and mechanisms to customize the behavior of the GraphQL server, including error handling, logging and request execution. This allows developers to tailor the server's behavior to their specific needs.

---

3. https://ghostdogpr.github.io/caliban/

- **Documentation and tooling**: The library comes with support for automatic generation of documentation from the GraphQL schema, making it easier for frontend developers to understand and use the API. It also supports GraphQL IDEs like GraphiQL out-of-the-box, for easy testing and exploration of the GraphQL API.

The following are the use cases for Caliban:

- **Building GraphQL APIs**: Caliban is primarily designed for building robust, type-safe GraphQL backends in Scala. It is suitable for a wide range of applications, from simple **Create, Read, Update, and Delete** (**CRUD**) applications to complex systems with real-time data requirements.

- **Microservices architectures**: Given its support for Scala and functional programming patterns, Caliban fits well into microservices architectures, especially those already leveraging the Scala ecosystem.

- **Real-time applications**: With support for subscriptions, Caliban is an excellent choice for applications requiring real-time data updates, such as chat applications, live dashboards, or collaborative tools.

- **Scala GraphQL clients**: Developers using Scala to consume GraphQL services can benefit from Caliban's client generation capabilities, ensuring type-safety and reducing boilerplate when interacting with GraphQL APIs.

The following is an example of using Caliban library to expose graphQL endpoint:

Setting up dependencies: First, ensure you have the necessary dependencies in your **build.sbt** file. You might need to adjust the versions depending on the latest releases, as follows:

```
1. libraryDependencies ++= Seq(
2.   "com.github.ghostdogpr" %% "caliban" % "1.3.1",
     // Use the latest version of Caliban
3.   "com.github.ghostdogpr" %% "caliban-http4s" % "1.3.1",
     // HTTP4S adapter for Caliban
4.   "org.http4s" %% "http4s-blaze-server" % "0.23.6",
     // HTTP server
5.   "org.http4s" %% "http4s-circe" % "0.23.6",
     // Circe support for HTTP4S (JSON)
6.   "io.circe" %% "circe-generic" % "0.14.1",
     // Circe library for JSON
7.   "org.typelevel" %% "cats-effect" % "3.3.0"
     // Cats-effect for effect management
8. )
```

GraphQL schema

In Caliban, the GraphQL schema is defined using Scala case classes and sealed traits. The following is an example:

```
1.  import caliban.GraphQL.graphQL
2.  import caliban.RootResolver
3.  import caliban.schema.GenericSchema
4.  import zio._
5.
6.  object CalibanExample extends GenericSchema[Any] {
7.    // Define a case class that represents the GraphQL "Query" type
8.    case class Character(name: String, age: Int)
9.
10.   // Define a resolver that provides data for the GraphQL queries
11.   case class Queries(allCharacters: List[Character])
12.
13.   // Sample data
14.   val characters = List(
15.     Character("Luke Skywalker", 53),
16.     Character("Darth Vader", 45)
17.   )
18.
19.   // Implement the resolver
20.   val queries = Queries(characters)
21.
22.   // Create the GraphQL API from the resolver
23.   val api = graphQL(RootResolver(queries))
24. }
```

Setting up server

You will need to setup an HTTP server to serve the GraphQL API.

The following example uses **http4s** with **blaze** as the server backend:

```
1.  import caliban.Http4sAdapter
2.  import org.http4s.server.blaze.BlazeServerBuilder
3.  import org.http4s.implicits._
4.  import zio.interop.catz._
5.  import zio._
6.
7.  object Server extends CatsApp {
8.    override def run(args: List[String]): URIO[zio.ZEnv, ExitCode] = {
```

```
9.      // Define the GraphQL route
10.     val route = Http4sAdapter.makeHttpService(CalibanExample.api)
11.     // Setup and start the server
12.     BlazeServerBuilder[Task]
13.       .bindHttp(8088, "localhost")
14.       .withHttpApp(route.orNotFound)
15.       .resource
16.       .toManagedZIO
17.       .useForever
18.       .exitCode
19.   }
20. }
```

This server listens on **localhost:8088** and serves the GraphQL API you defined. The **Http4sAdapter.makeHttpService** method creates an **http4s** service from the Caliban GraphQL API, which is then used to setup the server.

Caliban distinguishes itself in the Scala ecosystem with its focus on type-safety, ease of use, and seamless integration with the Scala functional programming model, particularly with the ZIO library. It is an excellent choice for Scala developers looking to either expose a GraphQL API or consume one with the benefits of Scala's type system and functional programming paradigms.

Circe

Circe[4] is a JSON library for Scala and Scala.js that provides powerful and simple tools for parsing, transforming, and printing JSON data. It is built on top of Cats, a functional programming library for Scala, which allows Circe to offer a purely functional, type-safe approach to dealing with JSON data. Circe's design emphasizes simplicity, robustness, and performance, making it a popular choice in the Scala ecosystem for working with JSON.

The following are the key features of Circe:

- **Automatic derivation**: Circe can automatically derive encoders and decoders for case classes and sealed trait hierarchies, significantly reducing boilerplate when working with JSON serialization and deserialization.

- **Type-safety**: With Circe, JSON handling is type-safe, which means that many common errors are caught at compile time. This approach minimizes runtime errors related to JSON parsing and encoding.

- **Custom encoders or decoders**: While Circe provides automatic derivation, it also allows for the easy definition of custom encoders and decoders. This flexibility is crucial for dealing with complex or non-standard JSON structures.

---

4. https://circe.github.io/circe/

- **Immutability and functional programming**: Circe is designed with immutability and functional programming principles in mind, making it a good fit for Scala applications that prioritize these approaches.

- **Interoperability**: Thanks to its foundation on Cats, Circe integrates well with other libraries in the Scala functional programming ecosystem, facilitating the development of robust and scalable applications.

- **Performance**: Circe is designed to be efficient, with performance that is competitive with other Scala JSON libraries. This makes it suitable for applications that require high-performance JSON parsing and generation.

The following is the use cases for Circe:

- **Web services and APIs**: Circe is commonly used in the development of web services and APIs, where JSON is the standard data interchange format. It is particularly useful in RESTful and GraphQL services built with Scala.

- **Configuration files**: Circe can parse configuration files written in JSON, allowing applications to load configuration data in a type-safe manner.

- **Data processing**: Applications that need to process JSON data, such as logs or messages from message queues, can use Circe to parse and transform JSON in a functional and type-safe way.

- **Frontend-backend communication**: For full-stack Scala applications (e.g., those using Scala.js for the frontend), Circe ensures seamless and type-safe data exchange between the server and client sides.

Working with Circe

Working with Circe typically involves defining case classes that represent the data structures you expect to encode or decode. Circe can then automatically derive the necessary encoders and decoders for these classes, or you can manually define them for more complex scenarios.

The following is an example of how you might decode a JSON string into a Scala case class and then encode it back to a JSON string:

```
1. import io.circe.generic.auto._, io.circe.parser._, io.circe.syntax._
2.
3. case class User(name: String, age: Int)
4.
5. val jsonString: String = """
6. {
7.   «name»: «John Doe»,
8.   «age»: 30
9. }
```

```
10. """
11.
12. // Decode the JSON string to a User instance
13. val decodedUser: Either[io.circe.Error, User] = decode[User]
    (jsonString)
14.
15. // Encode a User instance to a JSON string
16. val user = User("Jane Doe", 25)
17. val encodedJsonString: String = user.asJson.noSpaces
18.
19. println(decodedUser)
20. println(encodedJsonString)
```

In this example, **decode[User](jsonString)** attempts to parse the JSON string into a **User** instance, and **user.asJson.noSpaces** converts a **User** instance back into a compact JSON string.

Circe's integration with Cats and its emphasis on functional programming make it a powerful tool for Scala developers who need to work with JSON data in a type-safe, expressive, and efficient manner.

ZIO scheduling

ZIO is a powerful Scala library for asynchronous and concurrent programming, designed to make it easier to write robust, scalable, and efficient software. It provides a comprehensive set of features for functional effects, asynchronous programming, and dependency injection. While ZIO itself is not solely a scheduling library, it includes robust capabilities for scheduling asynchronous tasks, among many other features.

The following are the key features of ZIO related to scheduling:

- **Fiber-based concurrency**: ZIO uses fibers, which are lightweight threads of execution managed by the ZIO runtime rather than the underlying JVM threads. This allows for efficient execution of a large number of concurrent operations. Fibers can be used to schedule parallel or sequential tasks in a resource-efficient manner.

- **Scheduling asynchronous tasks**: ZIO provides various combinators to perform scheduling of tasks, such as **ZIO.sleep** (duration) which can delay the execution of a task for a specified duration. These can be combined with other ZIO effects to build complex scheduling logic without blocking threads.

- **Repeating and retrying effects**: ZIO includes powerful abstractions for repeating or retrying effects with complex policies. For example, retry and repeat combinators can be used with a schedule to define how and when to retry or repeat an effect, such as exponential backoff retrying of a failed network request.

- **Schedule**: ZIO schedule is a composable way to express complex scheduling logic, such as repeating an action every hour or retrying with a delay that increases exponentially. Schedules can be combined, making it possible to express sophisticated policies in a declarative and type-safe manner.

- **Resource safety**: ZIO ensures that resources are managed safely, which is critical for long-running applications and services. It provides guarantees that resources will be released when they are no longer needed, even in the presence of errors or interruptions.

The following is an example demonstrating how to use ZIO to schedule a repeating task:

```
1.  import zio._
2.  import zio.Console._
3.  import scala.concurrent.duration._
4.
5.  object ZioSchedulingExample extends ZIOAppDefault {
6.
7.    val repeatedTask: ZIO[Any, Nothing, Unit] =
8.      printLine("Hello, ZIO!").repeat(Schedule.fixed(1.second))
9.
10.   def run: ZIO[Any, Throwable, Unit] =
11.     repeatedTask.exitCode
12. }
```

In this example, **printLine("Hello, ZIO!")** is a simple ZIO effect that prints a message to the console. The **repeat(Schedule.fixed(1.second)** part specifies that the effect should be repeated every second. This demonstrates how ZIO can be used to schedule recurring tasks in a non-blocking manner.

PureConfig

PureConfig[5] is a Scala library designed to simplify the process of reading configuration files. It allows developers to map configuration files directly to Scala case classes, effectively leveraging Scala's type system to ensure configurations are both correct and easy to work with. PureConfig supports various formats but is most commonly used with **Human-Optimized Config Object Notation (HOCON)**, which is the default configuration format for Lightbend Config, widely used in Akka and Play framework applications.

The following are the key features of PureConfig:

- **Automatic derivation**: PureConfig can automatically derive the necessary code to read your configuration into Scala case classes without requiring explicit boilerplate code. This significantly simplifies the process of handling configurations.

---

5. https://pureconfig.github.io/

- **Type-safety**: By mapping configuration directly to Scala case classes, PureConfig ensures that configurations adhere to the expected types at compile time, reducing runtime errors and enforcing correctness in the application's configuration.

- **Support for collections and nested structures**: PureConfig naturally handles collections and nested case class structures, making it straightforward to work with complex configurations.

- **Customizable**: While PureConfig works out-of-the-box for many use cases, it also offers mechanisms to customize the behavior for specific types or to handle custom parsing logic.

- **Support for various types**: PureConfig comes with built-in support for many Scala and Java types, including primitive types, collections, dates, and more. This extensive support makes it easy to get started without needing to define custom parsing logic for common types.

- **Modular**: PureConfig is designed to be modular, allowing developers to pull in only the parts of the library they need. This modularity helps in keeping the application dependencies lean.

The following are the use cases for PureConfig:

- **Application configuration**: PureConfig is ideal for loading application configurations, such as database settings, API keys, service URLs and other operational parameters that need to be externalized from the application code.

- **Microservices**: In microservices architectures, managing configuration can become complex due to the number of services and environments. PureConfig simplifies this by providing a consistent and type-safe way to load configurations across services.

- **Complex configurations**: For applications that require complex configurations involving nested structures, lists, or custom types, PureConfig provides a robust solution that leverages Scala's type system for clarity and safety.

Assuming you have an application configuration defined in HOCON format. The following is an example for using PureConfig:

```
1. app {
2.   name = "MyApp"
3.   version = "1.0"
4.   database {
5.     url = "jdbc:postgresql://localhost/mydb"
6.     user = "dbuser"
7.     password = "dbpass"
8.   }
9. }
```

Corresponding Scala case classes can be defined for configuration, as follows:

```
1.  case class AppConfig(app: AppDetails)
2.  case class AppDetails(name: String, version: String, database:
    DatabaseConfig)
3.  case class DatabaseConfig(url: String, user: String, password: String)
4.  And then load the configuration with PureConfig:
5.
6.  import pureconfig._
7.  import pureconfig.generic.auto._
8.
9.  object ConfigLoader {
10.   def loadConfig: AppConfig = ConfigSource.default.loadOrThrow[AppConfig]
11. }
```

In this example, **loadOrThrow[AppConfig]** will either return an **AppConfig** populated with the values from the default configuration source (typically **application.conf**), or it will throw an exception if the configuration does not match the expected structure or types.

PureConfig's seamless integration with Scala's type system and its ability to reduce boilerplate code make it a valuable tool for managing application configurations in a type-safe and maintainable manner.

Functional Streams for Scala

Functional Streams for Scala (**FS2**[6]) is a compositional, streaming I/O library for Scala. It allows developers to build and evaluate descriptions of streaming computations, which can then be executed to process streams of data in a functional, type-safe, and lazy manner. FS2 stands out for its powerful and flexible approach to stream processing, enabling both synchronous and asynchronous data processing, resource management, and effects integration, primarily through its integration with the Cats Effect library.

The following are the key features of FS2:

- **Compositional**: FS2 streams are built using pure functional programming concepts, allowing complex stream processing pipelines to be constructed from simple, composable parts.

- **Type-safe**: Leveraging Scala's strong typing system, FS2 provides compile time guarantees about the correctness of stream operations and transformations.

- **Lazy and asynchronous processing**: Streams in FS2 are lazily evaluated, meaning computation on stream elements happens only when necessary. FS2 also supports asynchronous and concurrent stream processing, making it suitable for I/O-bound and CPU-bound tasks alike.

---

6. http://fs2.io/

- **Resource safety**: FS2 ensures safe acquisition and release of resources, which is crucial for working with external resources like files, network connections, or database connections.

- **Back-pressure**: FS2 streams naturally support back-pressure, allowing producers and consumers to operate at different speeds without overwhelming system resources.

- **Integration with Cats and Cats Effect**: FS2 is designed to work seamlessly with Cats and Cats Effect, offering a unified approach to functional programming in Scala, including handling effects and asynchronous computations.

The following is the basic usage:

To use FS2 in a project, you need to include it in your **build.sbt** file. Ensure that you check the latest version on the official FS2 GitHub repository or Maven Central.

```
1. libraryDependencies ++= Seq(
2.    "co.fs2" %% "fs2-core" % "3.x.x", // Use the latest version
3.    "co.fs2" %% "fs2-io" % "3.x.x" // For I/O operations
4. )
```

The following is an example demonstrating how to create a stream, apply some transformations, and run it:

```
1. import cats.effect.{IO, IOApp}
2. import fs2.Stream
3.
4. object Fs2Example extends IOApp.Simple {
5.
6.   val run: IO[Unit] = {
7.     // Define a stream of integers
8.     val stream: Stream[IO, Int] = Stream.emits(Seq(1, 2, 3, 4, 5))
   .covary[IO]
9.
10.    // Apply a transformation
11.    val processedStream = stream
12.      .map(_ * 2) // Double each number
13.      .evalMap(n => IO(println(n))) // Print each number
14.
15.    // Compile and run the stream
16.    processedStream.compile.drain
17.  }
18. }
```

This example multiplies each number in the stream by two and then prints it. The **evalMap** operation is used to apply an effectful function (printing to the console in this case) to each element of the stream.

FS2 sub projects

The following are the sub projects of FS2:

- **FS2 Core**: The core module provides the primary abstractions and functionality for stream creation, transformation, and evaluation. It includes the `Stream` and `Pull` data types, among others.

    - **Dependency**: `"co.fs2" %% "fs2-core" % "version"`

- **FS2 I/O:** This module adds support for input/output operations, including file I/O, network I/O (Sockets), and more. It is crucial for applications that deal with streaming data from files or over the network.

    - **Dependency**: `"co.fs2" %% "fs2-io" % "version"`

The following are the benefits:

- **Composability**: FS2 streams are highly composable, allowing developers to build complex data processing pipelines from simple, reusable components. This composability stems from the library's foundation in functional programming principles, making it easier to reason about code, reduce duplication, and improve maintainability.

- **Type-safety**: One of the core advantages of FS2 is its emphasis on type-safety. FS2 leverages Scala's strong type system to catch errors at compile time, reducing runtime exceptions related to stream processing. This feature ensures that transformations and operations on streams are correct according to their types, which is invaluable in building reliable applications.

- **Resource safety**: FS2 provides robust resource management, ensuring that resources like file handles, network sockets, or database connections are properly acquired and released, even in the face of errors. This automatic and safe management of resources helps prevent common issues such as resource leaks, making FS2 ideal for applications that interact with external systems or perform long-running operations.

- **Asynchronous and concurrent processing**: FS2 natively supports asynchronous and concurrent stream processing, enabling efficient handling of I/O-bound and CPU-bound tasks. It integrates seamlessly with Cats Effect, which provides a powerful model for effectful and concurrent programming. This capability allows FS2 to perform non-blocking operations, manage parallel processing, and handle synchronization without the complexity often associated with concurrency.

- **Back-pressure**: FS2 streams inherently support back-pressure, a mechanism that prevents overwhelming producers or consumers when they operate at different speeds. Back-pressure ensures that the system remains responsive and stable under varying loads, making FS2 suitable for real-time data processing applications.

- **Interoperability with the functional programming ecosystem**: FS2 is part of the Typelevel ecosystem, designed to work seamlessly with other functional programming libraries in Scala, such as Cats and Cats Effect. This interoperability allows developers to leverage a consistent and powerful set of abstractions for functional programming across their applications, from stream processing with FS2 to effect management with Cats Effect and more.

- **Lightweight core with modular extensions**: FS2's core library focuses on stream processing, keeping dependencies minimal. Additional functionality, such as I/O operations, is available through modular extensions, allowing developers to include only what they need. This modular design keeps applications lean and focused.

- **Extensive documentation and community support**: FS2 benefits from comprehensive documentation and a vibrant community. Newcomers can find numerous resources, examples, and guides to help them get started, while experienced users can contribute to and draw from a wealth of community knowledge and support.

FS2 is a powerful library for stream processing in Scala, offering a robust set of features for handling complex streaming data flows in a functional and type-safe way. It is particularly well-suited for applications that require sophisticated data processing pipelines, resource safety and integration with functional programming patterns in Scala. A lot of integration available with FS2 which makes it suitable to use.

Cats collection

Cats collection[7] is a Cats sub project which provides list of data structures which can be used with functional programming following all the principles of functional programming. Some provide more safety and improvements in existing Scala standard library.

The following are the data structures available:

- **Binary heap**: It is purely a functional binary heap. Its implementation depends upon mutable arrays in order to gain in performance.

  The following are the supported operations:

  o   **Add**: It adds a value to heap.

  o   **Remove**: Remove a value from heap.

  o   **(--) operator**: It removes a minimum value from heap.

  o   **Min**: It provides a minimum value.

  o   **toList**: It gives a list of sorted values in heap.

---

7. https://typelevel.org/cats-collections/index.html

- **Deque**: It is a double ended queue. It offers constant time to push value of either end. It offers amortized constant time to pop a value off from left or right of list.

- **Diet**: It is a discrete interval encoding tree.

- **Discrete**: It provides discrete operation that can be performed on any type.

- **Disjoint sets**: It is a purely functional implementation of union-find-collection. It is set of sets where the intersection of any two sets is empty.

- **Predicate**: Function that return Boolean value if parameter satisfies the condition.

- **Range**: It represents a range of values that can be generated using discrete operations.

- **AVL Set**: It is a tree-based set which stores elements in **Adelson-Velsky and Landis (AVL)** balanced binary tree.

Cats retry

The Cats retry[8] library provides an idiomatic way to perform retries in Scala applications using the Cats and Cats Effect libraries. It is especially useful for operations that can intermittently fail due to external factors, such as network requests, database operations, or any I/O operations. By leveraging the functional programming paradigms provided by Cats, Cats retry offers a flexible and composable approach to adding retry logic to your applications.

The following are the key features:

- **Policies**: Define retry policies such as constant delay, exponential backoff, or a custom policy.

- **Jitter**: Apply jitter strategies to add randomness to the retry delays, helping to smooth the load on the system being called.

- **Error filtering**: Choose which errors should trigger a retry and which should not, using partial functions or predicates.

- **Maximum retries**: Limit the number of retries with a maximum count or a maximum duration.

- **Algebraic data types**: Use **algebraic data types** (**ADTs**) for composing complex retry policies in a readable and maintainable way.

- **Integration with Cats Effect**: Seamlessly works with Cats Effect types like **IO**, making it easy to integrate with existing Cats Effect-based applications.

---

8. **https://cb372.github.io/cats-retry/docs/**

Setting dependency

To use Cats retry, add the following dependency to your **build.sbt** file. Make sure to check for the latest version on the project's GitHub page or Maven Central, as follows:

```
1. libraryDependencies += "com.github.cb372" %% "cats-
   retry" % "3.1.0" //, check for the latest version
```

The following is an example demonstrating how to use cats-retry to implement retry logic for a hypothetical network request:

```
1. import cats.effect.{IO, IOApp}
2. import retry._
3. import retry.CatsEffect._
4. import scala.concurrent.duration._
5.
6. object RetryExample extends IOApp.Simple {
7.
8.   // A mock function representing a network request that might fail
9.   def networkRequest: IO[String] = IO {
10.     if (scala.util.Random.nextBoolean()) throw new Exception
   ("Network error")
11.     else "Success"
12.   }
13.
14.   // Retry policy: exponential backoff starting at 100ms, doubling
   each retry
15.   val policy: RetryPolicy[IO] = RetryPolicies.exponentialBackoff[IO]
   (100.milliseconds)
16.
17.   // Only retry on certain exceptions
18.   val isWorthRetrying: Throwable => Boolean = {
19.     case _: Exception => true
20.     case _            => false
21.   }
22.
23.   // The retrying logic
24.   val retriedNetworkRequest: IO[String] = retryingOnSomeErrors(
25.     policy = policy,
26.     isWorthRetrying = isWorthRetrying,
27.     onError = (e: Throwable, details: RetryDetails) =>
   IO(println(s"Retrying due to ${e.getMessage}. Details: $details"))
28.   )(networkRequest)
```

```
29.
30.   def run: IO[Unit] = retriedNetworkRequest.flatMap(result =>
      IO(println(s"Result: $result")))
31. }
```

The following are the details of above code snippet:

- **networkRequest**: This represents a potentially failing operation. For the sake of the example, it randomly throws an exception to simulate a failure.

- **policy**: Defines the retry strategy. Here, we are using an exponential backoff strategy starting with a 100 milliseconds delay, doubling the delay with each retry.

- **isWorthRetrying**: A function to determine if a thrown exception is worth retrying. In this example, we retry for any exception.

- **retriedNetworkRequest**: Applies the retry logic to **networkRequest** using the **retryingOnSomeErrors** method. It logs retry attempts and their reasons.

- **run**: Executes the retried operation and prints the final result.

Cats retry is a powerful tool for adding retry logic with minimal boilerplate, leveraging the type-safe and functional programming capabilities of Scala with Cats and Cats Effect.

Conclusion

In this chapter, we learned different functional tools available focusing on common problems and providing efficient, composable, functional and battle tested implementation which can be used directly without reinventing the wheel and put our effort and energy to our specific problems. The tools discussed here are common tools which gets used in day-to-day coding. There are other tools like web or database implements required when dealing with web APIs or reading or writing data to database. Standard solutions are also available in those space but we will look into those at length in our next chapters.

In next chapter, we will learn web implementation in functional way, where we focus on web development using pure functions (no side effects), composable and working with immutable data which provides improved modularity, enhanced testability, composability, easier concurrency and scalability, better maintainability and easier state management.

Join our Discord space

Join our Discord workspace for latest updates, offers, tech happenings around the world, new releases, and sessions with the authors:

https://discord.bpbonline.com

CHAPTER 9

Web Implementation in Functional Way

Introduction

We have learned a lot about functional programming now. There is always some new learning, each learning helps us to be stronger and steadier in functional programming. In this chapter, we will learn all functional programming benefits with web development. We will see how immutability, composability, and other functional benefits in web implementation. We will also learn all the tools available in Scala for functional web development.

Structure

In this chapter, we will cover the following topics:

- Functional web
- Advantages of functional web
- http4s
- Tapir
- ZIO HTTP
- sttp
- Sample web application

Objectives

By the end of this chapter, we will learn how we can develop all web using functional libraries. We see how composability works and how it provides ways to write modular code.

Functional web

The term functional web in the context of functional programming does not refer to a specific technology or framework, but rather to an approach or philosophy for building web applications and services using the principles of functional programming. Functional programming is a paradigm that treats computation as the evaluation of mathematical functions and avoids changing state and mutable data. It emphasizes functions as a first-class citizen that produce consistent outputs for given inputs, immutability, and the use of higher order functions.

When we talk about the functional web or applying functional programming principles to web development, we look at how these concepts can be applied to the design and implementation of web applications.

This can involve several aspects, as follows:

- **Immutability**: Data is not modified once it is created. Instead, any changes produce new data structures. This approach can simplify state management and improve the predictability of the application.

  Immutability refers to the idea that once a data structure is created, it cannot be changed. Any modification to an object results in creating a new object with the desired changes, leaving the original object unaltered. This approach has several implications and benefits for web development.

- **Predictability and simplicity**: It revolves around creating web systems that are both intuitive and reliable, ensuring a seamless user experience while maintaining functional efficiency.

  The following are the features which increases the reasoning and its predictability:

  o **Easier state management**: Managing the application state becomes more predictable when state changes are explicit and do not affect the original state. This can significantly simplify debugging and reasoning about the application, as each state is a distinct value that does not change over time.

  o **Reduced side effects**: Since data cannot be modified once created, the risk of unintended side effects from shared mutable state is minimized. Functions and components operate independently, improving code reliability and predictability.

- **Performance optimization**: It involves adopting practices that ensure code efficiency, scalability, and maintainability without compromising speed.

The following are the functional programming features which help to achieve performance:

- o **Efficient data structures**: Libraries that support immutability, such as Immutable.js for JavaScript, often use sophisticated data structures like tries for efficient storage and manipulation. These structures can make modifying large datasets much cheaper in terms of performance because they share a substantial portion of their structure between versions.

- o **Change detection**: In the context of web frameworks, particularly those that rely on a virtual **Document Object Model (DOM)** (like React), immutability can lead to more efficient change detection and rendering. When data structures are immutable, a simple reference check (===) can determine if a component needs to be re-rendered, instead of deep object comparison.

- **Functional techniques and patterns**: It uses functional programming techniques in web implementation to get functional correctness and its reasoning.

The following are the important techniques relevant for web implementation:

- o **Pure functions**: Embracing immutability encourages the use of pure functions, which depend solely on their input and produce no side effects. This makes functions more predictable and testable.

- o **Persistent data structures**: Functional programming languages and libraries offer persistent data structures that are optimized for immutability. These structures make it practical to work with immutable data in performance-critical applications.

- **Easier concurrency**: Immutability eliminates issues related to concurrent mutations of shared state, which is a common source of bugs in traditional mutable systems. This makes it inherently easier to write applications that perform well under concurrent access or that run in distributed environments.

The following are the challenges:

While immutability brings several benefits to the functional web, it also presents challenges. Developers must become familiar with patterns and practices for effectively managing and updating immutable state, which can have a learning curve. Performance considerations, particularly in JavaScript environments, may require careful management of object creation and garbage collection to prevent memory issues.

For example, copying data instead of modifying can be expensive in terms of memory and CPU cycles in case of large objects, as follows:

```
1. Val list = List(1,2,3) // assume it as a large object that need
   to be modified
2. val updatedList = list :+ 4 // this create again a new object
   by copying the original one and 4 included which takes memory
   allocation and CPU cycles to process
```

So, it is recommended to focus on usage of persistent data structure and structure sharing so that only a change part operating system copied and other structure is shared.

Here, we can used **Vector** which allows fast upend and updates *O(1)* amortize:

```
1. Val vec = Vector(1,2,3)
2. Val updatedList = vec :+ 4
```

Functional web implementation

In practice, immutability in the functional web is facilitated through languages that enforce immutability (like Elm), libraries that provide immutable data structures (like Immutable.js), or by convention and discipline in languages like JavaScript, where immutability is not enforced by the language but can be achieved through patterns and practices (using const, avoiding mutations, etc.).

The following are the ways to achieve immutability by implementing the patterns:

- **Pure functions**: Functions that have no side effects and return the same output for the same inputs, making them easier to reason about and test.

- **Function composition**: Building complex operations out of simpler functions, improving modularity and reusability.

The following is how functional composition works:

Functional composition relies on the mathematical principle that if you have two functions, f and g, you can combine them into a new function h such that $h(x) = f(g(x))$. In this setup, the output of function g becomes the input for function f. This can be extended to any number of functions, enabling developers to build up complex behavior from simple, focused functions.

The following are the benefits of web development:

- **Modularity**: By decomposing features into smaller functions that do one thing and do it well, code becomes more modular and easier to understand. Each function can be developed, tested, and debugged independently before being composed into larger application features.

- **Reusability**: Small, generic functions can be reused across different parts of an application or even across projects. This reduces code duplication and the potential for bugs, while also speeding up development.

- **Testability**: Smaller functions that perform a single responsibility are easier to test. When functions are pure (having no side effects and depending only on their inputs), tests can be more straightforward and less prone to errors introduced by shared state or side effects.

- **Readability and maintainability**: Composing software from well-named functions can make code more readable and easier to maintain. Developers can more easily understand the flow of data and the transformations applied, leading to quicker debugging and enhancements.

The following are the applications in the functional web:

- **Frontend development**: In frameworks like React, functional composition is used to build components. Hooks, for instance, are composable functions that allow you to add functionality to functional components. **Higher order components (HOCs)** and render props are patterns that also rely on functional composition to share logic between components.

- **State management**: Libraries like Redux embody functional programming principles, where reducers (pure functions) are composed to handle actions and update the application state in a predictable manner.

- **Functional libraries aid**: JavaScript libraries such as Ramda or lodash/fp provide help that facilitate functional composition, offering functions like compose and pipe. It is possible to achieve without these libraries but these provides best practices implemented so we should focus on business logic instead of specific technical details. These allow developers to easily chain and combine functions to create new functionality.

- **Backend development:** In server-side development with languages like Elixir (using Phoenix) or Haskell (using Yesod), functional composition is a core part of organizing logic and building request handling pipelines. Middleware in Node.js, though not always purely functional, can also be seen as a form of composition, where each middleware function has the opportunity to operate on the request and response objects before passing control to the next function in the chain.

- **Higher order functions**: Functions that can take other functions as arguments or return them as results. This is useful for creating flexible and reusable code patterns.

- **Declarative programming**: Describing what the program should accomplish rather than detailing the control flow explicitly. This often leads to more concise and readable code.

In the context of web development, these principles can be applied in both the frontend and backend, as follows:

- **Frontend**: JavaScript, with its support for first-class functions and closures, allows for a functional style of programming. Libraries and frameworks like React (especially with hooks) encourage functional programming concepts, enabling developers to manage state and side effects in a more functional manner.

- **Backend**: Functional programming languages like Haskell, Elixir (with the Phoenix framework), and F# (with the Giraffe framework for .NET) can be used to build backend services. These languages and frameworks encourage or enforce functional programming principles, leading to applications that are robust, scalable, and easy to maintain.

Using the functional programming approach in web development can lead to more predictable, maintainable, and scalable applications. However, it requires a shift in mindset from the more traditional imperative and **object-oriented programming** (**OOP**) paradigms that dominate web development.

Advantages of functional web

The following are the benefits of using a functional approach to web development over more traditional imperative or object-oriented approaches:

- **Immutability and state management**: By avoiding mutable state, functional web applications can become more predictable and easier to debug. Immutability makes it simpler to understand how data flows through the application, reducing side effects and making state management more straightforward.

- **Easier to reason about**: Functional code, by relying on pure functions (functions that always produce the same output for the same input and have no side effects), can be easier to understand and reason about. This can lead to more reliable code and fewer bugs.

- **Concurrency and scalability**: Functional programming's emphasis on immutability makes it inherently more suitable for concurrent execution. Since data is not modified but rather new data is created, it is easier to execute tasks in parallel, leading to potentially better performance and scalability in web applications, especially under high load.

- **Code reusability and modularity**: Functions in functional programming are designed to be small, composable, and reusable, which can lead to more modular code. Smaller, purpose-specific functions are easier to test and can be combined in various ways to achieve complex functionality without repeating code.

- **Better testing and debugging**: The predictability of pure functions makes unit testing more straightforward. Since pure functions have no side effects and only depend on their inputs to produce outputs, tests can be run in isolation without the need for mocking a context or state.

- **Declarative code style**: Functional programming often encourages a more declarative style of coding, where you express what you want to achieve rather than how to achieve it. This can lead to more readable and concise code.

- **Functional reactive programming for UIs**: Applying functional programming to web UI development can simplify the handling of asynchronous events and data streams. Libraries and frameworks that support **functional reactive programming** (**FRP**) concepts, such as Elm or Redux (used with React), offer robust solutions for building dynamic user interfaces in a functional style.

While the functional web and its approach offer several benefits, it is important to recognize that the best choice of programming paradigm depends on the specific project requirements, team expertise, and other factors. Traditional web development approaches continue to be valid and powerful, especially when they incorporate elements of functional programming where it makes sense.

http4s

http4s[1] is a Scala library for building HTTP services. It is designed to provide a functional way to construct HTTP servers and clients, embracing the principles of functional programming that are central to Scala, particularly those from the Typelevel ecosystem. http4s uses a purely functional programming model to handle HTTP requests and responses, offering a composable and expressive way to define web services.

The following are the key features and concepts of http4s:

- **Functional and type-safe**: http4s builds upon purely functional libraries like Cats and FS2 to represent computations and streaming data as first-class citizens, and all effects in it are managed using a functional effect type, such as **IO** from Cats Effect, ensuring purity.

- **Immutability and side-effect management**: http4s encourages using immutable data structures and functional patterns to manage side effects, aligning with functional programming principles.

- **Type-safety**: Leveraging Scala's strong type system, http4s helps catch errors at compile time, reducing runtime exceptions and improving the reliability of web applications.

- **Streaming**: http4s is built on FS2, a streaming library that provides for processing and emitting large payloads in constant space and implementing WebSocket.

- **Cross-platform**: http4s cross-builds for Scala.js and Scala Native. Share code and deploy to browsers, Node.js, native executable binaries, and the JVM.

- **Based on Cats and Cats Effect**: http4s is built on top of Cats and Cats Effect, two prominent libraries in the Scala ecosystem that provide abstractions for functional programming and dealing with effects (e.g., **IO** operations), respectively. This integration allows http4s to offer a powerful and flexible foundation for asynchronous and non-blocking **IO** operations, which is crucial for scalable web applications.

- **Declarative DSLs**: http4s offers **domain-specific languages** (**DSLs**) for both client and server-side HTTP programming. These DSLs provide a declarative way to define routes, handle requests, and produce responses, making the code more expressive and concise.

---

1. **https://http4s.org/**

- **Integrations**: http4s integrates well with various JSON libraries (e.g., Circe for JSON encoding and decoding) and can be used with a variety of Scala HTTP clients and server backends (such as Blaze for high-performance network I/O).

To provide a clearer understanding of using http4s for creating a web service in Scala, the following is a basic example:

This example will demonstrate setting up an http4s server and defining a simple route that responds to GET requests. http4s uses a purely functional model for HTTP services, leaning heavily on Cats Effect and FS2 for managing effects and streams, respectively.

The following are the steps for implementation for the example:

1. **Add dependencies**:

   First, ensure your Scala project's **build.sbt** file includes the necessary dependencies for http4s, Cats Effect, and FS2, as follows:

   Note: **That versions may change, so please check for the latest versions on their respective websites.**

```
1.  libraryDependencies ++= Seq(
2.    "org.http4s" %% "http4s-blaze-server" % "0.23.6",
3.    "org.http4s" %% "http4s-circe"        % "0.23.6",
4.    "org.http4s" %% "http4s-dsl"          % "0.23.6",
5.    "io.circe" %% "circe-generic" % "0.14.1",
6.    "io.circe" %% "circe-literal" % "0.14.1",
7.    "org.typelevel" %% "cats-effect" % "3.3.0"
8.  )
```

2. **Define a simple service**:

   Next, let us define a simple HTTP service that responds to GET requests on the root path (**/**) with a plain text greeting.

   The following example uses http4s's DSL for constructing routes and responses:

```
1.  import cats.effect._
2.  import org.http4s._
3.  import org.http4s.dsl.io._
4.  import org.http4s.server.blaze._
5.  import org.http4s.implicits._
6.
7.  object Http4sExample extends IOApp {
8.
9.    val helloWorldService = HttpRoutes.of[IO] {
10.     case GET -> Root =>
```

```
11.      Ok("Hello, world!")
12.    }.orNotFound
13.
14.  override def run(args: List[String]): IO[ExitCode] = {
15.    BlazeServerBuilder[IO]
16.      .bindHttp(8080, "localhost")
17.      .withHttpApp(helloWorldService)
18.      .serve
19.      .compile
20.      .drain
21.      .as(ExitCode.Success)
22.  }
23. }
```

The following are the details:

- **Imports**: The necessary imports from **http4s**, **cats-effect**, and the specific server implementation (Blaze in this case) are included at the top.

- **Service definition**: The **helloWorldService** uses the http4s DSL to define a route that matches **GET** requests at the root path (**/**). When matched, it responds with a 200 OK status and the text **"Hello, world!"**.

- **Server setup**: The **run** method uses **BlazeServerBuilder** to create and configure a Blaze server, specifying the port and host. The server is set to use the **helloWorldService** as its HTTP app.

- **Running the server**: The **serve** method starts the server, and the application is configured to keep running until terminated. The **compile.drain** pattern is used to run the FS2 stream representing the server indefinitely.

To run this example, you will need to have **sbt** and Scala setup on your machine. After adding the code to your Scala project, as follows:

- Open a Terminal in your project's root directory.

- Run the command **sbt run** to compile and start the server.

- Once the server is running, you can test the endpoint by navigating to **http:// localhost:8080/** in your web browser or using a tool like **curl**:

  curl http://localhost:8080/

You should receive a response saying **"Hello, world!"**.

This example provides a basic introduction to setting up a simple HTTP service using http4s. http4s offers a lot more functionality, including support for various HTTP methods, path parameters, query parameters, and producing/consuming JSON, among other features.

The following are the use cases:

http4s is suitable for creating all types of HTTP services in Scala, from simple RESTful APIs to complex web applications. It is particularly appreciated by developers who prefer a functional programming style and want to maintain type-safety and composability in their HTTP layer.

The following is an example of an **http4s** service that defines a simple **GET** route:

```
1. import cats.effect._
2. import org.http4s._
3. import org.http4s.dsl.io._
4. import org.http4s.HttpRoutes
5. import org.http4s.blaze.server.BlazeServerBuilder
6. import org.http4s.implicits._
7.
8. val helloWorldService = HttpRoutes.of[IO] {
9.   case GET -> Root / "hello" / name =>
10.    Ok(s"Hello, $name")
11. }.orNotFound
12.
13. val server = BlazeServerBuilder[IO]
14.   .bindHttp(8080, "localhost")
15.   .withHttpApp(helloWorldService)
16.   .resource
17.
18. def run(args: List[String]): IO[ExitCode] =
19.   server.use(_ => IO.never).as(ExitCode.Success)
```

This code snippet showcases a simple HTTP server that responds to requests to **/hello/ {name}** with a greeting message. It demonstrates http4s's use of Cats Effect for effectful programming, its DSL for defining HTTP routes, and its integration with the Blaze server for handling HTTP requests.

http4s is a potent tool for Scala developers looking to apply functional programming principles to web development, enabling the construction of concise, composable, and type-safe HTTP services.

Tapir

Typed API descRiptions (Tapir [2]), is an open-source library used in Scala to describe HTTP API endpoints in a type-safe manner. It stands out by allowing developers to describe their APIs at a higher abstraction level while maintaining type-safety, enabling them to automatically derive server endpoints, client calls, and OpenAPI (formerly **Swagger**) documentation from these descriptions. This approach contrasts with more traditional web development practices where these aspects are often handled separately, leading to potential inconsistencies and more boilerplate code.

---

2. **https://tapir.softwaremill.com/en/latest/**

The following are the key features of Tapir:

- **Type-safety**: Tapir heavily relies on Scala's strong typing system to ensure that the definitions of API endpoints are consistent with their implementations. This helps catch errors at compile-time rather than at runtime.

- **Declarative API definitions**: With Tapir, developers define their API endpoints in a declarative manner, specifying the input and output types, error types, and other relevant information. This abstract description can then be used to generate server-side logic, client-side calls, and documentation, ensuring consistency across these different components.

- **Integration with various libraries**: Tapir integrates well with multiple server backends (like Akka HTTP, http4s, and others) and client libraries in the Scala ecosystem. This flexibility allows developers to choose their preferred tools and libraries while still benefiting from Tapir's type-safe API descriptions.

- **Automatic documentation**: From the API endpoint descriptions, Tapir can automatically generate OpenAPI (Swagger) documentation, making it easier to document the API and share the documentation with front-end developers or API consumers.

- **Reduced boilerplate**: By using type-safe descriptions that can be shared between server and client code, as well as to generate documentation, Tapir reduces the amount of repetitive and boilerplate code developers need to write and maintain.

The following is an example:

When using Tapir, you first describe your endpoints in Scala, specifying the HTTP method, path, request and response formats, and any expected status codes. This description is independent of any specific HTTP server framework. Then, you can use the following description to:

- Generate server endpoints compatible with your chosen Scala HTTP server framework (e.g., Akka HTTP, http4s).

- Derive client calls to these endpoints, ensuring that the client and server implementations are in sync.

- Produce OpenAPI documentation automatically from these descriptions, ensuring that your documentation accurately reflects your API's current implementation.

To provide a practical understanding of how Tapir is used, let us walk through a simple example where we define an API endpoint for fetching a user by ID, assuming we were working within a Scala project.

The following example shows how to define the endpoint and how to use it to generate server logic and OpenAPI documentation:

Note: That to run this example, you will need to have Tapir and an appropriate server backend library (like http4s or Akka HTTP) added to your project dependencies.

1. **Add dependencies**:

   First, make sure your **build.sbt** file includes dependencies for Tapir and a server backend, such as **http4s**. The specific versions may change, so check for the latest versions, as follows:

   ```
   1.  libraryDependencies ++= Seq(
   2.    "com.softwaremill.sttp.tapir" %% "tapir-core" % "0.19.0",
   3.    "com.softwaremill.sttp.tapir" %% "tapir-http4s-
         server" % "0.19.0",
   4.    "com.softwaremill.sttp.tapir" %% "tapir-openapi-
         docs" % "0.19.0",
   5.    "com.softwaremill.sttp.tapir" %% "tapir-openapi-circe-
         yaml" % "0.19.0",
   6.    "org.http4s" %% "http4s-blaze-server" % "0.23.0",
   7.    "org.http4s" %% "http4s-circe" % "0.23.0",
   8.    "io.circe" %% "circe-generic" % "0.14.0"
   9.  )
   ```

2. **Define the API endpoint**:

   In this step, we describe the API endpoint. We define an endpoint for fetching a user by ID, where the ID is provided as a path parameter, and the endpoint returns a JSON response, as follows:

   ```
   1.  import sttp.tapir._
   2.  import sttp.tapir.json.circe._
   3.  import io.circe.generic.auto._
   4.
   5.  case class User(id: Int, name: String)
   6.
   7.  // Define the endpoint
   8.  val getUserEndpoint: Endpoint[Int, String, User, Any] =
         endpoint
   9.    .get
   10.   .in("user" / path[Int]("userId"))
   11.   .errorOut(stringBody)
   12.   .out(jsonBody[User])
   ```

3. **Implement the server logic**:

   Next, we will bind the endpoint description to server logic using **http4s**. The implementation will simply return a mocked user for demonstration purposes, as follows:

```
1. import sttp.tapir.server.http4s.Http4sServerInterpreter
2. import cats.effect.IO
3. import org.http4s.HttpRoutes
4.
5. val getUserLogic: Int => IO[Either[String, User]] = userId =>
6.    IO.pure(Right(User(userId, "John Doe"))) // Mocked user lookup
7.
8. val getUserRoutes: HttpRoutes[IO] = Http4sServerInterpreter
   [IO]().toRoutes(getUserEndpoint)(getUserLogic)
```

4. **Run the server and generate documentation**:

Finally, you can use **http4s** to run the server and serve the API. Additionally, you can generate OpenAPI (Swagger) documentation based on the endpoint definition, as follows:

```
1.  import org.http4s.blaze.server.BlazeServerBuilder
2.  import org.http4s.server.Router
3.  import sttp.tapir.docs.openapi._
4.  import sttp.tapir.openapi.circe.yaml._
5.  import scala.concurrent.ExecutionContext.global
6.
7.  // Generate OpenAPI documentation
8.  val openApiDocs = OpenAPIDocsInterpreter().toOpenAPI
    (getUserEndpoint, "User API", "1.0")
9.  val openApiYaml = openApiDocs.toYaml
10.
11. // Start the server
12. val allRoutes = Router("/" -> getUserRoutes).orNotFound
13.
14. BlazeServerBuilder[IO](global)
15.    .bindHttp(8080, "localhost")
16.    .withHttpApp(allRoutes)
17.    .resource
18.    .useForever
```

This example demonstrates defining a simple API endpoint with Tapir, implementing server logic using http4s, and generating OpenAPI documentation. This is a basic illustration; Tapir's capabilities allow for much more complex API designs and integrations.

Tapir offers a powerful abstraction for Scala developers building HTTP APIs, emphasizing type-safety, reduced boilerplate, and the automatic generation of consistent server endpoints, client calls, and documentation. By separating the API description from its implementation, Tapir encourages a more modular, maintainable, and collaborative approach to API development.

ZIO HTTP

ZIO HTTP[3] is a Scala library designed to build efficient, type-safe web applications and HTTP services. It leverages the ZIO library, which provides a powerful framework for asynchronous and concurrent programming in Scala, focusing on functional programming principles. ZIO HTTP aims to make web development more intuitive and productive by offering a simple yet expressive API, taking full advantage of ZIO's features for managing effects, errors, and context propagation in a purely functional way.

The following are the key features of ZIO HTTP:

- **High-performance**: ZIO HTTP is built for performance. It is designed to handle a high number of concurrent requests efficiently, making it suitable for building scalable applications.

- **Type-safety**: Leveraging Scala's strong type system, it ensures that many common errors are caught at compile time, promoting safer and more reliable web service development.

- **Functional programming**: By integrating tightly with ZIO, it encourages a functional programming model, making it easier to reason about code, manage side effects, and handle errors in a consistent manner.

- **Simple and expressive API**: ZIO HTTP provides a clean and expressive API that makes it straightforward to define routes, handle requests, and send responses, all while keeping boilerplate to a minimum.

- **Asynchronous and non-blocking**: Built on top of ZIO, it naturally supports writing asynchronous and non-blocking code, helping developers to write efficient I/O operations without the complexities typically associated with concurrency and parallelism.

- **Composable**: ZIO HTTP services are highly composable, allowing developers to easily modularize and reuse code across different parts of an application.

Let us discuss a detailed example of using ZIO HTTP to create a simple web application. This example will demonstrate handling different types of requests and paths, showcasing the flexibility and power of ZIO HTTP for building HTTP servers. Before running this example, ensure you have ZIO and ZIO HTTP dependencies added to your Scala project.

The following are the steps of the example:

1. **Setup dependencies**:

    First, make sure your **build.sbt** file includes ZIO and ZIO HTTP. Check for the latest versions on their respective websites or repositories.

---

3. **https://zio.dev/zio-http/**

The following is an example of how you might setup your dependencies:

```
1. libraryDependencies ++= Seq(
2.   "dev.zio" %% "zio" % "1.0.12",
3.   "io.d11" %% "zhttp" % "2.0.0-
   RC5" // Ensure to use the latest version
4. )
```

2. **Create the HTTP server**:

Next, let us write the Scala code to define our HTTP server. This server will respond to different paths and methods, illustrating the handling of various routes, as follows:

```
1. import zhttp.http._
2. import zhttp.service.Server
3. import zio._
4.
5. object MyApp extends ZIOAppDefault {
6.   val app: HttpApp[Any, Nothing] = Http.collect[Request] {
7.     case Method.GET -> !! / "text" =>
8.       Response.text("This is a plain text response")
9.
10.    case Method.GET -> !! / "json" =>
11.      Response.
   json("""{"message": "This is a JSON response"}""")
12.
13.    case Method.GET -> !! / "html" =>
14.      Response.html("<html><body><h1>Hello, ZIO HTTP!</h1></
   body></html>")
15.  }
16.
17.  override def run: ZIO[ZEnv with ZIOAppArgs, Any, Any] =
   Server.start(8080, app)
18. }
```

The following are the details of the code:

- **Imports**: We import necessary modules from ZIO and ZIO HTTP.

- **App definition**: **MyApp** extends **ZIOAppDefault**, providing a straightforward way to define an executable ZIO application. Inside, we define an app, which is a **HttpApp** that uses **Http.collect** to pattern match on incoming HTTP requests.

- **Routes**: We define several routes (**/text**, **/json**, **/html**) that demonstrate returning different types of responses: plain text, JSON, and HTML. Each case pattern matches on the HTTP method (**GET**) and the request path.

- **Server**: The run method uses **Server.start** to launch an HTTP server on port **8080**, serving the defined app.

The following are the steps for running the server:

1. Open a Terminal in your project's root directory.

2. Run the command **sbt run** to compile and start the server.

3. Once the server is up, you can access the endpoints (**/text**, **/json**, **/html**) using a web browser or tools like **curl**, as follows:

```
curl http://localhost:8080/text
curl http://localhost:8080/json
curl http://localhost:8080/html
```

Each command should return the respective response indicated by the route definition in the Scala code.

This example illustrates the basic setup and capabilities of ZIO HTTP for building web applications, demonstrating how to define a simple HTTP server that can respond to different types of requests with various response types. ZIO HTTP's model is highly composable and flexible, allowing for the construction of more complex web applications and services.

sttp

Scala HTTP (sttp)[4] client is a comprehensive, open-source library designed for creating and sending HTTP requests in Scala applications. It is a part of the broader Scala ecosystem that emphasizes functional programming principles, offering a flexible and expressive way to work with HTTP. sttp stands out for its backend-agnostic design, allowing developers to choose from a variety of backends to execute requests, including synchronous and asynchronous models, as well as support for various functional programming libraries.

The following are the key features of sttp:

- **Backend-agnostic**: sttp provides a unified API to send HTTP requests, which can be executed using multiple backends. This includes support for synchronous backends, Future-based, Scala.js, as well as functional effect types like Cats Effect IO, Monix Task, and ZIO.

- **Rich request building**: It offers a rich DSL for constructing HTTP requests, making it possible to easily set request parameters, headers, body content, and handling of responses.

- **Type-safe and functional**: sttp supports type-safe request and response handling, embracing Scala's functional programming capabilities. This includes support for decoding responses into custom types, error handling, and working with effects in a type-safe manner.

---

4. https://sttp.softwaremill.com/en/latest/

- **Support for various body types**: sttp allows sending requests with various body types, including form data, multipart, text, binary, and more. It also supports streaming request and response bodies, compatible with the backend in use.

- **Composable**: Thanks to its functional nature, requests can be composed and reused across different parts of an application, enhancing modularity and reusability.

- **Interoperability**: sttp integrates well with popular JSON libraries for Scala, such as Circe, Json4s, and others, allowing for seamless serialization and deserialization of JSON bodies.

The following is an example demonstrating how to use **sttp** to make a GET request and handle the response:

```
1.  import sttp.client3._
2.
3.  object SttpExample extends App {
4.    // Define a simple GET request to httpbin.org
5.    val request = basicRequest
6.      .get(uri"https://httpbin.org/get")
7.
8.    // Choose a backend (here, the synchronous backend)
9.    val backend = HttpURLConnectionBackend()
10.
11.   // Send the request
12.   val response = request.send(backend)
13.
14.   // Print the response body
15.   println(response.body)
16. }
```

This example uses the synchronous backend, but **sttp** supports various asynchronous and functional effect-based backends, allowing it to fit naturally into Scala applications using different concurrency models.

Getting started

To use **sttp** in your Scala project, you will need to add the **sttp** library dependency to your **build.sbt** or equivalent build configuration. Make sure to check for the latest version of **sttp** to use, as follows:

```
1.  libraryDependencies += "com.softwaremill.sttp.
    client3" %% "core" % "3.x.x"
```

Replace **3.x.x** with the latest version available.

sttp is a powerful tool for Scala developers looking to perform HTTP operations with an emphasis on functional programming practices, offering flexibility, type-safety, and an expressive API.

Sample web application

Let us take an example of to-do list and try to implement the same using details we got in above sections using ZIO HTTP.

Creating a simple to-do list web application with ZIO HTTP involves setting up a ZIO HTTP server that can handle HTTP requests to add, view, and delete tasks.

The following is an example that demonstrates how to build a minimalistic To-Do list application. The following steps will keep the tasks in-memory, so restarting the server will reset the data:

1. **Setting up the project**:

    First, ensure you have Scala and **sbt** installed. Then, create a new **sbt** project and add ZIO and ZIO HTTP dependencies to your **build.sbt** file:

    ```
    1.  name := "zio-http-todo-list"
    2.
    3.  version := "0.1"
    4.
    5.  scalaVersion := "2.13.6"
    6.
    7.  libraryDependencies ++= Seq(
    8.    "dev.zio" %% "zio" % "1.0.9",
    9.    "io.d11" %% "zhttp" % "1.0.0-
       RC17" // Use the latest version
    10. )
    ```

2. **Implementing the to-do list logic**:

    Create a Scala file for your application logic, for example, **TodoApp.scala**. Define a simple model for your tasks and a service to manage them, as follows:

    ```
    1.  import zio._
    2.  import scala.collection.mutable
    3.
    4.  case class TodoItem (id: Long, title: String, completed: Boolean)
    5.
    6.  object TodoService {
    7.    private val todoItems = mutable.ListBuffer.empty[TodoItem]
    8.
    9.    def addTodo(title: String): UIO[TodoItem] = ZIO.succeed {
    10.     val newTodo = TodoItem (todoItems.length + 1L, title, false)
    11.     todoItems += newTodo
    12.     newTodo
    13.   }
    14.
    ```

```
15.  def getTodos: UIO[List[TodoItem]] =
   ZIO.succeed(todoItems.toList)
16.
17.  def deleteTodo(id: Long): UIO[Boolean] = ZIO.succeed {
18.    todoItems.indexWhere(_.id == id) match {
19.      case -1 => false
20.      case idx =>
21.        todoItems.remove(idx)
22.        true
23.    }
24.  }
25. }
```

3. **Setting up HTTP Server with ZIO HTTP**:

Now, integrate **TodoService** with ZIO HTTP to handle HTTP requests. Update your **TodoApp.scala** or create a new file for the web server part, as follows:

```
1.  import zhttp.http._
2.  import zhttp.service.Server
3.  import zio._
4.  import zio.json._
5.
6.  object TodoApp extends zio.ZIOAppDefault {
7.
8.    implicit val todoEncoder: JsonEncoder[TodoItem] =
   DeriveJsonEncoder.gen[TodoItem]
9.    implicit val todoDecoder: JsonDecoder[TodoItem] =
   DeriveJsonDecoder.gen[TodoItem]
10.
11.    private val app = Http.collectZIO[Request] {
12.      case req @ Method.POST -> !! / "todos" =>
13.        for {
14.          todo <- req.body.asString.map(_.fromJson[TodoItem])
   .flatMap {
15.            case Left(_)       => ZIO.fail(new Exception
   ("Invalid JSON"))
16.            case Right(todo) => TodoService.addTodo (todo.title)
17.          }
18.          response <- ZIO.succeed(Response.json(todo.toJson))
19.        } yield response
20.
21.      case Method.GET -> !! / "todos" =>
22.        for {
23.          todos <- TodoService.getTodos
24.          response <- ZIO.succeed(Response.json(todos.toJson))
```

```
25.        } yield response
26.
27.      case Method.DELETE -> !! / "todos" / LongVar(id) =>
28.        for {
29.          success <- TodoService.deleteTodo (id)
30.          response <- ZIO.succeed(
31.            if (success) Response.status(Status.NO_CONTENT)
32.            else Response.status(Status.NOT_FOUND))
33.        } yield response
34.  }
35.
36.  override def run = Server.start(8080, app)
37. }
```

4. **Running your application**:

   Run your application using **sbt,** as follows:

   sbt run

Your simple to-do list application is now set up and should be running on **localhost:8080**. You can interact with it using HTTP requests to add, view, and delete tasks.

The following are the ways for implementing the same using http4s:

- **Define the to-do model**: Start by defining a simple case class to represent a to-do item, as follows:

  ```
  case class TodoItem(id: String, title: String, completed: Boolean)
  ```

- **Create a repository**: Implement a basic repository for managing to-do items. For simplicity, this example uses an in-memory store, as follows:

  ```
  1. object TodoRepository {
  2.   private var todos: List[TodoItem] = List()
  3.
  4.   def add(todo: TodoItem): TodoItem = {
  5.     todos = todos :+ todo
  6.     todo
  7.   }
  8.
  9.   def getAll: List[TodoItem] = todos
  10.
  11.   def delete(id: String): Option[TodoItem] = {
  12.     val (toBeDeleted, remain) = todos.partition(_.id == id)
  13.     todos = remain
  14.     toBeDeleted.headOption
  15.   }
  16. }
  ```

- **Setting Up the HTTP routes**: Define the HTTP routes needed for your to-do list service. This includes routes to create, list, and delete to-do items. The implementation of these routes will vary depending on the HTTP library you choose.

The following is an example using **http4s**:

```
1.  import cats.effect._
2.  import org.http4s._
3.  import org.http4s.dsl.io._
4.  import org.http4s.implicits._
5.  import org.http4s.server.blaze._
6.  import org.http4s.circe._
7.  import io.circe.syntax._
8.  import io.circe.generic.auto._
9.
10. object TodoApp extends IOApp {
11.   val todoRoutes = HttpRoutes.of[IO] {
12.     case GET -> Root / "todos" =>
13.       Ok(TodoRepository.getAll.asJson)
14.
15.     case req @ POST -> Root / "todo" =>
16.       for {
17.         todo <- req.as[TodoItem]
18.         added = TodoRepository.add(todo)
19.         resp <- Ok(added.asJson)
20.       } yield resp
21.
22.     case DELETE -> Root / "todo" / id =>
23.       TodoRepository.delete(id) match {
24.         case Some(todo) => Ok(todo.asJson)
25.         case None => NotFound()
26.       }
27.   }
28.
29.   val httpApp = todoRoutes.orNotFound
30.
31.   override def run(args: List[String]): IO[ExitCode] = {
32.     BlazeServerBuilder[IO](runtime.compute)
33.       .bindHttp(8080, "localhost")
34.       .withHttpApp(httpApp)
35.       .serve
36.       .compile
```

```
37.        .drain
38.        .as(ExitCode.Success)
39.  }
40. }
```

Note: Ensure you have the necessary dependencies in your build.sbt. This example uses in-memory storage for simplicity. It depicts the feature and it is not as-is usable for production implementation.

The following is a simplified example of creating a to-do list application using Tapir, **http4s** as the server backend, and Circe for JSON serialization. This example will cover defining a basic API for adding, listing, and deleting to-do items:

1. **Adding dependencies**: First, you need to add the necessary dependencies to your **build.sbt** for Tapir, **http4s**, and Circe, as follows:

```
1.  libraryDependencies ++= Seq(
2.    "com.softwaremill.sttp.tapir" %% "tapir-core" % "0.19.0",
3.    "com.softwaremill.sttp.tapir" %% "tapir-http4s-
      server" % "0.19.0",
4.    "com.softwaremill.sttp.tapir" %% "tapir-json-
      circe" % "0.19.0",
5.    "com.softwaremill.sttp.tapir" %% "tapir-openapi-
      docs" % "0.19.0",
6.    "com.softwaremill.sttp.tapir" %% "tapir-openapi-circe-
      yaml" % "0.19.0",
7.    "org.http4s" %% "http4s-blaze-server" % "0.21.22",
8.    "org.http4s" %% "http4s-circe" % "0.21.22",
9.    "io.circe" %% "circe-generic" % "0.13.0",
10.   "io.circe" %% "circe-literal" % "0.13.0"
11. )
```

Ensure that you check for the latest versions of these libraries.

2. **Defining the to-do model and repository**: Define a simple case class for your to-do items and a mock repository, as follows:

```
1.  import java.util.concurrent.atomic.AtomicLong
2.  import scala.collection.concurrent.TrieMap
3.
4.  case class TodoItem(id: Long, title: String, completed: Boolean)
5.
6.  object TodoRepository {
7.    private val items = TrieMap.empty[Long, TodoItem]
8.    private val idGenerator = new AtomicLong()
9.
10.   def add(item: TodoItem): TodoItem = {
```

```
11.     val id = idGenerator.incrementAndGet()
12.     val newItem = item.copy(id = id)
13.     items.put(id, newItem)
14.     newItem
15.   }
16.
17.   def list(): Iterable[TodoItem] = items.values
18.
19.   def delete(id: Long): Option[TodoItem] = items.remove(id)
20. }
```

3. **Defining endpoints with Tapir**: The following is the code for defining endpoints with Tapir:

```
1.  import sttp.tapir._
2.  import sttp.tapir.json.circe._
3.  import io.circe.generic.auto._
4.
5.  object TodoEndpoints {
6.    val baseEndpoint = endpoint.in("todos")
7.
8.    val addTodo: Endpoint[TodoItem, Unit, TodoItem, Any] =
9.      baseEndpoint.post
10.       .in(jsonBody[TodoItem])
11.       .out(jsonBody[TodoItem])
12.
13.   val listTodos: Endpoint[Unit, Unit, List[TodoItem], Any] =
14.     baseEndpoint.get
15.       .out(jsonBody[List[TodoItem]])
16.
17.   val deleteTodo: Endpoint[Long, Unit, Unit, Any] =
18.     baseEndpoint.delete
19.       .in(path[Long]("id"))
20.       .out(emptyOutput)
21. }
```

4. **Implementing the server logic**: The following are the ways for combining your endpoints with business logic using **http4s**:

```
1.  import cats.effect._
2.  import sttp.tapir.server.http4s._
3.  import org.http4s.server.blaze._
4.  import org.http4s.implicits._
5.
6.  object TodoServer extends IOApp {
```

```
7.
8.    val addTodoRoute = TodoEndpoints.addTodo.toRoutes
      (TodoRepository.add)
9.    val listTodosRoute = TodoEndpoints.listTodos.toRoutes
      (_ => Right(TodoRepository.list().toList))
10.   val deleteTodoRoute = TodoEndpoints.deleteTodo.
      toRoutes(id => Right(TodoRepository.delete(id)))
11.
12.   val allRoutes = addTodoRoute <+> listTodosRoute <+>
      deleteTodoRoute
13.
14.   val httpApp = Http4sServerInterpreter[IO]().toRoutes
      (allRoutes).orNotFound
15.
16.   override def run(args: List[String]): IO[ExitCode] = {
17.     BlazeServerBuilder[IO](runtime.compute)
18.       .bindHttp(8080, "localhost")
19.       .withHttpApp(httpApp)
20.       .resource
21.       .use(_ => IO.never)
22.       .as(ExitCode.Success)
23.   }
24. }
```

5. **Running the application**: You can now run your server, and it will start listening for HTTP requests based on the defined endpoints. You have created endpoints to add a to-do item, list all to-do items, and delete a to-do item by its ID.

Conclusion

In this chapter, we learned how we can use functional constructs and apply it in web development and create web application easily using matured functional libraries available like ZIO HTTP (under ZIO umbrella), http4s and Tapir by creating endpoints definitions indifferent of what web functional libraries we have been using. These libraries provide routes concepts which are again a layer on top of features as handles and featuring composability so that these features could be integrated with other with all ease and no extra effort of integrations. All concurrency features come free because of immutability in its core. These are all the benefits we reap out of the basic fundamental core of functional programming. We implemented the web layer in this chapter but did not try to store the to-do items we created in any database.

In the next chapter, we will learn how to use database layer to be used with functional core and all libraries helping our journey smoother.

CHAPTER 10

DB Implementation in Functional Way

Introduction

We have learned many concepts to deploy functional programming concepts till now but there is one very important aspect which gets employed in every real-world implementation which is **database (DB)** programming. When implementation is done end-to-end, then this aspect gets very crucial to implement in functional way to reap the full benefit of functional programming in our implementation. In this chapter, we look into this aspect and will learn what is functional means in DB, which libraries available to help functional implementation of DB programming and their hands-on to get our hand dirty with functional DB implementations.

Structure

In this chapter, we will cover the following topics:

- DB in functional style
- Slick
- Quill
- Doobie
- Skunk

- Choosing library
- Sample to-do application

Objectives

By the end of this chapter, readers will learn how to implement DB implementation in functional way. We will see how composability works and how it provides ways to write modular code.

DB in functional style

In functional programming, the approach to DB differs from the traditional imperative style found in languages like Java or Python. The focus in functional programming is on immutability, statelessness, and pure functions as first-class citizens. This means when interacting with DBs, the goal is to maintain these principles as much as possible. Let us explore how DBs can be used in a functional programming context.

Pure functions and side effects

One of the core principles of functional programming is the use of pure functions, which means the function's output is solely dependent on its input, without any side effects like modifying DB. However, DB operations inherently involve side effects. The solution in functional programming is to isolate and control these side effects. This can be done through the following approaches:

- **Monads**: In languages like Haskell, monads are used to encapsulate side effects. A monad like **IO** can be used to perform DB operations, ensuring that the impure actions are contained and managed within a functional framework.

- **Functional reactive programming (FRP)**: FRP libraries like RxJava in the Java world or Reactive Extensions in .NET, handle asynchronous streams of data, which can include DB operations, in a functional manner.

Immutability and databases

While DBs themselves are mutable, their state changes over time, functional programming handles this through immutable data structures and pure functions. This means that instead of modifying a DB record directly, a functional approach will be able to do, as follows:

- Retrieve the record (as an immutable data structure)
- Transform it with pure functions
- Save the new version back to the DB

This approach helps in maintaining the predictability and ease of reasoning about the code, which are hallmark benefits of functional programming.

The following is an example:

- **Querying a DB in functional programming style**: Consider a hypothetical functional language or a library that allows us to interact with a DB. The code will be as follows:

```
1.  // Assume a fictional functional programming library for
    DB operations
2.  def getUserByEmail(email: String): IO[Option[User]] = {
3.      // IO encapsulates the side effect of querying the DB
4.      sql"SELECT * FROM users WHERE email = $email".query[User]
    .option.transact(xa)
5.  }
6.
7.  def updateUserAge(userId: Int, newAge: Int): IO[Unit] = {
8.      sql"UPDATE users SET age = $newAge WHERE id = $userId"
    .update.run.transact(xa).map(_ => ())
9.  }
10.
11. // Using the functions
12. for {
13.   userOption <- getUserByEmail("example@example.com")
14.   _ <- userOption match {
15.     case Some(user) => updateUserAge(user.id, 42)
16.     case None => IO.unit // Do nothing if the user is not found
17.   }
18. } yield ()
```

In this Scala example, **IO** is a type that represents a computation that might produce side effects like a DB call and will eventually return a value of type **Option[User]** or **Unit** in the case of **updateUserAge**. The **transact** method is where the side effect (DB interaction) is actually executed, but it is neatly contained within the **IO** monad.

Slick

Slick[1] is a modern DB query and access library for Scala, designed to be a functional alternative to traditional SQL libraries and **object-relational mapping** (**ORMs**). It allows you to work with DB queries in a way that feels natural to Scala, leveraging its strong functional programming features. With Slick, DB queries can be written in Scala itself, instead of embedding strings of SQL code. This provides a type-safe way to query and manipulate DBs, which can reduce runtime errors and improve developer productivity.

---

1. **https://scala-slick.org/**

The following are the core features of Slick:

- **Functional and reactive**: Slick is designed to work well within Scala's functional programming paradigm and integrates smoothly with reactive streams for asynchronous DB operations.

- **Type-safety**: Queries in Slick are checked at compile-time for type correctness, reducing the risk of SQL syntax errors and type mismatches at runtime.

- **Composable**: Slick queries are built using a **functional relational mapping (FRM)** approach, enabling query composition using Scala's for-comprehensions and monadic operations.

Basic concepts

The following are the basic concepts to save data in persistent storage (disk) and execute queries to read the data from that storage:

- **Tables and queries**: In Slick, you define your tables as Scala classes, and queries are represented as Scala collections. This allows you to work with DB operations in a very similar way to working with in-memory collections like **List** or **Seq**.

  Refer to the following code:

```
1. import slick.jdbc.H2Profile.api._
2.
3. final case class User(id: Int, name: String, age: Int)
4.
5. class Users(tag: Tag) extends Table[User](tag, "USERS") {
6.   def id = column[Int]("ID", O.PrimaryKey)
7.   def name = column[String]("NAME")
8.   def age = column[Int]("AGE")
9.   def * = (id, name, age).mapTo[User]
10. }
11.
12. val users = TableQuery[Users]
```

- **Executing queries**: With Slick, you execute your queries asynchronously, returning Future results that you can compose and work within a non-blocking manner.

  Refer to the following code:

```
1. val db = Database.forConfig("mydb")
2. val action = users.filter(_.age > 18).result
3. val future: Future[Seq[User]] = db.run(action)
4.
5. future.onComplete {
6.   case Success(users) => users.foreach(println)
```

```
7.    case Failure(e) => e.printStackTrace()
8. }
```

Functional programming with Slick

When using Slick in a functional programming context, you will often focus on composing operations and working with immutable data.

The following are some ways Slick supports functional programming:

- **Immutability**: Even though you are working with a mutable DB, the objects you retrieve and work with in Scala are immutable by default.

- **Monadic operations**: Slick's DB actions can be composed using for-comprehensions and other monadic operations, making it easy to chain DB operations in a clean and readable way.

- **Asynchronous and non-blocking**: By returning Futures, Slick allows you to write non-blocking DB code, which is essential for scalable and reactive applications.

Handling side effects

Although functional programming prefers pure functions without side effects, real-world applications often need to interact with DBs, which are inherently side effecting. Slick deals with this by isolating side effects in DB actions, which are executed asynchronously and only produce side effects when run against a DB object. This approach allows you to write your DB interaction code in a way that is composable and consistent with functional programming principles, while still interacting with the outside world.

In summary, Slick offers Scala developers a powerful tool kit for working with DBs in a way that is both functional and type-safe. It bridges the gap between the relational DB world and the functional programming paradigm, allowing developers to write concise, composable, and correct DB access code.

Sample working with Slick

Let us create a small example using Slick to illustrate how you can perform basic DB operations in Scala in a functional and type-safe manner. We will setup a simple **User** table, insert same data into it, and then query the data. This example assumes you have Slick and a DB driver, for example, H2 for an in-memory DB added to your project dependencies.

The following are the steps:

1. **Add dependencies**: First, ensure you have the necessary dependencies in your **build.sbt** file. For an H2 in-memory DB and Slick, you might have entries, as follows:

```
1. libraryDependencies ++= Seq(
2.   "com.typesafe.slick" %% "slick" % "3.3.3",
3.   "com.typesafe.slick" %% "slick-hikaricp" % "3.3.3",
4.   "com.h2database" % "h2" % "1.4.200"
5. )
```

2. **Define a table**: Define a case class for your entity and a corresponding Slick table, as follows:

```
1. import slick.jdbc.H2Profile.api._
2.
3. case class User(id: Int, name: String, age: Int)
4.
5. class Users(tag: Tag) extends Table[User](tag, "USERS") {
6.   def id = column[Int]("ID", O.PrimaryKey)
7.   def name = column[String]("NAME")
8.   def age = column[Int]("AGE")
9.   // Projection to map columns to the case class
10.  def * = (id, name, age).mapTo[User]
11. }
12.
13. val users = TableQuery[Users]
```

3. **DB configuration**: For simplicity, we will use H2 in-memory DB. You typically configure your DB in the **application.conf** file, but for this example, we will directly create a DB instance, as follows:

```
1.
   val db = Database.forConfig("mydb", ConfigFactory.parseString("""
2.   mydb = {
3.     url = «jdbc:h2:mem:test;DB_CLOSE_DELAY=-1",
4.     driver = «org.h2.Driver",
5.     connectionPool = disabled,
6.     keepAliveConnection = true
7.   }
8. """))
```

4. **Creating the Schema and inserting data**: We will now create the **User** table schema and insert some sample data, as follows:

```
1. val setup = DBIO.seq(
2.   // Create the table
3.   users.schema.create,
4.   // Insert some users
5.   users += User(1, "Alice", 28),
6.   users += User(2, "Bob", 25)
```

```
7.  )
8.
9.  val setupFuture = db.run(setup)
```

5. **Querying DB**: Finally, let us write a query to select all users and print them out, as follows:

```
1.  import cats.effect.IO
2.  val queryFuture = db.run(users.result).map(_.foreach {
3.    user => println(s"Id: ${user.id}, Name: ${user.name},
    Age: ${user.age}")
4.  })
5.
6.  // Don't forget to properly handle the future results and
    shutdown the database
7.  queryFuture.onComplete {
8.    case Success(_) => IO.println("Query successful!")
9.    case Failure(e) => e.printStackTrace()
10. }
11.
12. // Import necessary for Await
13. import scala.concurrent.Await
14. import scala.concurrent.duration.Duration
15.
16. // Await the futures for demonstration purposes
    (avoid in production code)
17. Await.result(setupFuture, Duration.Inf)
18. Await.result(queryFuture, Duration.Inf)
19.
20. // Properly shut down the database
21. db.close()
```

This example provides a basic illustration of how to use Slick for DB operations in Scala. Slick allows you to work with DBs in a way that feels natural in Scala, leveraging functional programming principles for type-safety, composability, and immutability. Remember, for real-world applications, you will need to handle futures more gracefully, likely in the context of an application framework like Play, which can manage asynchronous operations and lifecycle events more effectively.

Quill

Quill[2] is another library that facilitates DB access in Scala, emphasizing compile-time language integrated query. Like Slick, Quill offers a functional programming approach to interacting with DBs, but it distinguishes itself with its compile-time query generation and a more straightforward interface for composing and executing queries. This can lead

---

2. **https://zio.dev/zio-quill/**

to more efficient execution and easier debugging since errors in query syntax or type mismatches are caught at compile-time rather than at runtime.

The following are the core features of Quill:

- **Compile-time query generation**: Quill translates Scala code to SQL at compile-time, offering immediate feedback on errors and potentially more optimized queries.

- **Type-safety**: Provides strong compile-time checks for queries, reducing runtime errors related to data access and manipulation.

- **Minimal boilerplate**: Quill aims to reduce the amount of boilerplate code needed to map between Scala objects and DB tables.

- **Support for multiple DBs**: Quill supports various DBs, including PostgreSQL, MySQL, SQLite, and more, as well as different modes of interaction such as synchronous, asynchronous, and reactive streams.

- **Handling futures and async operations**: Quill also supports asynchronous DB operations through different contexts like `AsyncPostgresJdbcContext` for PostgreSQL. Using an async context, your queries would return Future[T] or other asynchronous results suitable for non-blocking applications.

Quill offers a powerful yet straightforward approach to integrating DB operations into Scala applications, with a strong emphasis on compile-time safety and efficiency. Its API encourages functional programming patterns, allowing developers to write concise, composable, and type-safe DB queries. Quill's compile-time approach provides immediate feedback on the correctness of queries, reducing runtime errors and potentially improving query performance.

Sample working with Quill

Let us put together a simple working example of using Quill to perform DB operations in a Scala application. This example will focus on setting up a minimal project using Quill with an H2 in-memory DB, defining a case class to represent a table, inserting some data, and then querying it.

The following are the steps:

1. **Setup your build environment**: First, make sure you have Scala and **sbt** installed on your machine. Then, create a new **sbt** project and add the following dependencies to your **build.sbt** file, as follows:

```
1.  scalaVersion := "2.13.8"
2.
3.  libraryDependencies ++= Seq(
4.    "io.getquill" %% "quill-jdbc" % "3.15.0",
```

```
5.     "com.h2database" % "h2" % "1.4.200"
6.  )
```

2. **Define your case class and context**: Create a Scala file, let us say **Main.scala**, and define your case class and a context. We will use the **H2JdbcContext** and the **SnakeCase** naming strategy, which is common for SQL DBs, as follows:

```
1. import io.getquill._
2.
3. case class Person(id: Int, name: String, age: Int)
4.
5. object Main extends App {
6.   lazy val ctx = new H2JdbcContext(SnakeCase, "ctx")
7.   import ctx._
8.
9.   // Define your database operations here
10. }
```

Your **application.conf** (located in **src/main/resources/application.conf**) should contain H2 DB configuration, as follows:

```
1. ctx.dataSourceClassName = "org.h2.jdbcx.JdbcDataSource"
2. ctx.dataSource.url = "jdbc:h2:mem:testdb;DB_CLOSE_DELAY=-1"
3. ctx.dataSource.user = "sa"
4. ctx.dataSource.password = ""
```

3. **Insert and query data**: Within your **main** object, let us define methods to insert and query data in the **Person** table. You may need to manually create the table in your H2 DB if you have not setup automatic schema generation, as follows:

```
1. def main(args: Array[String]): Unit = {
2.   // Example schema creation (you might handle this outside
     your application)
3.   val createTable = quote {
4.     querySchema[Person]("Person").schema.createIfNotExists
5.   }
6.   ctx.run(createTable)
7.
8.   // Insert some people
9.   val insertPeople = quote {
10.     query[Person].insert(lift(Person(1, "Alice", 30)),
     lift(Person(2, "Bob", 32)))
11.   }
12.   ctx.run(insertPeople)
13.
14.   // Query all people
15.   val allPeople = quote {
16.     query[Person]
```

```
17.  }
18.
19.  val people = ctx.run(allPeople)
20.  people.foreach(println)
21. }
```

This **main** method demonstrates creating a **Person** table if it does not exist, inserting a couple of entries into it, and then querying and printing all entries.

The following is how you run the example:

Execute your application by running **sbt run** from the terminal in your project directory. You should see the inserted **Person** entries printed out, demonstrating that Quill successfully interacted with the H2 DB.

Doobie

Doobie[3] is a pure functional **Java Database Connectivity (JDBC)** layer for Scala and Cats. It is not an ORM or a query **domain-specific language (DSL)** but rather a straightforward, principled way to interact with your DB directly with SQL. Doobie allows you to write SQL queries, analyze them at compile-time (to an extent), and safely map the results to case classes, all while integrating with Cats Effect types for managing side effects, such as DB interactions, in a functional way.

Doobie embraces functional programming principles and integrates tightly with Cats and Cats Effect. This makes it a go-to choice for Scala developers building applications that leverage these libraries for functional programming.

The following are the key features of doobie:

- **Type-safety**: While you write raw SQL, doobie allows for compile-time checking of query syntax against your DB schema (if using certain plugins) and provides strong type mapping between SQL types and Scala types.

- **Purely functional**: Leverages Cats and Cats Effect for functional programming constructs, ensuring effects like DB queries are encapsulated and managed effectively.

- **Composability**: Queries and their associated operations can be composed using for-comprehensions and Cats **flatMap**, making complex transactional operations more manageable and readable.

Sample working with doobie

Let us go through a simple example that demonstrates setting up a project with doobie, connecting to a DB, and performing some basic operations.

---

3. https://typelevel.org/doobie/

The following are the steps:

1. **Setup your project**: Add the following dependencies to your **build.sbt** for doobie, Cats Effect, and an H2 DB for testing purposes, as follows:

```
1.  scalaVersion := "2.13.8"
2.
3.  libraryDependencies ++= Seq(
4.    "org.tpolecat" %% "doobie-core"      % "1.0.0-RC1",
5.    "org.tpolecat" %% "doobie-h2"        % "1.0.0-
      RC1", // For H2 database
6.    "org.typelevel" %% "cats-effect"     % "3.3.11",
7.    "com.h2database" % "h2"              % "1.4.200"
8.  )
```

2. **Define a case class and a doobie transactor**: Create a Scala file, for example, **Main.scala**. Define a case class for your data model and setup a doobie transactor. The transactor is responsible for managing connections to your DB, as follows:

```
1.  import cats.effect.{IO, IOApp}
2.  import doobie._
3.  import doobie.implicits._
4.  import doobie.h2._
5.
6.  case class Person(id: Int, name: String, age: Int)
7.
8.  object Main extends IOApp.Simple {
9.
10.   val transactor: Transactor[IO] =
      H2Transactor.newH2Transactor[IO](
11.     "jdbc:h2:mem:test;DB_CLOSE_DELAY=-1", // In-memory database
12.     "sa", "", // User and password
13.     scala.concurrent.ExecutionContext.global
      // ExecutionContext for asynchronous execution
14.   ).unsafeRunSync() // Normally, you'd want to handle this
      in your IO program's composition root
15.
16.   def run: IO[Unit] = {
17.     // Your database operations go here
18.     IO.unit
19.   }
20. }
```

3. **Creating a table, inserting data, and querying**: Inside your **run** method, you can now define and execute some DB operations. Let us create a table, insert some data, and query it, as follows:

```
1. val createTable: doobie.ConnectionIO[Int] =
2.   sql"CREATE TABLE person (id INT, name VARCHAR, age INT)".update.run
3.
4. val insertPeople: doobie.ConnectionIO[Int] =
5.   sql"INSERT INTO person (id, name, age) VALUES (1, 'Alice', 30),
     (2, 'Bob', 32)".update.run
6.
7. val getPeople: doobie.ConnectionIO[List[Person]] =
8.   sql"SELECT id, name, age FROM person".query[Person].to[List]
9.
10. val program: IO[Unit] = for {
11.   _ <- createTable.transact(transactor)
12.   _ <- insertPeople.transact(transactor)
13.   people <- getPeople.transact(transactor)
14.   _ = people.foreach(println)
15. } yield ()
16.
17. override def run: IO[Unit] = program
```

The following is how to run the example:

Execute your application with **sbt run**. This will create an in-memory H2 DB, create a person table, insert two rows, and print out the results of a query to select all people.

This basic example introduces how to use doobie for DB operations in a purely functional Scala application. Doobie's tight integration with Cats and Cats Effect makes it an excellent choice for Scala developers committed to functional programming principles, providing a powerful, flexible way to perform DB I/O operations in a type-safe and compositional manner.

Skunk

Skunk[4] is a purely functional, type-safe Scala library for working with PostgreSQL. It is built on top of Cats and Cats Effect, adhering to functional programming principles. Skunk separates the concerns of program description from interpretation, allowing you to describe DB interactions as immutable values that can be run, tested, or mocked without requiring an actual connection to the DB until necessary. This approach promotes composability, testability, and robustness in applications that interact with PostgreSQL.

The following are the key features of Skunk:

- **Type-safety**: Skunk provides compile-time query checking, parameter and row encoding or decoding directly against your DB schema, and more.

---

4. https://typelevel.org/skunk/

- **Purely functional**: Leverages Cats and Cats Effect for managing side effects, encouraging a functional programming style.

- **Session management**: Skunk manages sessions for you, handling resource acquisition and release transparently.

- **Streaming**: Supports streaming results with backpressure, making it suitable for handling large datasets efficiently.

Sample working with Skunk

The following is a basic example to illustrate setting up a project with Skunk, defining a query, and running it:

1. **Setup your build**: Add Skunk and Cats Effect to your **build.sbt**. Make sure to replace the versions with the latest available ones, as follows:

```
1. scalaVersion := "2.13.6"
2.
3. libraryDependencies ++= Seq(
4.   "org.tpolecat" %% "skunk-core"   % "0.2.2",
5.   "org.typelevel" %% "cats-effect" % "3.3.0"
6. )
```

2. **Define a case class and session**: Create a Scala file, say **Main.scala**, to define a case class for **Person** and setup a Skunk session, as follows:

```
1. import cats.effect.{IO, IOApp}
2. import skunk._
3. import skunk.implicits._
4. import skunk.codec.all._
5. import natchez.Trace.Implicits.
   noop // Needed for tracing, even if not used
6.
7. case class Person(id: Int, name: String, age: Int)
8.
9. object Main extends IOApp.Simple {
10.
11.   val session: Resource[IO, Session[IO]] = Session.single(
12.     host = "localhost",
13.     port = 5432,
14.     user = "postgres",
15.     database = "yourdatabase",
16.     password = Some("yourpassword")
17.   )
18.
```

```
19.  def run: IO[Unit] = {
20.    // Database operations go here
21.    IO.unit
22.  }
23.}
```

3. **Querying the DB**: Let us define a simple query to fetch all **Person** entries from the **people** table and run it, as follows:

```
1. val query: Query[Void, Person] = sql"""
2.   SELECT id, name, age FROM people
3. """.query(int4 ~ varchar ~ int4).map {
4.   case id ~ name ~ age => Person(id, name, age)
5. }
6.
7. def run: IO[Unit] = session.use { s =>
8.   s.execute(query).flatMap { people =>
9.     IO(people.foreach(println))
10.  }
11.}
```

The following is how to run the example:

Executing **sbt run** will compile your Scala application and, assuming your PostgreSQL DB is accessible with the table and data expected, print out all **Person** entries in the **people** table.

This example offers a glimpse into using Skunk in a Scala application to interact with PostgreSQL in a type-safe and purely functional way. Skunk's tight integration with Cats Effect and its adherence to functional programming principles make it an attractive choice for Scala developers who prefer a functional approach to DB interaction.

Choosing library

Choosing a functional library for DB interaction in Scala depends on several factors, including your specific project requirements, your familiarity with functional programming concepts, the DB system you're using, and the level of type-safety you desire.

The following is a comparative overview of Slick, Quill, doobie, and Skunk to help guide your decision:

- **Slick**:

  o **DB support**: Broad support for multiple relational DBs.

  o **Type-safety**: Strong compile-time checking, but not as extensive as Skunk or doobie in terms of DB schema validation.

    o **Learning curve**: It has moderate learning curve. Familiarity with Scala's for-comprehensions and futures is helpful.

    o **Use case**: Good for applications requiring a balance between type-safety and the flexibility to work with various RDBMS.

- **Quill**:

    o **DB support**: Supports multiple DBs including relational and non-relational.

    o **Type-safety**: Compile-time query generation and checking. Uses **Quoted DSL (QDSL)** for queries.

    o **Learning curve**: It has moderate learning curve. Requires understanding of Quill's DSL and compile-time quotations.

    o **Use case**: Suited for projects that need compile-time query generation and support for both SQL and NoSQL DBs.

- **Doobie**:

    o **DB support**: Focused on relational DBs via JDBC, without direct support for any specific RDBMS dialect.

    o **Type-safety**: Offers strong compile-time checking of queries against DB schema with certain plugins.

    o **Learning curve**: Higher for those not familiar with Cats and functional programming.

    o **Use case**: Ideal for projects where pure functional programming is a priority and the application interacts with the DB in a type-safe manner. Great fit for teams comfortable with Cats Effect.

- **Skunk**:

    o **DB support**: Exclusively for PostgreSQL.

    o **Type-safety**: Very high, with compile-time checking of queries and DB schema.

    o **Learning curve**: Similar to doobie, requires familiarity with functional programming concepts and Cats Effect.

    o **Use case**: Best choice for PostgreSQL users seeking the highest level of type-safety and are committed to pure functional programming.

Decision factors

The following are the factors to select which library is best suited for specific scenario:

- **DB compatibility**: If you are using PostgreSQL and deeply value type-safety, Skunk is an excellent choice. For broader RDBMS support, Slick or Quill might be more appropriate.

- **Type-safety and compile-time checks**: If compile-time query validation against your schema is critical, consider doobie or Skunk.

- **Functional programming paradigm**: If your team is proficient in Scala's functional programming model and uses Cats Effect, doobie or Skunk will integrate well into your codebase. For a more general approach, Slick and Quill are still functional but might feel more familiar to those transitioning from imperative or mixed paradigms.

- **Learning curve and development speed**: Slick and Quill might offer a quicker start, especially for simple **Create, Read, Update, and Delete** (**CRUD**) operations. doobie and Skunk require a deeper dive into functional programming but reward you with powerful type-safety and expressiveness.

In summary, the best library depends on your project's specific needs, your team's familiarity with Scala and functional programming, and the DB system you are using. It is also perfectly reasonable to prototype with a couple of these libraries to see which one fits your project and workflow best.

Sample to-do application

Creating a simple to-do application using Skunk for DB interactions in Scala involves several steps.

The following are the steps using a PostgreSQL DB:

1. **Environment setup**: Ensure you have Scala and sbt installed on your system. Also, make sure PostgreSQL is installed, running, and accessible.

2. **DB setup**: Create a new DB for your application, for example, **todo_app** and setup a table for to-do items. You can use the following SQL commands:

   ```
   1. CREATE DATABASE todo_app;
   2. - Switch to the newly created database before running the
      following command
   3. CREATE TABLE todos (
   4.     id SERIAL PRIMARY KEY,
   5.     task VARCHAR(255) NOT NULL,
   6.     completed BOOLEAN NOT NULL DEFAULT FALSE
   7. );
   ```

3. **Scala project setup**: Create a new Scala project. You can do this manually or through an IDE. Then, add the following dependencies to your **build.sbt** file to include Skunk and Cats Effect:

   ```
   1. scalaVersion := "2.13.6"
   2.
   3. libraryDependencies ++= Seq(
   ```

```
4.    "org.tpolecat" %% "skunk-core"      % "0.3.1",
5.    "org.typelevel" %% "cats-effect"    % "3.3.11"
6. )
```

4. **Implementing the to-do application**: Create a Scala file, e.g., **ToDoApp.scala**, and implement the to-do application.

The following is a simplified version that includes creating a task and listing all tasks:

```
1. import cats.effect.{IO, IOApp}
2. import skunk._
3. import skunk.implicits._
4. import skunk.codec.all._
5. import natchez.Trace.Implicits.noop
6. import cats.effect.Resource
7.
8. case class Todo(id: Int, task: String, completed: Boolean)
9.
10. object ToDoApp extends IOApp.Simple {
11.
12.   val session: Resource[IO, Session[IO]] = Session.single(
13.     host = "localhost",
14.     port = 5432,
15.     user = "yourUsername",
16.     database = "todo_app",
17.     password = Some("yourPassword")
18.   )
19.
20.   val codec: Codec[Todo] = (int4 ~ varchar ~ bool).gimap[Todo]
21.
22.   def addTodo(task: String): Command[skunk.Void] =
23.     sql"INSERT INTO todos (task) VALUES ($varchar)".command
24.
25.   def listTodos: Query[Void, Todo] =
26.     sql"SELECT id, task, completed FROM todos".query(codec)
27.
28.   def run: IO[Unit] = session.use { s =>
29.     for {
30.       _ <- s.prepare(addTodo("Learn Skunk")).use(_.execute(Void))
31.       todos <- s.execute(listTodos)
32.       _ <- IO(todos.foreach(println))
33.     } yield ()
34.   }
35. }
```

This sample application demonstrates the following:

- **Establish a session with your PostgreSQL DB**: Define encoders and decoders for mapping between Scala case classes and DB rows.

- **Implement basic CRUD operations**: Adding a new to-do and listing all to-do.

- **Running the application**: Run your application using **sbt**. If everything is setup correctly, it should add a new to-do item to your DB and then list all the to-do.

- **Expanding the application**: This example covers the basics. You can extend it by implementing additional features like updating and deleting to-do, filtering based on completion status, and adding error handling. As you develop the application further, you will explore more of Skunk's capabilities, including transaction management and streaming large datasets.

Above code sample uses placeholders like **yourUsername** and **yourPassword**, change it according your choice and run it to get a practical implementation of a sample application which is using Skunk as DB functional library.

Conclusion

In this chapter, we learned how we can apply the functional concepts in DB programming to get all benefits of functional programming. We also tried to learn the different libraries available, their feature, and a quick hands-on for those libraries. We also compared those libraries against their key features and learned which should be the good to use based on the available scenario where it matters most about the team familiarity for the concepts. This chapter equips us to add one more block (DB programming) of real-world implementation to work in functional programming.

In the next chapter, we will understand streams concept which is a powerful abstraction for working with sequences of data in a lazy, composable, and resource-efficient manner and enable us to handle large or even infinite datasets, real-time data, and resource-intensive tasks efficiently.

Join our Discord space

Join our Discord workspace for latest updates, offers, tech happenings around the world, new releases, and sessions with the authors:

https://discord.bpbonline.com

CHAPTER 11
Functional Streams for Scala

Introduction

We have learned many concepts to deploy functional programming concepts till now. We are going to learn a new concept stream which allow us to handle a flow of data and how to process this flow in a functional way. In functional programming, streams are a powerful abstraction for working with sequences of data in a lazy, composable, and resource-efficient manner. Unlike traditional data structures such as arrays or lists, which are typically eager and require storing all elements in memory, streams process data incrementally, producing and consuming elements on demand.

Streams enable us to handle large or even infinite datasets, real-time data, and resource-intensive tasks efficiently. By decoupling data production from consumption, streams allow for better control of resource usage, scalability, and composability, making them a fundamental tool in functional programming.

It also makes us capable to handle an infinite amount of data to be process with limited resources. This plays a very important role in microservices-based implementation where event-driven programming is implemented to solve a real-world problem.

Structure

In this chapter, we will cover the following topics:

- Streams
- Stream in functional style
- FS2
- ZIO stream
- Comparing different stream implementations

Objectives

By the end of this chapter, readers learn about what streams is, how it could be categorized and its use cases. We see how composability works and how it provides ways to write modular code. We will further look into how streams could be realized in a functional way in Scala using different available libraries like **Functional Streams for Scala** (**FS2**), ZIO and also understand the difference in their implementations.

Streams

The term **stream** refers to a concept used in several contexts, each related to the handling and processing of data sequences.

The following is a breakdown of the primary uses of streams in computer science:

- **Continuous data**: A stream in this context represents a continuous sequence of data elements that are available over time. This is common in scenarios where data is produced or received incrementally rather than all at once, and needs to be processed in a similar incremental manner. Common examples include real-time analytics, sensor data processing, and ongoing user input.

  - **Characteristics**: Streams in this sense are often unbounded in size, with no clear start or end, and are processed element by element. The focus is on real-time processing, often with latency requirements that dictate how quickly data must be processed after it arrives.

    Now when data is available as unbounded in size or continuous data, it is somehow need to be used. This is where stream processing comes into picture.

  - **Purpose**: This involves algorithms and software frameworks designed for high-throughput, low-latency processing of continuous data streams. Stream processing engines like Apache Kafka, Apache Storm, and others provide tools to manage, analyze, and act on real-time data without requiring it to be first stored in a database.

- o **Applications**: Used in applications such as event monitoring, fraud detection in transactions, live traffic monitoring, and real-time advertising.

To categorize this further based on if data is sent or ingested, it is of the following types:

- **Input streams**: These are used to read data from a source, which could be a file, network connection, keyboard, etc. The data flows from the source into your program.

- **Output streams**: These are used for writing data to a destination, like a file, network connection, or console. The data flows from your program to the specified destination.

The following are the characteristics of streams:

- **Sequential access**: Streams provide data one piece at a time in a specific order, typically starting at the beginning and moving to the end. This sequential access is ideal for certain types of data processing, where earlier data can be processed independently of later data.

- **Buffering**: Many streams perform some form of buffering to optimize I/O operations. Buffering involves storing a block of data temporarily while it is being transferred.

- **Blocking versus non-blocking**: Streams can be blocking, where the execution stops until the data becomes available, or non-blocking, where the execution continues even if the data is not immediately available.

- **Asynchronous operations**: Modern systems often support asynchronous stream operations, allowing a program to perform other tasks while waiting for stream operations to complete.

We understood what a stream is meant for and its characteristics. Now, the question comes about its use cases.

The following are the common use cases of streams:

- **File I/O**: Reading from or writing to files is a common operation using streams. This allows programs to handle large files or perform efficient data processing.

- **Network communications**: Streams are essential for sending and receiving data over networks. HTTP responses and requests, for instance, use streams to handle potentially large volumes of data.

- **Inter-process communication**: Streams can connect different processes, allowing them to communicate by sending data to each other sequentially.

- **Streaming media**: This is a technique used to transfer data such that it can be processed as a steady and continuous stream. Streaming media allows users to start playing video or audio before the entire file has been transmitted. This concept leverages data buffering, adaptive bitrate streaming technologies, and other techniques to provide smooth playback over various network conditions.

Each of these uses of stream shares the common theme of handling data in a continuous or sequential manner, which is crucial for efficiency in storage, processing, and communication tasks in computing environments.

Programming with streams

In many programming languages, there are built-in libraries for working with streams, as follows:

- **Java**: Java provides a rich set of classes for dealing with streams under the **java.io** package, such as **InputStream** and **OutputStream** for byte streams, and **Reader** and **Writer** for character streams.

- **Python**: Python has file objects that support reading and writing (**open()** function), and it supports more abstract streams through libraries like **io**, for example, **StringIO** for in-memory stream processing.

- **Node.js**: In Node.js, streams are a fundamental part of the environment, supporting efficient handling of files, network communications, and other data flows with streams implemented under various core modules (**fs** for file streams, **http** for HTTP streams, etc.).

Streams are a powerful concept in computer science, enabling efficient and manageable handling of data in various forms, whether it is large files, real-time data, or network communications.

Streams in functional style

Streams in functional programming are an abstract concept used to model a sequence of data that can be computed on demand and potentially handled as an infinite sequence. They are particularly useful in situations where data elements need to be processed sequentially, and where it is impractical or impossible to store the entire sequence in memory at once due to size constraints or because the total length is unknown or infinite.

The following are the key features of streams:

- **Laziness**: Streams are lazy, that is, they compute their elements only when those elements are specifically requested. This is important for working with large or infinite datasets, allowing the program to consume as much data as needed without overwhelming system resources.

- **Immutability**: As with many constructs in functional programming, streams are immutable. Once a stream is created, it cannot be altered. All operations that transform a stream return a new stream without affecting the original.

- **Functional operations**: Streams support functional operations such as `map`, `filter`, `reduce`, and `more`. These operations allow for expressive ways to handle data transformation and aggregation.

- **Mapping**: Transforming each element of a stream using a function.

- **Filtering**: Selecting elements from a stream-based on a predicate.

- **Reducing**: Aggregating the elements of a stream into a single value.

- **Folding**: Similar to reducing, but with an initial value.

- **Zip**: Combining two streams element-wise into a new stream.

- **Concatenation**: Joining multiple streams into a single stream.

The following are the key concepts of Stream composability:

- **Modularity**: Streams can be broken down into discrete operations that can be combined in various ways. Each operation typically performs a small, well-defined task. This modularity makes streams easier to understand, test, and maintain.

- **Building blocks**: Stream libraries often provide a set of fundamental operations like `map`, `filter`, `reduce`, and `flatMap`. These operations can be used as building blocks to construct more complex behaviors.

- **Chainability**: Stream operations often return another stream. This allows the operations to be chained together in a fluent style, facilitating the transformation of data in a step-by-step manner.

- **Lazy evaluation**: Streams typically employ lazy evaluation, meaning computations are only performed when required, usually at the point of producing a final result or side effect. This can lead to performance optimizations, such as avoiding unnecessary computations.

- **Higher order functions**: Streams leverage higher order functions, meaning that functions are treated as first-class citizens and can be passed to other functions as arguments. This is useful for defining operations like `map` and `filter`.

Buffering

Stream processing involves an entity called **producer** which continuously produces data and other entity named consumer which consumes the and do the required processing but there could be many scenarios where stream processing could be impacted due to dynamic processing.

Example:

- Rate mismatch between producer and consumer.

- Consumer get failed then produced data would get unprocessed.

- Batch processing is not possible to increase the throughput.

Buffering helps to increase the stream processing where a temporary storage (memory/disk) is employed between producer and consumer which disconnects the producer and consumer and temporary stores the data produced by produces. This increases the reliability in stream processing by supporting any scenario if:

- Consumer is temporarily unavailable

- Rate is maintained by storing the extra produced data

- Batch processing is possible by collection a group the data which gets processed by consumer

Stream composability with buffering provide resilient processing of data streams by tackling complex scenarios by composing different streams together using functional programming and then buffering adds resiliency in case of any error scenarios.

The following are the benefits of stream composability:

- **Flexibility**: Developers can build custom operations by combining existing ones, allowing for a high degree of flexibility in processing data streams.

- **Readability**: Chains of operations on streams can be more readable and expressive, closely mirroring the problem domain.

- **Reusability**: Common patterns of data processing can be encapsulated into reusable components.

- **Performance**: By composing operations and utilizing lazy evaluation, programs can be more performance-efficient, avoiding unnecessary computations.

The following is how a simple stream, infinite stream of Fibonacci numbers, might be used in Haskell and Scala for clarity:

```
1. // Define the infinite stream of Fibonacci numbers
2. val fibs: Stream[BigInt] = BigInt(0) #:: BigInt(1) #:: fibs.zip(fibs.
   tail).map(n => n._1 + n._2)
3.
4. // Take the first 10 Fibonacci numbers
5. fibs.take(10).toList.foreach(println)
```

Usage in functional programming

Streams in functional programming are powerful tools for handling sequences of data in a lazy, efficient manner. They enable the processing of potentially infinite lists without loading the entire dataset into memory. This feature is particularly useful in scenarios such as data processing pipelines, where large datasets or infinite data sources like sensor data or continuous input are involved.

The following is a closer look at how streams are used in functional programming across various applications and scenarios:

- **Processing large or infinite datasets**: Streams are ideal for working with large or infinite datasets because they allow for operations on data without requiring all of it to be present in memory at once. This is particularly useful for applications, as follows:

    o **Log file processing**: Reading and processing large log files that could be gigabytes in size.

    o **Real-time data feeds**: Handling data from real-time sources like financial tickers, IoT sensors, or social media feeds.

- **Functional transformations**: Streams support all typical functional transformations, such as `map`, `filter`, `fold`, and many more. These transformations are applied lazily, meaning computations only occur when the results are actually needed. This enables the following:

    o **Data cleaning and preparation**: Efficiently preparing and cleaning data for analysis or processing.

    o **Complex transformations**: Applying multiple transformations in sequence without creating intermediate collections that consume memory.

- **Concurrent data processing**:

    Many functional programming languages that support streams also provide easy ways to parallelize stream processing. This can dramatically speed up data processing tasks, as follows:

    o Parallel processing of streams in Scala can be achieved using the **par** method, which converts a collection into a parallelizable form.

    o Asynchronous stream processing, such as using Akka Streams in Scala, allows for non-blocking backpressure streams.

- **Building reactive applications**:

    Streams are fundamental in building reactive applications, which require non-blocking, asynchronous data flows. Frameworks like Akka Streams in Scala and Project Reactor in Java are built around the concept of streams, as follows:

    o **Backpressure handling**: Managing data flow in an application so that no part of the system gets overwhelmed.

    o **Resilient data handling**: Creating robust systems that can handle failures and continue processing.

- **Integration and middleware services**:

    Streams are used extensively in middleware and integration services, which often need to handle data from various sources and formats in a reliable, scalable manner. Examples are as follows:

- Message processing systems: Services that consume and process messages from queues or topics can use streams to handle varying loads of data efficiently.

- Data pipelining: Connecting different data sources and sinks through transformation stages, which can be implemented as a series of stream transformations.

The following is an example of Scala:

It uses **LazyList** (the modern replacement for stream as of Scala 2.13), as follows:

```
1. val fibonacci: LazyList[BigInt] = BigInt(0) #:: BigInt(1)
   #:: fibonacci.zip(fibonacci.tail).map(n => n._1 + n._2)
2.
3. println(fibonacci.take(10).toList)  // Outputs the first 10
   Fibonacci numbers
```

In these examples, the Fibonacci sequence is defined recursively and computed lazily. Only the necessary parts of the sequence are computed when they are actually required, such as when taking the first 10 elements of the sequence. This approach is memory efficient and allows for handling sequences that would be impractical to generate in a non-lazy, eager manner.

FS2

FS2[1] is a prominent library designed for purely functional, compositional, and declarative data stream processing in Scala. The library is built on the concept of describing streaming computations as pure functions and uses typeful and compositional primitives to ensure safety and expressiveness.

The following are the core concepts of FS2:

- **Streams and pure functional programming**: FS2 provides a robust foundation for building stream processing applications in a functional programming style. It allows for the building of complex data pipelines that are both type-safe and maintainable.

- **Resource safety**: One of the key features of FS2 is its focus on resource safety, ensuring that resources are properly managed and released, even in the presence of errors or interruptions.

- **Backpressure**: FS2 handles backpressure implicitly. Streams produced and consumed using FS2 naturally respect backpressure without the need for explicit management from the developer.

- **Modularity and composability**: FS2 streams are highly modular and composable. Operations on streams can be combined in a declarative manner, which promotes code reusability and clarity.

---

1. **https://fs2.io/**

- **Integration with Cats and Cats Effect**: FS2 is tightly integrated with the Cats and Cats Effect libraries, providing support for functional abstractions like **IO**, **Resource**, and other type classes that facilitate asynchronous and effectful programming.

The following is an example demonstrating how to use FS2 to create a stream, apply transformations, and run it. This example assumes you have Cats Effect and FS2 added to your Scala project:

```
1.  import cats.effect.{IO, IOApp}
2.  import fs2.Stream
3.
4.  object Fs2Example extends IOApp.Simple {
5.
6.    // A simple FS2 stream that emits integers from 1 to 5
7.    val stream: Stream[IO, Int] = Stream.emits(1 to 5)
8.
9.    // A transformation that filters even numbers and maps them
      to strings
10.   val processedStream: Stream[IO, String] = stream
11.     .filter(_ % 2 == 0)
12.     .map(n => s"Even number: $n")
13.
14.   // The main logic that runs the stream and prints out results
15.   def run: IO[Unit] =
16.     processedStream
17.       .evalMap(str => IO(println(str)))   // Using evalMap to
      perform side-effecting operations
18.       .compile
19.       .drain  // Compiles the stream to an IO, which when
      executed will run the stream and discard results
20.
21. }
```

The following are the key operations in FS2:

- **Transformations** (**map**, **filter**, **flatMap**, etc.) allow for changing the stream's content and structure.

- **Merging and joining streams** (**merge**, **interleave**, etc.) to combine multiple streams into one.

- **Error handling mechanisms** (**handleErrorWith**, **attempt**, etc.) to deal with exceptions in a functional way.

- **Resource management** (**bracket**, **onFinalize**, etc.) to ensure proper acquisition and release of resources.

Use cases

FS2 is a library designed for constructing and evaluating complex streaming computations in a purely functional manner. It excels in environments and applications where backpressure, resource safety, and compositionality are critical.

The following are several key use cases where FS2 can be effectively employed:

- **Real-time data processing**: FS2 is a well-suited for applications that require the processing of data in real-time, such as streaming analytics from sensors, financial tick data, or social media feeds. Its ability to handle backpressure ensures that the system can adapt to fluctuating input rates without overwhelming memory and processing resources.

  The following is an example:

  A system that monitors and aggregates metrics from multiple IoT devices in real-time, applying transformations and producing alerts based on certain thresholds.

- **CEP**: In scenarios where events must be correlated over time, FS2 streams can be used to create **complex event processing** (**CEP**) systems. FS2's time-based operations and ability to manage stateful computations make it a strong choice for applications that need to detect patterns over sliding windows of time.

  The following is an example:

  Detecting fraudulent banking transactions by analyzing sequences of operations across multiple accounts and geographies in near real-time.

- **Data integration and ETL jobs**: FS2 can orchestrate **extract, transform, and load** (**ETL**) processes where data is ingested from various sources, transformed, and loaded into different sinks. FS2's support for resource safety and asynchronous processing makes it ideal for handling large datasets that require transformations or need to be joined from multiple sources.

  The following is an example:

  An automated data pipeline that periodically extracts data from a distributed log system, transforms the data, for example, filtering, aggregation, and loads it into a data warehouse or analytical database.

- **Network servers and clients**: FS2 can be used to implement both servers and clients in networked applications. The streaming nature of FS2 is a natural fit for handling continuous data flows found in network streams, and its strong type system helps ensure that network protocols are implemented correctly.

  The following is an example:

  Building a lightweight HTTP server that streams large files or video content to clients, handling multiple connections efficiently without blocking.

- **Concurrent and parallel processing**: FS2 leverages the Cats Effect library, which supports high-level abstractions for concurrency and parallelism. This makes FS2 a good choice for scenarios where tasks need to be processed in parallel or in a non-blocking manner.

  The following is an example:

  A service that processes incoming requests concurrently, each performing I/O operations such as database queries or external API calls, and aggregating the results.

- **Reactive and asynchronous applications**: Applications requiring a high degree of responsiveness and resilience under load can benefit from FS2's reactive streams. The ability to handle backpressure and failures elegantly allows developers to build applications that remain responsive under varying loads and recover gracefully from errors.

  The following is an example:

  A reactive stock trading dashboard that updates UI components in real-time as new stock prices are streamed from a market data service.

- **Resource-aware computations**: The resource safety guarantees of FS2 ensure that file handles, network sockets, and other resources are properly managed, avoiding leaks and ensuring that resources are released promptly after use.

  The following is an example:

  A file processing system that needs to read and process multiple files simultaneously, ensuring that all file handles are closed, even if errors occur during processing.

FS2's comprehensive support for functional programming paradigms, combined with its deep integration with Scala and the Cats ecosystem, makes it a robust tool for building complex, scalable, and resilient streaming applications.

ZIO stream

ZIO streams[2] is a powerful library within the ZIO ecosystem designed for building scalable, resilient, and performant stream processing applications in Scala. It provides developers with tools to build both simple and complex data pipelines using purely functional programming. ZIO streams are part of the broader ZIO library, which is a zero-dependency library for asynchronous and concurrent programming in Scala.

The following are the core features of ZIO streams:

- **Backpressure**: ZIO streams are designed to handle backpressure automatically, ensuring that faster producers do not overwhelm slower consumers. This is crucial for maintaining system stability and efficiency.

---

2. https://zio.dev/reference/stream/

- **Resource safety**: ZIO streams guarantee the safe acquisition and release of resources, even in the face of errors or premature termination. This makes them ideal for working with file streams, network connections, and other I/O operations.

- **Composability**: Streams in ZIO can be composed both horizontally (e.g., merging or zipping streams) and vertically (e.g., chaining operations on a stream). This composability is a hallmark of functional design, allowing for modular and maintainable code.

- **Integration with ZIO ecosystem**: ZIO streams are seamlessly integrated with other parts of the ZIO ecosystem, such as ZIO fibers for concurrency, ZIO environment for dependency injection, and ZIO error for robust error handling.

- **Scalability**: Leveraging the asynchronous, non-blocking nature of ZIO streams can process a high volume of data efficiently and scale across multiple cores or machines.

Core abstractions

The core abstractions in ZIO streams help manage complex streaming operations, ensuring efficiency and type-safety.

The following are the primary components:

- **ZStream**: `ZStream[R, E, A]` is the fundamental abstraction in ZIO streams. It represents an asynchronous and possibly infinite stream of data. A `ZStream[R, E, A]` has three type parameters, as follows:

  o **R**: The environment type that the stream requires to run. This can be any dependency, such as a database connection or configuration data.

  o **E**: The error type that the stream might fail with.

  o **A**: The type of elements produced by the stream.

  The design of **ZStream** allows for sophisticated streaming operations, including transformations, filtering, merging, and more, while integrating deeply with other parts of the ZIO ecosystem.

- **ZSink**: `ZSink[R, E, A0, A, B]` is another core component used in ZIO streams for consuming streams. It represents a composable consumer of elements from a stream, as follows:

  o **R**: Environment required by the sink.

  o **E**: Error type that the sink might fail with.

  o **A0**: The initial input type that the sink can accept (allowing for contravariant input types).

  o **A**: The type of input the sink consumes.

  o **B**: The type of output the sink produces.

Sinks are used to accumulate results from a stream, transform streams into a final result, or even to control backpressure by signaling when no more data should be accepted.

- **ZPipeline**: `ZPipeline[R, E, A, B]` is an abstraction used to transform elements in a stream from type **A** to type **B**, as follows:

    o **R**: Environment required by the pipeline.

    o **E**: Error type for failures that may occur in the pipeline.

    o **A**: Type of input elements.

    o **B**: Type of output elements.

    Pipelines can be thought of as stream transformers or operators that can be applied to a **ZStream**. They are useful for encoding common operations like **map**, **filter**, or more complex transformations.

The following are the common use cases for ZIO streams:

- **Real-time data streaming**: Ideal for applications that need to process data in real-time, such as streaming analytics platforms, real-time monitoring systems, or chat servers.

- **CEP**: ZIO streams can handle CEP by allowing various temporal or spatial operations on streaming data, useful in domains like finance (for trading systems) or IoT (for sensor data analysis).

- **Data integration and ETL**: The library can orchestrate ETL workflows where data is continuously ingested, transformed, and loaded into databases or data warehouses.

- **Network applications**: Building robust network servers and clients, including web servers and RESTful APIs, leveraging ZIO streams for handling request and response streams efficiently.

- **File processing**: ZIO Streams provide tools for efficiently processing large files, enabling operations like parsing, transformations, and aggregations without loading entire files into memory.

The following is an example of creating a stream that emits numbers, processes them, and prints the results:

```
1. import zio._
2. import zio.stream._
3.
4. object ZioStreamsExample extends App {
5.   val myStream: ZStream[Any, Nothing, Int] = ZStream.fromIterable(1 to 10)
6.
7.   val processedStream: ZStream[Any, Nothing, String] = myStream
```

```
8.      .filter(_ % 2 == 0) // Filter even numbers
9.      .map(n => s"Even number: $n") // Map to a string
10.
11.  override def run(args: List[String]): URIO[zio.ZEnv, ExitCode] =
12.    processedStream
13.      .foreach(str => Console.printLine(str)) // Print each string
14.      .exitCode
15. }
```

In this example, **ZStream.fromIterable** is used to create a stream of numbers from **1 to 10**. The stream is then processed to filter out odd numbers and convert even numbers into a descriptive string. Finally, the **foreach** method is used to print each item of the stream to the console.

ZIO streams offer a comprehensive, type-safe, and highly performant toolkit for building stream processing applications in Scala. It excels in environments where performance, reliability, and scalability are critical, and it leverages the functional programming capabilities of Scala to provide elegant solutions to complex streaming problems. Whether for simple data transformations or complex networked applications, ZIO streams provide a robust foundation for reactive and stream-based applications.

Comparing different stream implementations

When comparing FS2 and ZIO streams, it is important to recognize that both are powerful libraries for handling stream processing in Scala, but they come from different ecosystems and have different philosophical underpinnings and design goals.

The following is a detailed comparison based on several aspects:

- **Ecosystem and dependencies**:
    - **FS2**: FS2 is built on top of the Cats and Cats Effect libraries, which are widely used in the Scala community for functional programming. FS2's design is deeply integrated with the type classes and abstractions provided by these libraries, such as **IO**, **Resource**, and **Sync**.

    - **ZIO streams**: Part of the larger ZIO ecosystem, which provides its own set of abstractions for dealing with asynchronous and concurrent programming, including its own effect type (ZIO). ZIO is a self-contained ecosystem, which means using ZIO Streams often leads to adopting other parts of ZIO, like ZIO Environment for dependency injection and ZIO Test for testing.

- **Type-safety and API design**:
    - **FS2**: Emphasizes pure functional programming with strong type-safety and immutabili1ty. FS2's API is designed to be minimal yet expressive, relying heavily on Cats Effect's capabilities for effect management.

  o **ZIO streams**: Also, highly type-safe, ZIO streams incorporate more features directly into the stream type, such as environmental requirements and error types. This can lead to more expressive APIs where more behaviors can be inferred and checked by the compiler.

- **Backpressure handling**:

  o **FS2**: Handles backpressure implicitly. Producers and consumers are automatically balanced by the library without needing the user to manage it explicitly, which simplifies stream composition and operation chaining.

  o **ZIO streams**: Similar to FS2, backpressure is managed internally by the library. ZIO streams are designed to be highly responsive and efficient with backpressure mechanisms, preventing overwhelming of consumers by producers.

- **Concurrency and parallelism**:

  o **FS2**: Provides powerful primitives for concurrency, such as `parJoin` and `race`, and integrates smoothly with Cats Effect's concurrency model. It handles concurrent operations by providing schedulers and mechanisms to run tasks in parallel.

  o **ZIO streams**: Concurrency is built into the core of ZIO, including ZIO streams. ZIO's fiber-based model allows fine-grained control over concurrency with a rich set of operators for parallelism and resource management.

- **Resource safety**:

  o **FS2**: Focuses extensively on ensuring resource safety through the Cats Effect Resource type, which guarantees that resources are acquired and released correctly, even when streams are interrupted or errors occur.

  o **ZIO streams**: ZIO provides its own resource safety mechanisms with ZManaged, similar to Resource in Cats Effect. This is integrated into streams to manage lifecycle events of resources transparently.

- **Performance**:

  o **FS2**: Known for good performance in pure functional streaming, especially in the Scala ecosystem. Performance may vary based on the underlying effect type used for example, Cats Effect IO vs Monix Task.

  o **ZIO streams**: Often touted for very high performance, particularly in scenarios involving high concurrency and low-latency requirements. ZIO's performance optimizations are integral parts of its design.

- **Community and documentation**:

  o **FS2**: FS2 has a robust community, especially among users of the Typelevel ecosystem. Documentation is thorough, and there are many resources for learning and getting support.

  o **ZIO streams**: ZIO has a rapidly growing community and excellent documentation. The community is very active, with constant updates, improvements, and a wealth of learning resources.

The choice between FS2 and ZIO streams often depends on the larger context of your Scala application. If you are already using Typelevel libraries like Cats and Cats Effect, FS2 is a natural choice. If you prefer a cohesive, powerful framework that includes everything from concurrency to dependency injection, ZIO (and by extension, ZIO streams) may be more appealing. Both libraries offer strong guarantees around type-safety, resource management, and performance, making them excellent choices for functional stream processing in Scala.

Conclusion

In this chapter, we learned about streams and its functional implementations. We saw how traditional synchronous implementation got modified with streams implementations to able to process infinite amount of data with finite resources. We learned FS2 and ZIO streams implementation of stream in functional way and provides a lots of functional programming features available to streams. Composability and reasoning are one of those attributes. It also provides effectful implementation to allow effects processing with stream data. Now, we have learned many attributes of functional implementation and tools required to implement any real-world problem in functional way.

In the next chapter, we will try to use all these tools to implement a toy ecommerce site with all functional tools we learned till this chapter.

Join our Discord space

Join our Discord workspace for latest updates, offers, tech happenings around the world, new releases, and sessions with the authors:

https://discord.bpbonline.com

CHAPTER 12

Case Study on Functional Toy E-commerce Site

Introduction

We have learned all the necessary concepts for implementing functional programming in real-world scenarios. In this chapter, we will try to use all those learnings and create a working toy e-commerce site. It gives a way to use all our functional knowledge and tools and reaping out all the benefits of functional programming.

Structure

In this chapter, we will cover the following topics:

- E-commerce site requirement
- Design

Objectives

By the end of this chapter, readers will develop a new e-commerce site with all features of showing the product details, add to cart, checking out the selected product, and all non-functional requirements (security, analytics etc.) with employing all the functional tools.

E-commerce site requirement

Any project starts from its requirements and identifying the features needed for a real-world implementation. Creating functional requirements for an e-commerce site involves specifying what the system should do and the features it must support to meet user needs.

User management

The following tasks covers user management for the e-commerce site:

- **User registration and authentication**:
  - Users can register with an email and password
  - Users can log in with their registered email and password
  - Users can reset their password via email

- **User profile management**:
  - Users can view and update their profile information (name, email, address, etc.)
  - Users can manage multiple shipping addresses
  - Users can view their order history

Product management

The following tasks are related to product management including cataloging and searching:

- **Product catalog**:
  - Admins can add, update, and delete products.
  - Products have details such as name, description, price, **Stock Keeping Unit SKU,** category, brand, and images.
  - Products can have variants, for example, size, color.

- **Product search and browsing**:
  - Users can search for products by name, category, brand, etc.
  - Users can filter products by attributes such as price range, brand, rating, and availability.
  - Users can sort products by price, popularity, rating, and newest arrivals.

Shopping cart

The following tasks are cart-related in our toy e-commerce site:

- **Cart management**:
  - o Users can add products to the shopping cart
  - o Users can view the contents of their cart
  - o Users can update the quantity of items in the cart
  - o Users can remove items from the cart

- **Cart persistence**:
  - o The cart should persist between sessions for logged-in users
  - o The cart should be saved locally for guest users and persist within the session

Checkout and payment

The following tasks are for checking out the products in the cart which include payment:

- **Checkout process**:
  - o Users can proceed to checkout from the shopping cart
  - o Users can enter or select a shipping address
  - o Users can select a shipping method
  - o Users can review the order summary before placing the order

- **Payment integration**:
  - o The site should support multiple payment methods for example, credit card or debit card, PayPal, Stripe)
  - o Payment information should be processed securely
  - o Users should receive an order confirmation upon successful payment

Order management

The following are the order-related tasks, including order processing, notification, inventory management, etc.

- **Order processing**:
  - o Admins can view and manage orders
  - o Admins can update order statuses for example, pending, shipped, delivered, cancelled

- o Users can view the status of their orders
- **Order notifications**:
  - o Users receive email notifications for order confirmation, shipping, and delivery
  - o Admins receive notifications for new orders
- **Inventory management**:
  - o **Inventory tracking**:
    - ▪ The system tracks the stock levels of products
    - ▪ Stock levels are updated automatically when orders are placed and fulfilled
- **Low stock alerts**:
  - o Admins receive alerts when product stock levels are low

Reviews and ratings

The following tasks are related to reviews and ratings for products listed in the e-commerce site:

- **Product reviews**:
  - o Users can leave reviews and ratings for products they have purchase
  - o Users can edit or delete their reviews
- **Review moderation**:
  - o Admins can moderate reviews (approve, reject, or remove inappropriate content).

Promotions and discounts

The following are promotion and discount tasks:

- **Discount management**:
  - o Admins can create and manage discount codes
  - o Users can apply discount codes at checkout
- **Promotional offers**:
  - o Admins can create and manage promotional offers, for example, buy one get one free, percentage discounts

Reporting and analytics

The following tasks are related to reporting and analytics of order and customers:

- **Sales reports**:
  - Admins can generate sales reports for different time periods
  - Reports can be filtered by product, category, or customer

- **Customer analytics**:
  - The system tracks customer behavior and purchase history
  - Admins can generate reports on customer activity

Customer support

The following tasks are related to customer support:

- **Support tickets**:
  - Users can create support tickets for order related issues
  - Admins can manage and respond to support tickets

- **Live chat**:
  - Users can initiate live chat sessions with customer support

Security and compliance

The following are the tasks which implements security for our e-commerce site:

- **Data protection**:
  - User data is encrypted and stored securely
  - The system complies with relevant data protection regulations for example, GDPR

- **Access control**:
  - Only authorized users (admins) can access the admin panel
  - Different admin roles with varying levels of access can be defined

- **Prevent cross-site scripting (XSS)**:
  - XSS allows attackers to inject malicious scripts into your web app, stealing user data or performing unauthorized actions
  - Escape user input before rendering (use frameworks that auto-sanitize input)
  - Use **Content Security Policy (CSP)** to restrict script execution

- o Use HTTP-only, secure cookies to protect session tokens
- **Prevent Cross-Site Request Forgery (CSRF)**:
  - o CSRF tricks users into unintended actions (e.g., fund transfer)
  - o Use CSRF tokens for sensitive actions (login, payment, data modification)
- **Secure authentication and authorization**:
  - o Weak authentication can lead to account takeovers
  - o Never store passwords or tokens in **localStorage** (use HTTP-only cookies)
  - o Use OAuth 2.0/OpenID Connect for authentication
- **Secure API calls and data transmission**:
  - o Always use HTTPS (TLS encryption)
  - o Validate and sanitize API responses on both frontend and backend
  - o Use **cross-origin resource sharing** (**CORS**) properly to restrict origins (Access-Control-Allow-Origin)
  - o Avoid exposing API keys in frontend code (use environment variables or backend proxy)
- **Prevent clickjacking**:
  - o Clickjacking tricks users into clicking hidden UI elements
  - o Avoid embedding iframes from untrusted sources
- **Protect against data exposure**:
  - o Disable verbose error messages in production
  - o Remove console logs and debug tools before deployment
  - o Minify and obfuscate JavaScript to prevent reverse engineering
  - o Use environment variables instead of exposing secrets
- **Proper access control**:
  - o Restrict who can access what on the frontend
  - o Use **role-based access control** (**RBAC**) or **attribute-based access control** (**ABAC**)
  - o Hide admin components for non-admin users (**useEffect()** in React)
  - o Enforce backend authorization checks (frontend can be bypassed)

Mobile responsiveness

The following tasks enable our e-commerce website to be used easily with mobile and tablet screens due to its responsive design:

- **Responsive design**:
  - o The site is fully responsive and works on different devices (desktops, tablets, mobile phones)

- **Mobile app integration**:
  - o If there is a mobile app, it should seamlessly integrate with the site's backend

Localization

The following task allows our e-commerce site to be internationally by providing multi-language and multi-currency support:

- **Multi-language support**:
  - o The site supports multiple languages
  - o Users can select their preferred language

- **Currency support**:
  - o The site supports multiple currencies
  - o Users can select their preferred currency

Wishlist

The following task enable our website to increase the leads as it would record the potentials orders as wishlists:

- **Wishlist management**:
  - o Users can add products to a wishlist
  - o Users can view and manage their wishlist
  - o Users can move items from the wishlist to the shopping cart

These functional requirements cover a wide range of features necessary for a comprehensive e-commerce site. Each individual requirement then breaks down into more details for behavior based on customer specific business and expectations. Depending on specific business needs, additional features might be required, or some of these features might be adjusted.

As we have been focusing on toy implementation so we will cover a part of the above requirements and focus on its implementation to use our functional knowledge we grasp throughout this book.

After requirement closure, the next step is to design the solution. Let us now focus on design of our e-commerce site.

Design

Designing software for an e-commerce platform with the aforementioned functional requirements involves creating a comprehensive architecture that covers all necessary components. A high-level software design outline addresses the requirements.

Architecture overview

We will use a layered architecture with the following layers:

- **Presentation layer**: Handles user interactions, UI components, and client-side logic.

- **Business logic layer**: Contains the core functionality and rules of the application.

- **Data access layer**: Manages interactions with the database.

- **Integration layer**: Manages interactions with external services, for example, payment gateways, email services.

- **Infrastructure layer**: Handles system concerns like security, logging, and configuration.

Technology stack

Our e-commerce site will use many technologies to implement all the tasks we discussed above.

The following are the list of all those technologies or libraries for different tasks:

- **Frontend**: React.js or Angular for a building scalable and maintainable frontend

- **Backend**: Scala with Play Framework or Akka HTTP

- **Database**: PostgreSQL or MySQL for relational data; Redis for caching

- **ORM**: Skunk for interacting with PostgreSQL in a type-safe manner

- **Authentication**: JWT for stateless authentication

- **Payment**: Stripe or PayPal SDK for payment processing

- **Deployment**: Docker and Kubernetes for container orchestration

Module breakdown

Our e-commerce site is implemented in layers where each layer is responsible and targeting to its core tasks.

The following are those layers that comprise all the tasks we discussed in above section to cover an end-to-end feature-rich e-commerce site:

- **Presentation layer**:
  - o **Web UI**: Developed using React.js or Angular
  - o **Mobile app**: Optional, built with React Native or Flutter
  - o **API gateway**: Manages API requests and routes them to appropriate services
- **Business logic layer**:
  - o **User management**:
    - ▪ Registration service
    - ▪ Authentication service
    - ▪ Profile management service
- **Product management**:
  - o Product catalog service
  - o Product search service
- **Shopping cart**:
  - o Cart management service
  - o Cart persistence service
- **Checkout and payment**:
  - o Checkout service
  - o Payment integration service
- **Order management**:
  - o Order processing service
  - o Order tracking service
- **Inventory management**:
  - o Inventory tracking service
  - o Low stock alert service
- **Review and ratings**:
  - o Review management service
  - o Moderation service
- **Promotions and discounts**:
  - o Discount management service
  - o Promotional offer service

- **Reporting and analytics**:
  - o Sales reporting service
  - o Customer analytics service

- **Customer support**:
  - o Support ticket service
  - o Live chat service

- **Security and compliance**:
  - o Data protection service
  - o Access control service

- **Wishlist**:
  - o Wishlist management service

- **Data access layer**:
  - o Repositories for each entity (User, product, order, etc.)
  - o Unit of Work pattern to handle transactions

- **Integration layer**:
  - o Payment gateway integrations (Stripe, PayPal)
  - o Email service integration (SendGrid, Mailgun)
  - o SMS gateway integration (Twilio)

- **Infrastructure layer**:
  - o Logging service (log4cats, SLF4J)
  - o Configuration management (Typesafe Config)
  - o Security (JWT, OAuth)
  - o Caching (Redis)

Detailed service design

Each layer we discussed above comprises services which encapsulates all the logic for that specific aspect.

The following are the services with its details that will be used in those layers:

- **User management**:
  - o **User service**:
    - ▪ Methods: `Register`, `login`, `updateProfile`, `changePassword`

- ▪ **Validations**: Email format, password strength, uniqueness of email
  - o **Profile service:**
    - ▪ Methods: `getProfile`, `updateProfile`
    - ▪ **Validations:** Profile data correctness
- **Product management**:
  - o **Product service:**
    - ▪ Methods: `addProduct`, `updateProduct`, `deleteProduct`, `getProductById`, `searchProducts`
    - ▪ **Validations**: Product data correctness, SKU uniqueness
  - o **Catalog service:**
    - ▪ Methods: `getProductsByCategory`, `getFeaturedProducts`
- **Shopping cart:**
  - o **Cart service:**
    - ▪ Methods: `addToCart`, `removeFromCart`, `updateCartItem`, `viewCart`
    - ▪ **Persistence**: Store cart in database for logged-in users, localStorage/ sessionStorage for guests
- **Checkout and payment:**
  - o **Checkout service:**
    - ▪ Methods: `startCheckout`, `confirmOrder`, `applyDiscountCode`
    - ▪ **Validations:** Stock availability, payment method validation
  - o **Payment service:**
    - ▪ Methods: `processPayment`, `refundPayment`
    - ▪ **Integrations**: Stripe, PayPal
- **Order management:**
  - o **Order service:**
    - ▪ Methods: `placeOrder`, `cancelOrder`, `getOrderById`, `getOrdersByUser`
    - ▪ **Validations**: Order state transitions (pending, shipped, delivered, canceled)
- **Inventory management:**
  - o **Inventory service:**
    - ▪ Methods: `adjustStock`, `checkStockLevels`
    - ▪ **Alerts:** Send low stock alerts to admins

- **Review and ratings**:
  - o **Review service**:
    - ▪ **Methods**:`addReview,updateReview,deleteReview,getReviewsByProduct`
    - ▪ **Moderation**: Flagging inappropriate content
- **Promotions and discounts**:
  - o **Promotions service**:
    - ▪ **Methods**: `createDiscount, applyDiscount, validateDiscountCode`
    - ▪ **Validations**: Expiry dates, usage limits
- **Reporting and analytics**:
  - o **Reporting service**:
    - ▪ **Methods**: `generateSalesReport, generateCustomerReport`
    - ▪ **Analytics**: Track customer behavior, sales trends
- **Customer support**:
  - o **Support service**:
    - ▪ **Methods**: `createTicket, updateTicket, closeTicket`
    - ▪ **Integrations**: Live chat system, for example, *Intercom*

Database schema design

Our e-commerce site need many persistent data regarding different aspects of site. It stores product, customer etc. And all supported entities which is browsed and worked upon during interaction with site. We need a database schema design for all these entities where we will save data.

The following are the entities or tables used for implementing e-commerce site:

- **Users**:
  - o **Columns**: `id, email, password_hash, name, address, created_at, updated_at`
- **Products**:
  - o **Columns**: `id, name, description, price, sku, category_id, brand_id, stock_quantity, created_at, updated_at`
- **Categories**:
  - o **Columns**: `id, name, description`
- **Orders**:
  - o **Columns**: `id, user_id, status, total_price, created_at, updated_at`

- OrderItems:
  - Columns: `id`, `order_id`, `product_id`, `quantity`, `price`
- Carts:
  - Columns: `id`, `user_id`, `created_at`, `updated_at`
- CartItems:
  - Columns: `id`, `cart_id`, `product_id`, `quantity`
- Reviews:
  - Columns: `id`, `product_id`, `user_id`, `rating`, `comment`, `created_at`, `updated_at`
- Discounts:
  - Columns: `id`, `code`, `description`, `percentage`, `expiry_date`
- Support tickets:
  - Columns: `id`, `user_id`, `status`, `subject`, `description`, `created_at`, `updated_at`
- Wishlists:
  - Columns: `id`, `user_id`
- WishlistItems:
  - Columns: `id`, `wishlist_id`, `product_id`

API endpoints design

As our e-commerce site is modular, composable and testable, its callable actions are triggered with API.

The following are those APIs covering different section of our e-commerce site:

- User management:
  - `POST/api/register`
  - `POST/api/login`
  - `GET/api/profile`
  - `PUT/api/profile`
  - `POST/api/password/reset`
- Product management:
  - `GET/api/products`
  - `GET/api/products/:id`
  - `POST/api/products`
  - `PUT/api/products/:id`
  - `DELETE/api/products/:id`

- **Shopping cart:**
    - POST/api/cart
    - GET/api/cart
    - PUT/api/cart/:itemId
    - DELETE/api/cart/:itemId

- **Checkout and payment:**
    - POST/api/checkout
    - POST/api/payment

- **Order management:**
    - GET/api/orders
    - GET/api/orders/:id
    - POST/api/orders
    - PUT/api/orders/:id
    - DELETE/api/orders/:id

- **Reviews and ratings:**
    - POST/api/products/:id/reviews
    - GET/api/products/:id/reviews
    - PUT/api/reviews/:id
    - DELETE/api/reviews/:id

- **Promotions and discounts:**
    - POST/api/discounts
    - GET/api/discounts
    - PUT/api/discounts/:id
    - DELETE/api/discounts/:id

- **Customer support:**
    - POST/api/support/tickets
    - GET/api/support/tickets
    - PUT/api/support/tickets/:id
    - DELETE/api/support/tickets/:id

- **Wishlist:**
    - POST/api/wishlist
    - GET/api/wishlist
    - DELETE/api/wishlist/:productId

This design outline provides a structured approach to building an e-commerce platform. Each module and service is designed to handle specific responsibilities, promoting maintainability and scalability. As development progresses, this design can be refined and expanded to accommodate new requirements and optimizations.

Class details with class diagram

A class diagram for the entire e-commerce site involves identifying key entities across different modules (user management, product management, order management, etc.), their attributes, methods, and relationships.

The following is a comprehensive class diagram for the e-commerce site:

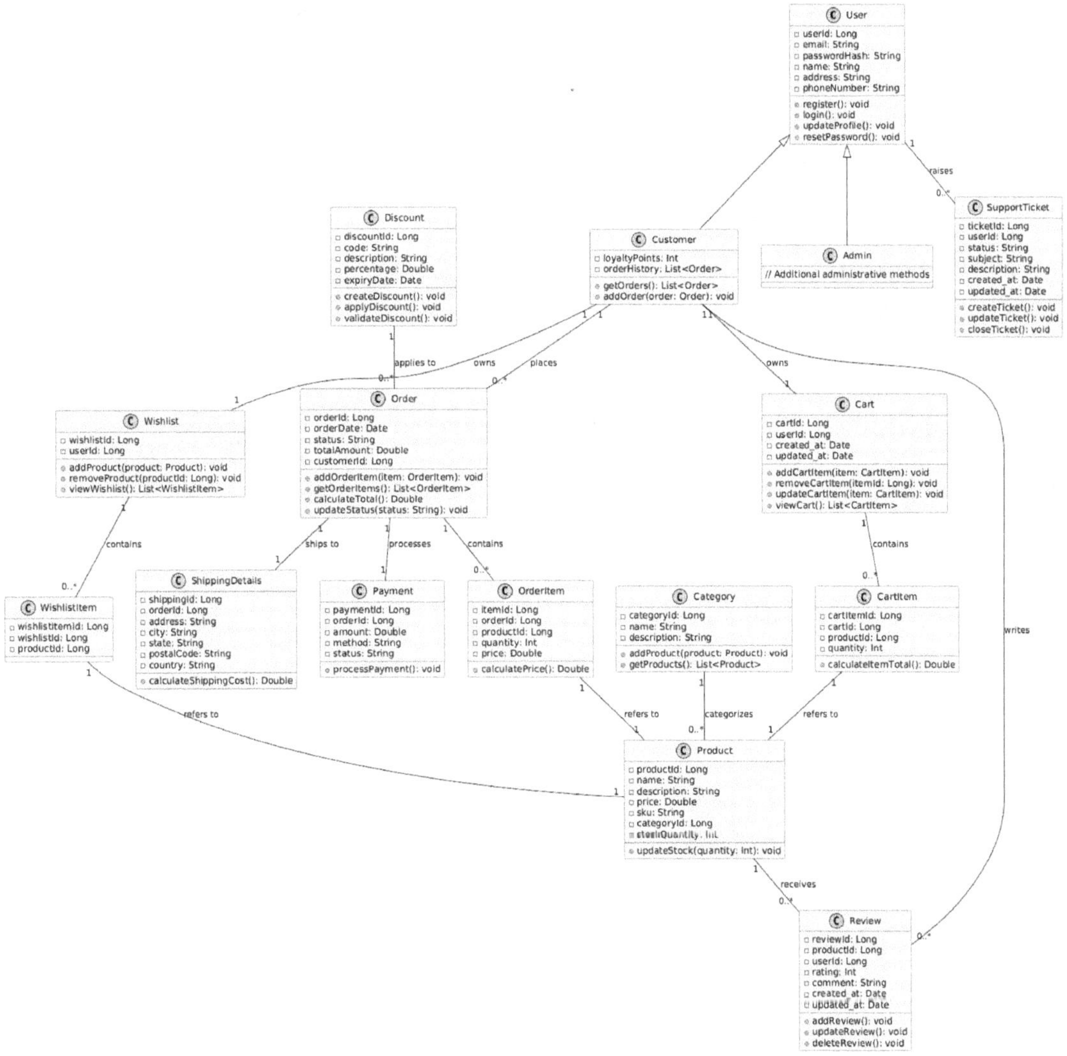

Figure 12.1: class diagram for involved entities

The following are the key classes which represent each entity in e-commerce site:

- `User`
- `Customer`
- `Admin`
- `Product`
- `Category`
- `Order`
- `OrderItem`
- `Payment`
- `ShippingDetails`
- `Cart`
- `CartItem`
- `Review`
- `Discount`
- `SupportTicket`
- `Wishlist`

Sequence details with sequence diagram

The following figure captures the typical flow of placing an order in an e-commerce system, highlighting the interactions between the customer and various components involved in the order placement process:

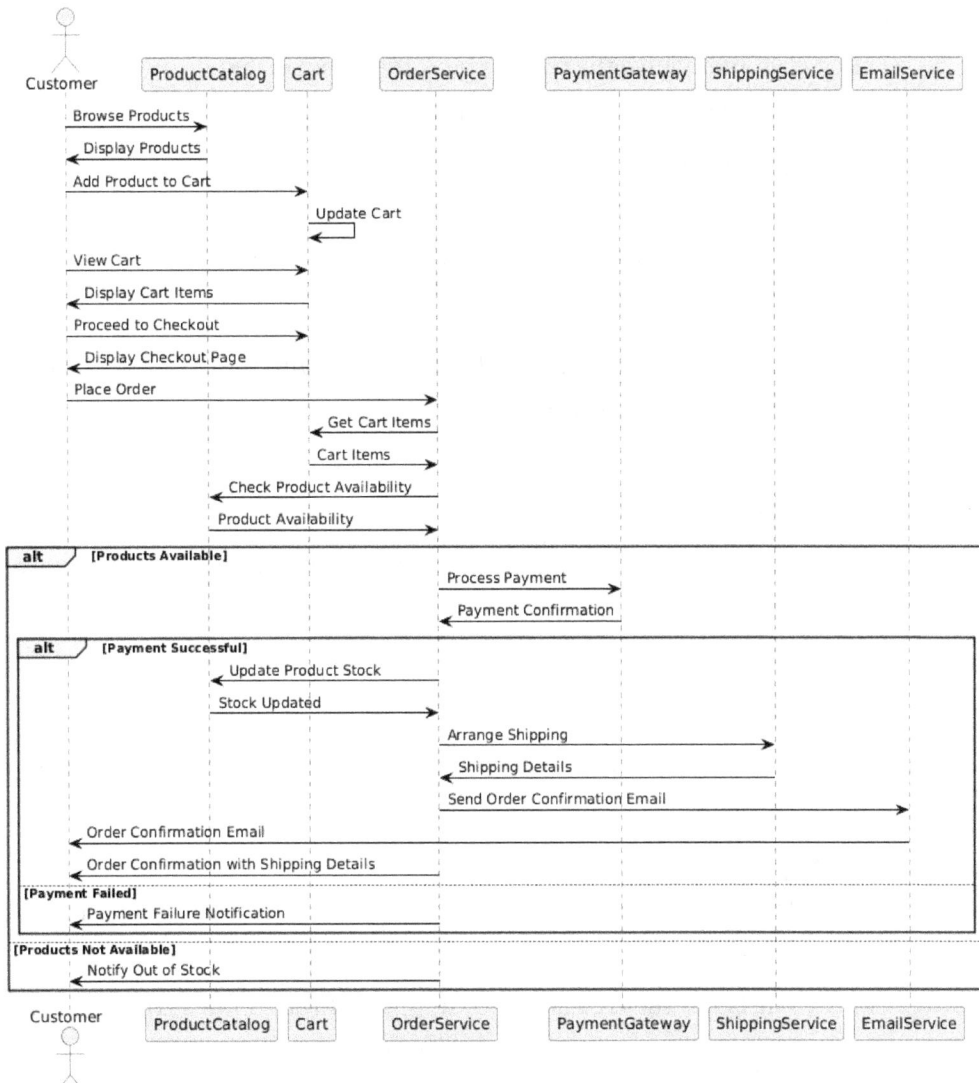

Figure 12.2: Sequence diagram for e-commerce site

The following is the sequence flow of ordering from a product from our e-commerce site:

1. **Browsing products:**

    a. The customer browses products from the `ProductCatalog`

    b. The `ProductCatalog` returns the list of available products to the customer

2. **Adding products to cart:**

    a. The customer adds a selected product to the cart

    b. The cart updates its items accordingly

3. **Viewing the cart**:
   a. The customer views the cart to check the selected items
   b. The cart displays the current items to the customer

4. **Proceeding to checkout**:
   a. The customer proceeds to checkout
   b. The cart displays the checkout page

5. **Placing the order**:
   a. The customer places the order by interacting with the `OrderService`
   b. The `OrderService` requests the cart items from the cart
   c. The cart returns the items to the `OrderService`

6. **Checking product availability**:
   a. The `OrderService` checks product availability with the `ProductCatalog`
   b. The `ProductCatalog` confirms the availability of the products

7. **Handling product availability**:
   a. **If the products are available**:
      i. The `OrderService` processes the payment through the `PaymentGateway`
      ii. The `PaymentGateway` returns a payment confirmation
   b. **If the payment is successful**:
      i. The `OrderService` updates the product stock in the `ProductCatalog`
      ii. The `ProductCatalog` confirms the stock update
      iii. The `OrderService` arranges shipping through the `ShippingService`
      iv. The `ShippingService` returns the shipping details
      v. The `OrderService` sends an order confirmation email through the `EmailService`
      vi. The `EmailService` sends the email to the customer
      vii. The `OrderService` confirms the order with shipping details to the customer
   c. **If the payment fails**:
      i. The `OrderService` notifies the customer of the payment failure
   d. **If the products are not available**:
      i. The `OrderService` notifies the customer that the products are out of stock

Activity details

The following figure provides a comprehensive overview of the order placement process on an e-commerce site, from browsing products to completing the purchase and handling various scenarios along the way:

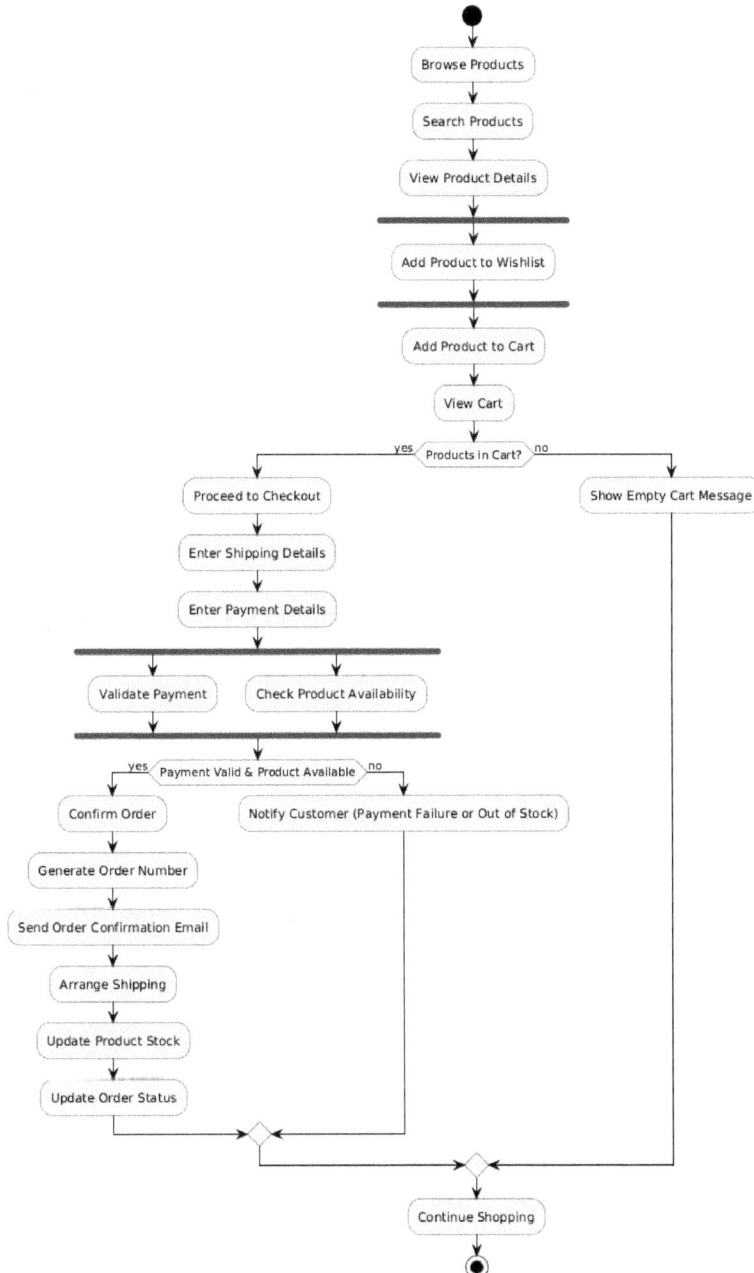

***Figure 12.3**: Actions diagram for e-commerce site*

The following steps are a part of user or admin interaction with e-commerce site:

1. **Browse products**: The user starts by browsing the products available on the e-commerce site.

2. **Search products**: The user may search for specific products.

3. **View product details**: The user views details of a selected product.

4. **Add product to wishlist**: Optionally, the user can add the product to their wishlist.

5. **Add product to cart**: The user adds the product to the cart.

6. **View cart**: The user views the cart to see the added products.

7. **Check products in cart**: The system checks if there are products in the cart.

8. **Proceed to checkout**: If there are products in the cart, the user proceeds to checkout.

9. **Enter shipping details**: The user enters shipping details.

10. **Enter payment details:** The user enters payment details.

11. **Validate payment and check product availability**: The system validates the payment and checks product availability concurrently.

12. **Confirm order**: If the payment is valid and the product is available, the order is confirmed.

13. **Generate order number**: The system generates an order number.

14. **Send order confirmation email**: The system sends an order confirmation email to the user.

15. **Arrange shipping**: The system arranges shipping for the order.

16. **Update product stock**: The system updates the product stock based on the order.

17. **Update order status**: The system updates the status of the order.

18. **Notify customer:** If the payment fails or the product is out of stock, the system notifies the user.

19. **Show empty cart message**: If there are no products in the cart, the system shows an empty cart message.

20. **Continue shopping**: The user can continue shopping after completing the current activities.

Database details

The following figure provides a comprehensive overview of the data structure for an e-commerce site, capturing the relationships between different entities and their attributes:

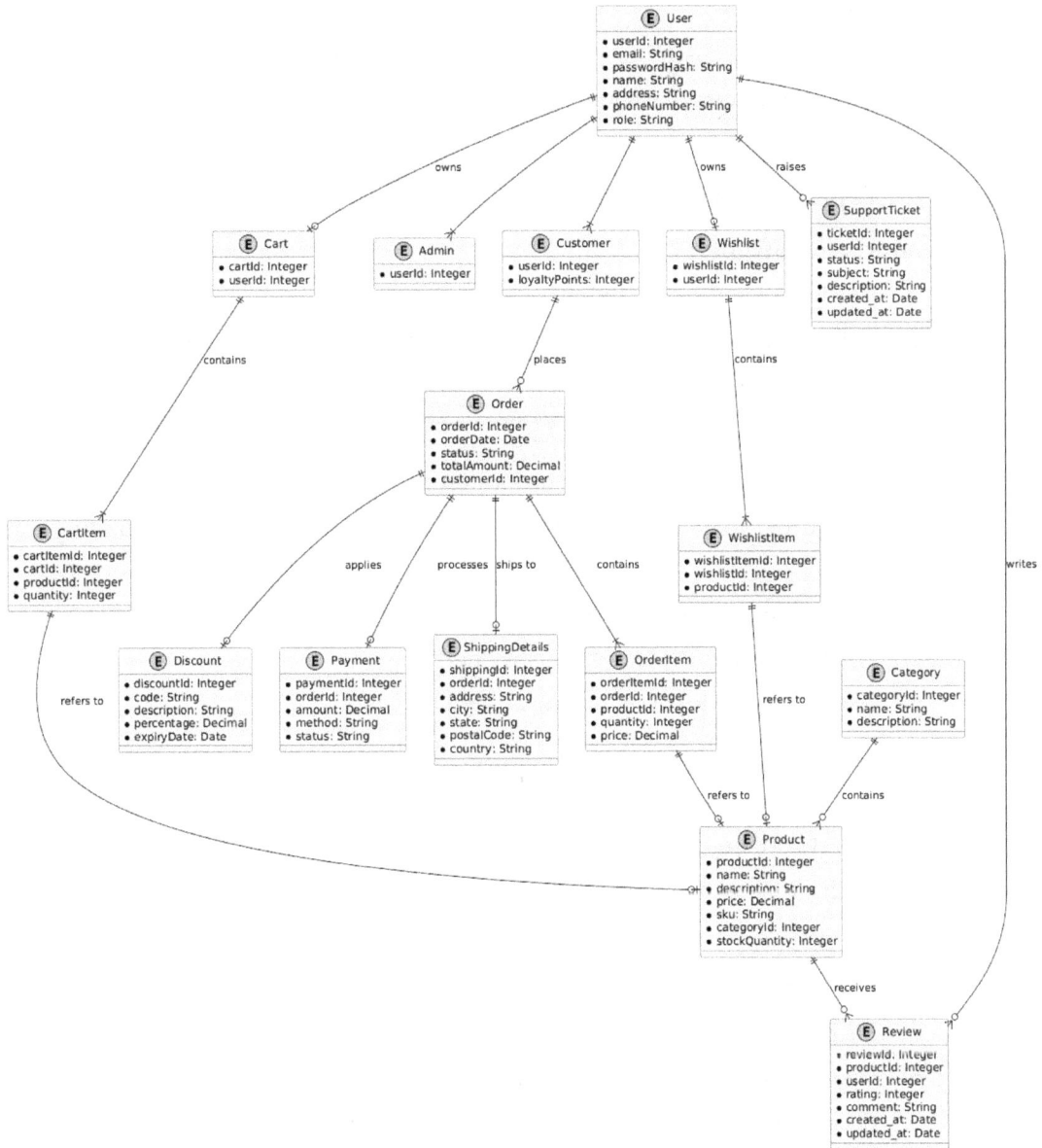

Figure 12.4: *Entity relationship among involved entities*

The following are all tables which are needed to save the state of each interaction with e-commerce site for product ordering:

- **User**:
  - Represents users of the system, including both customers and admins
  - Customers and admins inherit from user

- **Customer**:
  - Represents a customer with additional attributes like loyalty points
  - A customer can place many orders

- **Admin**:
  - Represents an admin user

- **Product and category**:
  - Products are categorized into categories
  - Each product has attributes like name, description, price, etc
  - Products belong to a category

- **Order and OrderItem**:
  - An order contains multiple order items
  - Each order item refers to a product and contains attributes like quantity and price

- **Payment and ShippingDetails**:
  - An order is associated with a payment
  - An order has shipping details

- **Cart and CartItem**:
  - A user owns a cart
  - A cart contains multiple cart items
  - Each cart item refers to a product

- **Review**:
  - Users can write reviews for products
  - Each review has attributes like rating, comment, and timestamps
  - Discounts can be applied to orders
  - Each discount has attributes like code, description, percentage, and expiry date

- **SupportTicket**:
  - Users can raise support tickets
  - Each ticket has attributes like status, subject, description, and timestamps

- **Wishlist and WishlistItem**:
  - o Users can have a wishlist
  - o A wishlist contains multiple wishlist items
  - o Each wishlist item refers to a product

Conclusion

In this final chapter, we conclude our learnings of functional programming and its practical applications for solving real-world problems while reaping the benefits of functional programming. In this chapter, we discussed the real-world implementation of e-commerce site and saw its different aspect required to be implemented. We discussed its design very closely and magnified each minute details from technology aspects, functional aspects and how projects are delivered with all its design aspects with class design, sequence flow, activity flow and its database tables. Each activity is also detailed out during real implementation, for example, browsing products can still be drilled down and same for its sequence diagram but here we tried to understand the aspects and its implementation in a functional way.

Join our Discord space

Join our Discord workspace for latest updates, offers, tech happenings around the world, new releases, and sessions with the authors:

https://discord.bpbonline.com

Index